Human Factors in Information Systems:
The Relationship Between User Interface Design and Human Performance

Jane Carey, editor
Arizona State University West

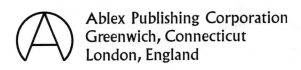

Ablex Publishing Corporation
Greenwich, Connecticut
London, England

Printed in the United States of America

Library of Congress Cataloging-in-Publication Data

Human factors in information systems : the relationship between user
    interface design and human performance / edited by Jane Carey.
            p.   cm. — (Human/computer interaction series)
    Papers originally presented at the Fourth Symposium on Human
Factors in Management Information Systems, held on Feb. 27–28, 1992,
Phoenix, AZ.
    Includes bibliographical references and index.
    ISBN 1-56750-285-7 (cloth)
    1. Human-computer interaction—Congresses. 2. User interfaces
(Computer systems)—Congresses. I. Carey, Jane M. II. Symposium
on Human Factors in Management Information Systems (4th : 1992 :
Phoenix, Ariz.) III. Series: Human/computer interaction (Norwood,
N.J.)
QA76.9.H85H8673 1996
005.3'01'9—dc20   96-25518
                                                                CIP

Ablex Publishing Corporation   Published in the U.K. and Europe by:
P.O. Box 5297   JAI Press Ltd.
55 Old Post Road #2   38 Tavistock Street
Greenwich, Connecticut 06830   Covent Garden
                                       London WC2E 7PB
                                       England

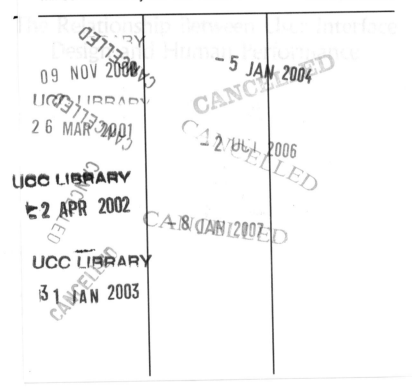

HUMAN FACTORS IN INFORMATION SYSTEMS

Jane Carey, editor

Volume 1: *Human Factors in Management Information Systems,* 1988
Volume 2: *Human Factors in Information Systems: An Organizational Perspective,* 1991
Volume 3: *Human Factors in Information Systems: Emerging Theoretical Bases,* 1995
Volume 4: *Human Factors in Information Systems: The Relationship Between User Interface Design and Human Performance,* 1997

For Victor

Contents

Preface   ix

Part I. Human/Computer Interaction

   1. *A Synergy of Theories on Human Information Processing in the User
       Interface,* Ellen D. Hoadley   3

   2. *An Empirical Evaluation of Spreadsheet and Database Task Performance
       Using Different Menu Styles,* Robert O. Jarman & Kirk P. Arnett   13

   3. *Group Interface Issues,* Robert Owen Briggs & Douglas R. Vogel   27

   4. *An Evaluation of Icon Performance Based on User Preferences,*
       Julieta K. Yamakawa, Nadalyn Miller & R. Dale Huchingson   35

Part II. Information Presentation

   5. *Design Implications of Children's Successes and Failures in Information
       Retrieval: A Case Analysis,* Paul Solomon   53

   6. *Assessing the Value of Information in a Decision Support System (DSS)
       Contest: A Simulation Study,* Ahmer S. Karim   67

Part III. System/User Communication

   7. *Cognitive Maps for Communication: Specifying Functionality and
       Usability,* Dov Te'eni, David G. Schwartz & Richard J. Boland, Jr.   83

   8. *Assessing the Use of an SQL Minimal Manual in Self-Instruction,*
       Ronald A. Guillemette & Minnie Yi-Miin Yen   101

Part IV. The Analyst

   9. *The Impact of Production Emphasis on Programmer Productivity,*
       Raghava G. Gowda & Donald R. Chand   111

  10. *Groupware, Teamwork, and Performance: Establishing the Links,*
       Peter Docherty, A.B. "Rami" Shani & James Sena   121

  11. *Conceptual Framework and Research Strategy Considerations: The
       Study of MIS Professional Ideology,* K. Gregory Jin   137

Part V. End User Involvement

12. *Importance of Familiarization for System Acceptance: The Case of Voice Mail,* Michel Plaisent & Prosper Bernard — 159

13. *A Task for Examining Information Channeling Under Time Pressure,* Manouchehr Tabatabai & James Hershauer — 171

14. *The Effects of Individual Differences on User Satisfaction,* Allison Harrison & Kelly Rainer — 183

15. *The Role of User Cognitive Skills in Information Display: A Follow Up Study,* Hulya Yazici — 199

Part VI. Methodological Issues

16. *Measurement Issues in the Study of Human Factors in Management Information Systems,* Peter R. Newsted, W. David Salisbury, Peter Todd & Robert W. Zmud — 211

Author Index — 243

Subject Index — 251

Preface

Fifteen of the chapters in this book are presentations from the Fourth Symposium on Human Factors in Information Systems (HFIS) conducted on February 27 and 28, 1992, in Phoenix, AZ at Arizona State University West. The symposium is part of an ongoing series of meetings dedicated to providing a forum for the exchange of ideas, conceptual work, and empirical research in the area of HFIS. The papers were subjected to a blind review process before being accepted. The other three chapters— "Groupware, Teamwork, and Performance: Establishing the Links," by Peter Docherty, A.B. (Rami) Shani, and James Sena; "A Conceptual Framework and Research Strategy Considerations in the Study of MIS Professional Ideology," by K. Gregory Jin; and "An Evaluation of Icon Performance Based on User Preferences," by Julieta K. Yamakawa, Nadalyn Miller, and R. Dale Huchingson—are invited papers that contribute to the content and theme of this book.

The first symposium was conducted at Texas A&M University in October 1986. Many of the original contributors have formed a nucleus group of researchers who are interested in the area of human factors and participated in subsequent symposia as reviewers and/or contributors. A second symposium was held in Sacramento, CA in February 1989, and a third symposium was held in Norman, OK in October 1990. A fifth symposium was held in Cleveland, OH at Case Western Reserve University.

In addition to the contributing authors, a group of reviewers played a significant part in assuring the quality of accepted papers. These reviewers have demonstrated an ongoing interest in HFIS and took time out of their busy schedules to aid in this endeavor. I would like to thank the following reviewers for their valuable input: Mel Martin, California State University, Sacramento; Peter Newsted, University of Calgary; James Trumbly, University of Texas, El Paso; Mohammed H.A. Tafti, Hofstra University; Kirk Arnett, Mississippi State University; Eugene Rathswohl, University of San Diego; Lorne Olfman, Claremont Graduate School; Kathleen E. Moffitt, California State University, Fresno; Jim Sena, California State Polytechnic University; Brenda Killingsworth, East Carolina University; Marilyn Kletke, Oklahoma State University; Barbara Beccue, Illinois State University; Ellen D. Hoadley, Loyola College in Maryland; Dan Stone, University of Illinois; and Raghava G. Gowda, University of Dayton.

I would also like to thank Ilene Sears, Arizona State University West, for her hard work and dedication. Ilene directed the arrangements for the symposium and also helped with the editing and production of the proceedings. She made my job as program director and host much easier.

Part I
Human / Computer Interaction

Chapter 1

A Synergy of Theories on Human Information Processing in the User Interface

Ellen D. Hoadley
Loyola College in Maryland

INTRODUCTION

Researchers in the field of information systems (IS) have long called for theory-based research (DeSanctis, 1984; Jarvenpaa, Dickson, & DeSanctis, 1985; Jenkins, 1983). The general lack of theory leads to a preponderance of inconclusive results and unreplicable findings that have no common underlying knowledge on which to build and test (Jarvenpaa et al., 1985). Those who strive to do theory-based research must have available existing theories developed in the area of IS or its reference disciplines on which to build, hypothesize, and test.

The purpose of this chapter is to make researchers in the field of human factors in IS aware of a theoretical body of knowledge developed by Dr. Valery Venda of Ukraine. The application of the body of knowledge is diverse, and it grounds our understanding of human/computer interface phenomena in explanatory and predictive theory. Furthermore, this chapter demonstrates the synergy of this theory with a Program of Research for Investigating Management Information Systems (PRIMIS) and application of the theory in empirical research already completed.

PRIMIS RESEARCH

Jenkins (1983) defined a *management information system* as "at least one *person* utilizing an *information system*, to undertake a *task* and the resulting *performance*" (p. 32). The four components of this definition and their interactions comprise the human/computer interface, the object of PRIMIS research. It is through this interface

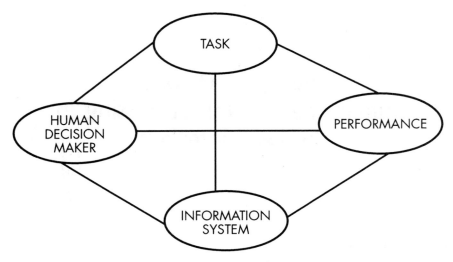

Figure 1.1.   Jenkins's Model of Human/Computer Interface.

that the user interacts with the system and uses the system to perform a task. The PRIMIS conceptual model of the human/computer interface (Figure 1.1) provides a global framework for conducting research concerning human/computer interaction.

The PRIMIS conceptual model has been used in numerous studies examining components of the human/computer interface in information extraction tasks (Addo, 1989; Hoadley, 1988, 1989, 1990; Hoadley & Jenkins, 1987; Joyner, 1989; Lauer, 1986). These tasks (answering questions using information presented in graphical or tabular formats) are fundamental to using information systems to support decision making such as in a decision support system (DSS) or executive information system (EIS). The functional relationship developed for this line of research was built on the rudimentary theory of Bertin (1983) and is stated as follows:

$$P = f(I, Q, F, C)$$

where:
P = Performance
I = Information Complexity
Q = Question Complexity
F = Form of Presentation
C = Color.

The factors of interest in PRIMIS for this chapter are not the studies themselves but this functional relationship derived from an underlying theoretical base—a base that dovetails into the Theory of Mutual Adaptation proposed by Venda.

In his book, *Higher Education and Computerisation* (Savelyev & Venda, 1989), Venda espouses a theory for understanding the phenomena of human/computer interaction. Venda's education and work experiences encompass the fields of both psychology and industrial engineering, providing him internal and external perspectives on human use of organizational tools. His theory addresses the problems of human/computer interaction efficiency at all levels of the organization—from first-line operational users to strategic managerial users. Venda's explanations of human/computer interaction and his Theory of Mutual Adaptation provide explanatory power to previously reported experimental data. It is this crossroad of theory and empirical observation that is reported on here.

THEORY OF MUTUAL ADAPTATION

Venda's theory of mutual adaptation is articulated as a collection of laws concerning the performance of humans using systems. The *Law of Mutual Adaptation* states that the highest level of efficiency, reliability, and safety of human performance with computers may be obtained by means of mutual adaptation of human beings and computer systems. Restating this law—the performance of a task is best when the capabilities of the computer match the cognitive skill structures and behavior strategies of the human user. The combination of the users' skill structures and behavior strategies are known as structure strategies. However, the efficiency to perform a task is subject to diminishing returns. As a user develops more advanced cognitive skill structures, additional strategies are open to the user to perform the same task. The "mutually adaptive" computer, especially through its interface, can support these new skills and strategies as well to achieve an even greater level of efficiency in performing the task.

The synergy of Venda's law of mutual adaptation and the PRIMIS research framework can be seen in Jenkins' conceptual model of the human/computer interface. Both Jenkins's model and Venda's law dictate that one cannot assess the effectiveness of an information system without some accounting for the user: Who is the user? What is the user trying to accomplish? What strategies does the user possess from which a most efficient strategy to use the system can be selected?

Yet even in recognizing the interdependence of the components of the human/computer interface, the experimental studies within PRIMIS most often examine performance using an information system but separate from the structure strategies available to the user for completing the task. One notable exception is with the studies (Hoadley, 1988, 1989, 1990, 1995; Hoadley & Jenkins, 1987) that examine the use of color. In these studies, the data collected from subjects who were colorblind were not included in the analysis. This exclusion recognized that users with particular cognitive structures would have to use different strategies to perform the task, that is, identifying the information to be extracted without the use of color. These different strategies were controlled for in the experiment in that no alternative strategy outside of the use of color was supported by the system.

APPLICATION TO USER LEARNING

Of further importance in issues involving human factors in IS is user learning and training. When we begin to look at learning, we can apply further laws proposed by Venda. The *Law of the Plurality of Structure Strategies* (relative to human activity) reads: "In the process of mutual adaptation between humans and their environment (the machine, other people), humans can realize a number of structure strategies of activity" (Savelyev & Venda, 1989, p. 162). Every structure-strategy has its own characteristic function curve (F) (see Figure 1.2). Over time (T), a human with a particular combination of an internal structure and behavioral strategy (S) can achieve a certain degree of efficiency (Q) in performing the activity. Efficiency is most often measured as the speed with which the activity can be performed. However, alternative human factors measures such as smoothness of motion and accuracy are not excluded from the theory.

An analogy can be drawn from one possible process of learning to read. In the beginning, a student may learn to read by reading a letter at a time putting them together to figure out the words (strategy Sa). As the student progresses, this reading skill may begin to encompass one word at a time (strategy Sb). Advanced readers finally may

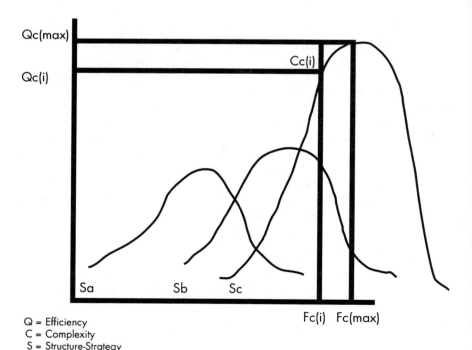

Q = Efficiency
C = Complexity
S = Structure-Strategy
F = Function
T = Time

Figure 1.2. Function Curve.

grasp groups of words in one glance to extract meaning from phrases and/or sentences (strategy Sc). For this activity—reading—the human uses these three distinct reading structure/strategies at different phases of learning.

Similarly, when using an information system, novice and expert users have different strategies for accomplishing their task. The question then becomes, in the process of using an information system, how does the user employ novice and/or expert strategies, and what impact do the strategies have on the user's efficient performance of the task? The *Law of Transformations* may be worded as follows: "Continuous transformation of one structure-strategy of a system into another may proceed through the system's state common to both structure-strategies and represented as an intersection of their characteristic curves" (Savelyev & Venda, p. 163).

In other words, as efficient performance using one structure strategy deteriorates due to its diminishing returns, a return to efficient performance can occur through application of a new and improved structure strategy. Using the reading analogy, reading word by word becomes inefficient as the reader improves and learns the reading process. At that point, a newly structured reader can begin using a new reading strategy such as reading in phrases to reach new levels of reading performance.

Think of novice users of spreadsheets who become slowed down, inefficient, and frustrated using menu-highlighting strategies and switch to the use of first-letter commands. The structure strategy of using menu selection becomes inefficient, and the use of first-letter commands has not been perfected. However, the switch to the new strategy is possible because the user now understands the first-letter command strategies, and the spreadsheet supports both structure strategies. The user is then capable of greater levels of performance using the spreadsheet because this transformation has been accomplished.

In addition, any transformation of one structure of the complex system to another can be done only through the common state of the system for both structures. That is, the user cannot move between structure strategies unless there is a common state between the two, a state where the user understands both strategies and switches from one to the other. Users do not jump from novice strategies to expert strategies. They employ intermediate structure strategies and move between them through states common to both. It is this need for common states that demands that information systems support multiple user strategies.

APPLICATION TO COMPLEXITY

A construct encountered within PRIMIS and the theory of mutual adaptation is that of complexity (C). With PRIMIS, complexity is an inherent component of information presentations and questions. Information presentations and questions with variations in prescribed characteristics have varying levels of complexity (Addo, 1989; Joyner, 1989; Lauer, 1986). Within the theory of mutual adaptation, complexity is the degree to which a user structure strategy is unable to achieve maximum efficiency. That is, it

Table 1.1.   Venda's Theory of Mutual Adaptation

Law of Mutual Adaptation
Law of Plurality of Structure Strategies
Law of Transformations

is the mutual adaptation between the user and the system that achieves the highest degree of efficiency in performing an activity. Anything less constitutes Venda's construct of complexity. It is impossible for Venda to view complexity as something separate from the collection of structure-strategies that an information processor uses. Users can reduce complexity by using different structure -strategies, and mutually adaptive systems can reduce complexity by presenting different system structures to support user strategies.

It is also true that the use of interface strategies presupposes a user with underlying structure strategies to start with. Basic skills of reading, problem -solving, thinking, reflection, and information extraction are presupposed as a base for users to begin with. It is this basic skill set that we expect the users to be taught before they come to the information systems environment. We as information professionals and academicians invest in our future users' abilities to use and develop information systems when we invest in basic skills education.

This brief restatement of Venda's Theory of Mutual Adaptation (see Table 1.1) including the laws of transformation provide us with an underlying theoretical base for continuing to develop and examine the human/computer interface. It is more than just a framework. It is a predictive and explanatory collection of theory that can be tested. In fact, much of the research that has been done in the field of human factors in IS demonstrates in some way the application of this theory. Work presented on the supplanting function of color is one example.

APPLICATION TO THE USE OF COLOR

The use of color in the human/computer interface continues to be a topic that generates interest in the field. Vendor claims about the importance of the use of color and the decreasing costs of color technology have made it available in most information systems. Continuing research is being conducted examining the functions of color in information processing (Hoadley, 1989) and the effectiveness of color in information extraction in a decision support or executive information system environment (Hoadley, 1990). One study on the use of color in information systems focused on the supplanting function of color.

When serving the supplanting function, color supersedes some portion of a covert mental operation that the information processor would otherwise have to activate (Salomon, 1972). This means that a cognitive process that would otherwise have been necessary need not be carried out. In previous research (Hoadley, 1995) when examining evidence to support the existence of the supplanting function of color, the following questions were addressed:

1. Do subjects perceive differences in the mental processes they use to extract information from presentations when the presentations are in color rather than in monocolor?
2. Do subjects verbalize specific mental operations that color assists, amends, adds, or replaces when extracting information from presentations?
3. Do subjects verbalize differences in supplanting among the types of information presentation (pie charts, bar graphs, line graphs, or tables)?

The results of this experiment demonstrate that 44 of the 51 subjects (86%) verbalized one or more mental processes that they went through during the experiment. There were different strategies employed to answer the question depending on whether the information was presented in color.

One example of a verbalized mental process reported by a subject is as follows: "I could group the companies [in a bar graph or pie chart] by color. Without it, I had to remember the order the companies were in."

This subject possessed the internal structures and was supported by the information system's internal structures to be able to use different strategies to extract information from the presentation depending on whether that presentation was made in color. If the subject's internal structures had differed, for example, if the subject were color blind, or if the information system structures had not presented the subject with the same presentations in both color and monocolor, the subject would not have used and reported different strategies for performing the task.

Subjects reported multiple performance strategies. Some counted the stripes in bars to determine which was larger. Some visualized a quantity by visualizing part of a bar or pie and comparing that quantity to another. Some referred to numbers on the y-axis to compare quantities. Different strategies for performing the task were reported based on the internal structures and preferences of the users. Yet most subjects had access to the internal fact that they had used different strategies and were able to articulate these strategies. Each user was striving to achieve the greatest level of efficiency, the lowest level of frustration, and the highest levels of speed and accuracy to perform the task.

CONCLUSIONS

Each of the differences in experimental subject strategies are explained and would be predicted by Venda's Theory of Mutual Adaptation. Its application in this environment surfacing in exchange between colleagues and in classroom explanation of various issues involving the human/computer interface demonstrates its robustness. The theory provides guidance in considering the user, the user structures, the system, the system structures, and the use strategies employed in performing the desired task. Systems need to be developed to support multiple structure strategies, and users need to be encouraged to develop cognitive skill structures and creative strategies to get the job done. Its the synergy of the two that improves productivity. It is the mutual adaptation of computer to human and human to computer that we are seeking to optimize in the human/computer interface.

Future research should be developed to examine user strategies in various task domains, whether it be using word processors, spreadsheets, graphical user interfaces, or pop-up menus within a mutual adaptation framework. In the various tasks, can user strategies be identified in a broader spectrum than just novice and expert? Are there intermediate levels a system might support that would better bridge the gap between novice and expert? Are there levels beyond expert that are yet to be supported? Are there internal skills that are more important than others in learning to perform a task? All such questions can be examined using the theoretical base presented here.

REFERENCES

Addo, T. B. A. (1989). *Development of a valid and robust metric for measuring question complexity in computer graphics experimentation.* Unpublished doctoral dissertation, Indiana University, Bloomington, Indiana.

Bertin, J. (1983). *The semiology of graphics,* Madison: University of Wisconsin Press.

DeSanctis, G. (1984). Computer graphics as decision aids: Directions for research. *Decision Sciences, 15*(4), 463–487.

Hoadley, E.D. (1995). The supplanting function of color in human information processing. *Human factors in information systems: emerging theoretical bases.* J.M. Carey, ed. Norwood, NJ. Ablex Publishing Corporation, 89–99.

Hoadley, E.D. (1990). Investigating the effects of color. *Communications of the ACM, 33*(2), 120–125, 139.

Hoadley, E.D. (1989). *The functions of color in human information processing* (Working Paper #WP0989.003 of the David D. Lattanze Center for Executive Studies in Information Systems). Baltimore: Loyola College.

Hoadley, E.D. (1988). *The effects of color on performance in an information extraction task using varying forms of information presentation.* Unpublished doctoral dissertation, Indiana University.

Hoadley, E.D., & Jenkins, A.M. (1987). *The effects of color in performance in an information extraction task using varying forms of information presentation* (Pilot Studies, IRMIS Working Paper #W713). Indiana University.

Jarvenpaa, S.L., Dickson, G.W., & DeSanctis, G. (1985). Methodological issues in experimental IS research: Experiences and recommendations. *MIS Quarterly, 9*(2), 141–156.

Jenkins, A.M. (1983). *MIS design variables and decision making performance.* Ann Arbor: University of Michigan Research Press.

Joyner, E.R. (1989). *The development of a metric for assessing the information complexity of time-series business graphs.* Unpublished doctoral dissertation, Indiana University,

Lauer, T.W. (1986). *The effects of variations in information complexity and form of presentation on performance for an information extraction task.* Unpublished doctoral dissertation, Indiana University,

Salomon, G. (1972). Can we affect cognitive skills through visual media? *AV Communication Review, 20*(4), 401–422.

Savelyev, A., & Venda, V. (1989). *Higher education and computerisation.* Moscow: Progress Publishers.

An Empirical Evaluation of Spreadsheet and Database Task Performance Using Different Menu Styles

Robert O. Jarman
Augusta College

Kirk P. Arnett
Mississippi State University

INTRODUCTION

The spreadsheet is given credit for introducing personal computers (PCs) to the business world. Today, spreadsheets and databases comprise the principle analytic and diagnostic tools for business PC users.

Menus have become a dominant interface style because of the constant need for spreadsheet and database users to choose among alternative actions and the menu's relative strengths of reducing memory requirements, training time, and erroneous selections. Despite the popularity of menus as an interface style, different implementations exist in the marketplace. For example, Borland International's Paradox™ database utilizes a scroll bar menu, whereas Ashton Tate's Dbase III+ employs combination scroll bar and pull-down menus.

This study offers hypotheses then reports laboratory findings from experiments that examine user performance with three different menu styles: traditional (full-screen), scroll bar (Lotus-like), and pull-down (partial screen window) for generic spreadsheet and database tasks. A theoretical background section introduces relevant menu-related research; an experiment description section discusses the subject selection techniques, demographics, experimental procedures, and performance analysis variables. Next, hypotheses, relevant treatments, and supporting statistics are reviewed. Finally, the summary and conclusions suggest reasons why the findings occurred as well as practical implications.

Theoretical Background: Menus

According to a survey by Mosier and Smith (1984), software design for the user interface can consume from 30% to 35% of the total design effort. Therefore, designers ride the horns of a dilemma: On the one hand, they must be concerned about the relatively high resource requirements for interface design, whereas on the other they must recognize that good interface design promotes more usage.

Menus have become the predominant interface style. This popularity results from menu advantages that include but are not limited to the menu's capability to: (a) reduce user memory requirements, (b) reduce user training time requirements, (c) reduce the latitude for error, (d) provide reasonable interaction speed, and (e) be easily incorporated into software products.

Empirical Research

Menu structure research examines several aspects of the human–computer interface. The basis for many of these studies lies in Card and Moran's (1980) keystroke-level model and their quantifying the many discrete steps required for an expert user to perform a given task. They view the model as a prototype tool that is easy to use and relieves systems designers of the need for psychological skills.

Perlman (1985) examined menu presentation format, the number of options, and how a user makes a selection. Interestingly, he found that: (a) users employ simple search strategies for normal size menus, (b) users are sensitive to menu length, and (c) sorted menus are simpler to search. Guidelines for menu design resulted from his research.

Norman (1987) built on earlier research to demonstrate the use of tradeoff analysis as a designer tool. Specifically, he looked at user satisfaction, menu-based systems, command language systems, and system workspace requirements within the context of a text editor environment. He concluded that "answers to design questions are heavily context dependent, being affected by the classes of users... types of applications... and the level of technology being employed" (p. 501).

The majority of menu-based systems are tree structured, that is, they are arranged in a hierarchy. Design options focus on (a) the number of selections per page (one video display screen), and (b) the number of levels that represent the hierarchy. The literature refers to these as depth/breadth issues.

As a segment of the depth/breadth interest, a series of experiments examined optimizing menu design and performance within an information retrieval context. Lee, Whalen, McEwen, and Latrémouille (1984) investigated the optimal design of menu pages for videotext systems. They concluded that (a) menu page indexes should be empirically tested prior to release to the general public, (b) design analysis can detect menu index faults and aid in their improvement, (c) added descriptors improve menus, and (d) naive users are consistent in their perception of good and bad menu indexes, whereas expert users are not.

Lee and MacGregor (1985) sought methods to minimize user search time (the time required to traverse a tree-structured menu and arrive at the correct selection for a given task). They based their analysis on components of the keystroke-level model and concluded that hierarchical menu indexes should contain between four and eight selections per page for optimal performance.

Paap and Roske-Hofstrand (1986) applied Lee and MacGregor's model in a more highly specified context. They empirically determined that the optimal number of selections per page can range from 16 to 78 when the user can limit the scope of the search based on "either experience with the menu panel or on the organization of the options on the panel" (p. 377).

MacGregor, Lee, and Lam (1986) extended their earlier research (to include the assertions of Paap) to propose and experimentally evaluate a criterion-based decision model. The model predicts the effect of the number of alternatives on the search process and resulting error patterns. Again, for naive users, the model indicates that the optimal number of selections per menu page is four or five.

The investigations mentioned here have provided the impetus and foundation for deeper analysis of subordinate issues. Schwartz and Norman (1986) specifically examined item distinctiveness. Their results are consistent with those of Lee et al. (1984).

Selection response, commonly performed via a keyboard, was evaluated by Shinar and Stern (1987) to ascertain if cursor pointing, keying a letter, or keying a digit all provide equivalent performance. Their results, derived from search time and error rates, suggest that a mnemonic device (a letter) is preferable.

A common theme throughout empirical research in the human–computer interface area is identification of factors contributing to optimal menu performance. For this study, cognitive, technical, and contextual issues were examined within an experimental framework of tree-structured menus. Independent variables included menu depth, breadth, and selection mechanisms. Dependent variables included response times and error rates—surrogate measures of performance. User-reported subjective ratings of menu structure preference and perceptions of ease-of-use also provided a basis for rating the different menu structures. These techniques and variables are consistent with the literature reviews discussed earlier and metrics proposed by Shneiderman (1980, 1986), Martin (1973), Lee and MacGregor (1985), as well as others.

Research Justification

The point of the preceding discussion is that, despite commercial adoption, empirical research is lacking regarding which, if any, technique is preferable to a traditional display or superior in performance. There is no clear preference for or dominance of a particular menu structure—each has gained a loyal following.

Note that many of the earlier classical research efforts were performed before the popularity of the PC and in mainframe computing environments. Thus the research might be questioned for generalizability on those grounds. Technological advances have simply outrun the limited community of researchers' ability to maintain pace. Carroll and McKendree (1987) expressed their concern for the gap between research and implementation in pointing out that "researchers have opted for a particular advisory style offering little or no empirical rationale" (p. 15). They further caution that "mere technological feasibility must be augmented by empirical study of whether and how people will find a new technology useful and tractable" (p. 14).

EXPERIMENTAL DESCRIPTION

This experiment evaluates computer users' performance using three menu structures for two different contextual settings. Different contexts were used to determine if a particular menu style contributes to better user performance within a given context as compared to alternative contexts. The contexts selected for this experiment were generic spreadsheet and database settings.

The menu structures are: (a) a standard tree-structure menu, (b) a scroll-bar menu, and (c) a pull-down menu. They are presented in order in Figures 2.1–2.3. Each menu structure is a different visual presentation of the same underlying tree structure. The access path to each terminal node in a tree structure is unique, requiring that the sub-

Document
File
Utilities
System

Figure 2.1. Traditional Menu.

Document File Utilities System
Edit Format Print Dictionary

Figure 2.2. Scroll-Bar Menu.

```
┌─────────────────────────────────────────┐
│                                         │
│   Document   File   Utilities   System  │
│   Edit                                  │
│   Format                                │
│   Print                                 │
│   Dictionary                            │
│                                         │
└─────────────────────────────────────────┘
```

Figure 2.3. Pull-Down Menu.

ject successfully traverse the structure to accomplish a subtask. The length of all access paths is the same for this experiment (three nodes).

In the case in which the subject has chosen an incorrect path, the path must be retraced, via the "Esc" key, to a junction suitable for branching to an alternate route. Pressing Esc will immediately return the subject to the next higher level of the menu hierarchy.

Subject Selection and Demographics

Shneiderman (1986) notes the importance of user profiles. Within the context of this research, a relevant user profile must address demographics (age, sex), typing expertise, spreadsheet and database software knowledge, computer courses taken, and routine computer use. This research did not, a priori, categorize computer users as did other major research in menu design and performance. Instead it relied on the selected methodology and concomitant variable (experience category) to introduce user classification into the analysis.

The sample consisted of 116 subjects enrolled at three institutions of higher learning in the southeastern United States. The subjects were undergraduate or graduate students enrolled as majors in a business school discipline, Computer Science, Management Information Systems, or MBA program. Of the sample, 55 (47.4%) were female and 61 (52.6%) were male. The average age was 25.6 years with a median age of 23 years. The youngest subject was 19 years of age, whereas the eldest was 55.

Experimental Procedures

Task sets represent common spreadsheet (database) operations encountered during a work session. One such task might be to save the current worksheet. Tasks were expressed in generic terms to avoid bias resulting from a subject's knowledge of a particular spreadsheet or database command set. Representative task sets are listed in Appendix A.

Subjects responded to a series of three sets of eight generic task directives, each referred to as a subtask. Each subtask required that the subject navigate through a menu to select the proper sequence of commands to ultimately accomplish the subtask. Recorded metrics were: (a) the time per subtask measured in units of "ticks" of the system clock (18.2 ticks per second), (b) whether the response was correct, and (c) the number of "escapes" entered (an "escape" represents an error in selection as perceived by the subject).

The software to drive the experiment, record the values for important variables, and record subject responses was included on a separate diskette for each subject. The disks were hand-shuffled before each experiment and before delivery to the subjects. This technique served to randomly disperse the order of menu presentations among the subjects to eliminate possible bias.

Skills Inventory

The last sequence of data developed a skills inventory for each subject. Skills surveyed included knowledge of leading specific spreadsheet and database products and self-reported skill ratings. Table 2.1 lists responses to a series of questions regarding spreadsheet and database familiarity respectively. The first question asked if the subject was familiar with a spreadsheet, the following four questions asked the same question about more popular spreadsheets, and the last asked about "another spreadsheet" for closure. The data categories include multiple responses and are not exclusive.

Table 2.1.   Context and Product Familiarity

Context	Response-Yes	Response-No
Familiar with a Spreadsheet	91 (78.4%)	25 (21.6%)
Specific Spreadsheet		
123 or clone	82 (70.7%)	34 (29.3%)
Supercalc	12 (10.3%)	104 (89.7%)
Multiplan	5 (4.3%)	111 (95.7%)
Another Spreadsheet	37 (31.9%)	79 (68.1%)
Familiar with a Database	77 (66.4%)	39 (33.6%)
Specific Database		
Dbase III or III+	58 (50.0%)	58 (58.0%)
R:base	10 (8.6%)	106 (91.4%)
Paradox	4 (3.4%)	118 (96.6%)
Another Database	31 (26.7%)	85 (73.3%)

Table 2.2. **Spreadsheet and Database Skill Ratings**

Skill Category	Observed	Minimum	Medium	Maximum
Spreadsheet				
Few Tasks	43	0	5	20
Some Tasks	16	21	30	40
Aver. # of Tasks	21	41	45	60
Most Tasks	23	61	70	80
About all Tasks	13	81	90	99
Database				
Few Tasks	45	0	20	20
Some Tasks	10	21	40	40
Aver. # of Tasks	21	41	60	60
Most Tasks	26	61	80	80
About all Tasks	14	81	99	99

Covariate Identification

For this particular research, individual expertise for spreadsheets, databases, and typing skills were candidate covariates to reduce the analysis of variance error term. Each contributes to a significant portion of user performance when timing metrics are used in the keystroke-level model.

Table 2.2 lists the self-reported categorical skill ratings and percentile placement within each category. That is, having selected the appropriate category, the subject rated his or her skills within a specific percentile range. Of the 116 subjects, 80 (68.9%) rated their individual spreadsheet and database skills to be average or better. Overall, spreadsheet and database skill ratings indicate approximately even coverage across the skill levels described. This is consistent with the high levels of familiarity reported earlier and also makes the point that one must not conclude breadth of familiarity equates to depth of knowledge. For example, although 91% reported familiarity with spreadsheets, only 49% assessed their skills as being average or better.

Performance Analysis

Table 2.3 lists, by context, descriptive statistics for the variable average time across the independent variable, menu style. Note that for both contexts the mean average time for the traditional menu is less than that for both the scroll-bar and pull-down menu.

ANACOVA was initially used to test for significance of the selected covariates. Covariate significance was not found so analysis continued using ANOVA techniques.

Table 2.3. Descriptive Statistics: Average Time by Context

Statistic	Traditional	Scroll Bar	Pull-Down
Spreadsheet			
No. of Cases	33	32	34
Minimum	169.13	85.63	42.75
Maximum	964.13	892.75	982.13
Mean	448.43	500.51	539.75
Stand. Dev.	170.21	200.03	201.62
Database			
No. of Cases	38	37	36
Minimum	160.88	225.88	155.88
Maximum	843.50	996.25	1039.63
Mean	463.93	568.93	579.62
Stand. Dev	179.44	219.05	217.03

HYPOTHESES TESTS

The first test experimental hypothesis appears as follows:

Ho1:   The average time required to complete the task for all menu designs
is the same.

Bartlett's test for homogeneity of variance and the Kolmorogov-Smirnov for goodness of fit validated the underlying assumptions of ANOVA: homogeneity of variance and a normal distribution of the dependent variable. Significance was found in the database context ($p = 0.031$) permitting rejection of the null hypothesis.

The next phase of this particular analysis, identification of those means (average time) that are significantly different across groups, was accomplished by using Tukey's highly significant difference (HSD) statistic. The results follow. Table 2.4 lists a matrix of pairwise comparison probabilities for the database context.

The traditional and pull-down menus show significant differences in the dependent variable average time ($p = 0.031$). One might also argue that marginal significance

Table 2.4. Tukey HSD Multiple Comparisons
Matrix of Pairwise Comparison Probabilities
Database: Average Time

	Traditional	Scroll Bar	Pull-Down
Traditional	1.000		
Scroll Bar	0.098	1.000	
Pull-down	0.031	0.868	1.000

($p = 0.098$) exists between the traditional and scroll-bar menus. Further discussion of these results is deferred until all experimental hypotheses have been tested.

Experimental Hypothesis 2 asserted that the number of errors does not vary with respect to menu style. Here again, the importance of the number of errors or its surrogates (error ratio, error rate, etc.) is evidenced by its wide use in related prior research:

Ho2:   The number of errors is the same for all menu designs.

An "escape" entry was defined previously as a willful attempt by the user to recover from a believed improper selection. Counting "escape" keystrokes was a part of the data collection process. This count is used for the evaluation of the second hypothesis. The aggregate escape counts were transformed in an attempt to achieve normality. The transformation did not produce a normal distribution, hence, a distribution-free methodology, Freidman's Two-Way Analysis of Variance, was applied.

Table 2.5 lists descriptive statistics (non-transformed data) for escape counts across menu styles. Note users exercised more escapes using the traditional menu for both the spreadsheet and database contexts.

The results of Freidman's Two-Way Analysis of Variance test appear in Table 2.6. The analysis permits rejecting the null hypothesis of equality in "escapes" for the database context ($p = 0.035$).

The third hypothesis asserted that users perform equally well across all menu styles. This hypothesis is in line with literature investigations of performance cited earlier:

Ho3:   The success level is the same for all menu designs.

The dependent variable "correct" was recorded as a success-level surrogate. Its values

Table 2.5. Descriptive Statistics: Escape by Context

Statistic	Traditional	Scroll Bar	Pull-Down
Spreadsheet			
No. of Cases	34	34	34
Minimum	0	0	0
Maximum	34	23	18
Mean	9.65	3.21	2.97
Stand. Dev.	10.70	5.07	4.46
Database			
No. of Cases	37	39	39
Minimum	0	0	0
Maximum	30	11	15
Mean	5.65	2.05	2.18
Stand. Dev.	8.11	2.80	3.78

Table 2.6. Friedman Two-Way Analysis of Variance
Dependent Variable: Escape

Dependent Variable	Rank Sum	Test Stat.	p
Spreadsheet			
Traditional	59.5		
Scroll Bar	72.0		
Pull-down	72.5	3.191	0.203
Database			
Traditional	73.5		
Scroll Bar	69.5		
Pull-down	91.0	6.705	0.035

Table 2.7. Descriptive Statistics: Correct by Context

Statistic	Traditional	Scroll Bar	Pull-Down
Spreadsheet			
No. of Cases	34	34	34
Minimum	0	0	0
Maximum	8	7	7
Mean	3.0	3.1	3.9
Stand. Dev.	2.5	2.3	2.5
Database			
No. of Cases	39	39	39
Minimum	0	0	0
Maximum	6	7	7
Mean	2.1	2.7	2.9
Stand. Dev.	1.9	2.1	2.0

were zero (incorrect selection path) or one (correct selection path). Correct is independent of time (as is the escape variable). Like the variable escape, correct is a frequency count. Data transformation did not achieve normality, thus Friedman's two-way test was used.

Table 2.7 lists descriptive statistics, and Table 2.8 lists results of Friedman's test. Little difference exists between mean values for the correct variable across menu styles, thus it would appear unlikely that the null hypothesis can be rejected.

Friedman's analysis listed in Table 2.8 confirms the previous suspicions: There is no basis for rejecting the null hypothesis of equal success levels across menu style for both the spreadsheet and database contexts.

Table 2.8. Friedman Two-Analysis of Variance
Dependent Variable: Correct

Dependent Variable	Rank Sum	Test Stat.	p
Spreadsheet			
Traditional	68.0		
Scroll Bar	71.0		
Pull-down	65.0	0.529	0.767
Database			
Traditional	82.0		
Scroll Bar	73.5		
Pull-down	78.5	0.936	0.626

Table 2.9. Friedman Two-Analysis of Variance
Dependent Variable: Preference

Dependent Variable	Rank Sum	Test Stat.	p
Spreadsheet			
Traditional	73.5		
Scroll Bar	67.5		
Pull-down	63.0	1.632	0.442
Database			
Traditional	89.0		
Scroll Bar	81.0		
Pull-down	64.0	8.359	0.015

A fourth hypothesis asserted that users are indifferent to menu styles. This hypothesis derives from earlier research that indicated that computer users are sensitive to interface performance times. Experimental Hypothesis 4 thus states:

Ho4:   User preference is the same for all menu styles.

Table 2.9 lists the results of Freidman's test for user-reported preference ratings. No differences in preference are evident for the spreadsheet context. Preference for the pull-down menu differs significantly ($p = 0.015$) from the other menu styles in the database context. The magnitude of rank sum values indicates a positive preference for the pull-down menu in comparison to others.

ANALYSIS OF RESULTS

Table 2.10 summarizes test hypotheses and the analytic results. Immediately obvious is a the lack of significance for all hypotheses in the spreadsheet context.

The spreadsheet context is dominated conceptually by the Lotus spreadsheet and its scroll-bar menu presentation. This is evident from other spreadsheet vendors' close following of Lotus's metaphor. Thus, it is reasonable to assert that a user's familiarity with the context mitigates any inherent effects of menu style for well-defined contexts.

Carrying the assertion one step further, one can hypothesize that the traditional menu is best suited for expert users because of its lower response times and negative correlation of average time to "errors" (Spearman rank correlation, $P = 0.025$); that is, longer response times were associated with a higher incidence of errors. This is consistent with Carroll's (1984) observation that experts prefer interfaces without menus, that is, direct command entry. The hypothesis is also supported by the notion of "chunking" information and trained response patterns. (When a Lotus user wants to save a copy of the current spreadsheet a "/FS<return>R" response is elicited without conscious consideration of each command—similar to a "mental macro.")

The database context varied little from spreadsheets in distribution of skill levels. An underlying difference does exist, however, by virtue of broader contextual coverage in terms of database products, associated conceptual models, and implementation of query facilities.

The database results are contrary to previous research. Although Rushinek and Rushinek (1986) reported that the time to complete a task is a contributor to satisfaction, a similar positive linkage between average completion and preference does not exist. That is, given equivalent success levels, database users preferred a menu style requiring more time but resulting in fewer errors. Hence, they appear to be willing to trade performance in terms of shorter times for reduced levels of frustration.

One other aspect of these results merits discussion. Because informational content of the scroll-bar and pull-down menus is identical, two other unrecorded factors appear to be at work: (a) horizontal versus vertical presentation styles, and (b) "animation" in the sense that the subordinate pull-down menu moved laterally in order to appear directly beneath each primary selection.

Anecdotal comments from subjects indicated that pull-down menus were "easier to read" and thereby more preferable. This suggests that interfaces using vertical lists

Table 2.10. Hypotheses and Analytic Results

Hypothesis No difference in	Spreadsheet	Database
Average Time	fail to reject	reject
Error Level	fail to reject	reject
Success Level	fail to reject	fail to reject
Preference	fail to reject	reject

are easier to discriminate than those with horizontal lists.

With regard to the second point, "animation" could conceivably evoke subliminal user satisfaction by the user's "having made something happen." It is then reasonable to hypothesize that users would prefer mobile and dynamic graphic interfaces to static, character-based ones. The preceding questions establish a logical connection between the two interface domains.

SUMMARY AND CONCLUSIONS

This chapter reports a recent study of menu performance for PC users conducting relatively simple and generic spreadsheet and database tasks. Much of the earlier work in this area was conducted in mainframe computer processing environments. This analysis is especially relevant for at least two reasons. First, there continues to be confusion and contention in the marketplace regarding interface issues (hardware and software requirements) in MS-DOS and OS/2-based systems. Next, software vendors are constantly introducing new or enhanced products with user-definable interfaces, seemingly no longer content to minimize the considerable resource requirements of the interface design efforts.

A secondary benefit of this research is the knowledge contributed to the process of learning to use the underlying software applications. Suppose for the moment that one or two interfaces dominate performance. A natural follow-up to this research is coupling the dominant interface(s) to other application software packages in different contexts to again evaluate performance while completing the underlying tasks.

Because the variety of interfaces in commercial application software ranges from cluttered, confusing displays to nearly blank screens devoid of visual clues, it is reasonable to experiment with interfaces that can positively contribute toward learning to use a software product. Thus the purpose of this experiment was not to extend inferences and causality to the population at large; rather, it was to explore carefully one aspect of human–computer interaction—computer user performance in combination with different menu styles. The result that average task completion time varies significantly across different menu designs and that computer users prefer certain menu styles builds a foundation for further research.

REFERENCES

Card, S.K., Moran, T.P., & Newell, A. (1980). The keystroke-level model for user
    performance time with interactive systems. *Communications of the ACM, 23,* 236–410.
Carroll, J.M., & McKendree, J. (1987). Interface design issues for advice-giving expert systems.
    Communications of the ACM, 30, 14–31.
Koved, L., & Shneiderman, B. (1986). Embedded menus: Selecting them in context.
    Communications of the ACM, 29, 312–318.
Lee, E., & MacGregor, J. (1985). Minimizing user search time in menu retrieval systems.
    Human Factors, 27, 157–162.

Lee, E., Whalen, T., McEwen, S., & Latremouille, S. (1984). Optimizing the design of menu pages for information retrieval. *Ergonomics, 27,* 1051–1069.

MacGregor, J., Lee, E., & Lam, N. (1986). Optimizing the structure of database menu indexes: A decision model of menu search. *Human Factors, 28,* 387–399.

Martin, J. (1973). *Design of man–computer dialogues.* Englewood Cliffs, NJ: Prentice-Hall.

Monk, A. (1987a). How and when to collect behavioural data. In A. Monk (Ed.), *Fundamentals of human–computer interaction* (pp. 69–79)., London: Academic Press.

Mosier, J.N., & Smith, S.L. (1984). The user interface to computer-based information systems: A survey of current software design practice. *Behaviour and Information Technology, 3,* 195–203.

Norman, D.A. (1987). Some observations on mental models. In R. Baecker & W. Buxton (Eds.), *Readings in human-computer interaction* (pp. 241–244). Los Altos, CA: Kaufmann.

Paap, K.R., & Roske-Hofstrand, R.J. (1986). The optimal number of menu options per panel. *Human Factors, 28,* 377–385.

Perlman, G. (1985). Making the right choices with menus. In R. Baecker and W. Buxton (Eds.), *Readings in Human-computer Interaction* (pp.451–455), Los Altos, CA: Kaufmann.

Rushinek, A., & Rushinek, S.F. (1986). What makes users happy? *Communications of the ACM, 29,* 594–598.

Schwartz, J.P., & Norman, K.L. (1986). The importance of item distinctiveness on performance using a menu selection system. *Behavior and Information Technology, 5,* 173–182.

Shinar, D., & Stern, M.I. (1987). Alternative option selection methods in menu driven computer programs. *Human Factors, 29,* 453–459.

Shneiderman, B. (1980). *Software psychology.* Cambridge MA: Winthrop.

Shneiderman, B. (1986). *Designing the user interface.* Reading, MA: Addison-Wesley.

Willeges, B.H., & Willeges, R.C. (1984). Dialogue design considerations for interactive computer systems. *Human Factors Review, 26,* 167–209.

APPENDIX A

A sample set of eight spreadsheet and database subtasks follows. Each subject responded to three such task sets, one set per menu style.

Spreadsheet Tasks	Database Tasks
1. Set colors for a graph	Erase an existing database view.
2. Perform an operation on a block of data.	Change an existing index.
3. Change the destination of a report.	Load 1-2-3 data into a database.
4. Load a worksheet.	Examine a list of queries.
5. Erase a worksheet.	Compute the sum of predetermined fields.
6. Execute a Search/Replace command.	Reorder the current database.
7. Change a column's width.	Edit a specific record.
8. Reset a worksheet layout to the default values.	Execute a report.

Group Interface Issues

Robert Owen Briggs
Douglas R. Vogel
University of Arizona

INTRODUCTION

Electronic Meeting Systems (EMS) and other applications meant for use by groups pose unique problems for interface designers. This chapter examines these challenges and offers suggestions for overcoming them.

EMS is a relatively new form of computer application specifically targeted toward making groups more productive (Nunamaker, Dennis, Valacich, Vogel, & George, 1991). An EMS facility supplies participants with a network of workstations, typically one for each participant. The EMS software helps groups to overcome communication barriers intrinsic to meetings. For instance, in a traditional meeting only one person can speak at a time. In an EMS meeting, all participants can "talk at once" by typing their ideas into the system. The system instantaneously passes each contribution to all other participants.

Evaluation apprehension is another barrier to meeting communication. People are sometimes reluctant to make an unusual or unpopular contribution, particularly if the boss is in the room. EMS can facilitate the free and frank exchange of ideas by permitting anonymous exchanges when they are appropriate. EMS software also focuses group thinking by offering structured processes for idea generation and organization, alternative evaluation, or issue exploration, and supports group information needs by reducing the cost of acquiring, storing, or retrieving group information.

The issues relating to good interface designs for single user applications—low error rates, rapid task performance, high user satisfaction, and so on. (Shneiderman, 1987)—are also critical for group tools. However, groups face special constraints not experienced by single users. Application developers must attend to these issues in order to produce interfaces acceptable for group settings.

CONSTRAINTS ON COMPUTER USE BY GROUPS

Groups Are Distracted

Work teams form because no single person has all the information, all the experience, or all the insight to accomplish a task alone. Teams accomplish their goals by exchanging information, thinking about that information, and reporting the results of their thinking to other team members. Teams commonly use meetings to achieve their goals.

However, a meeting is a process in conflict with itself. People cannot pay attention to everything at once, and in a meeting their attention is divided three ways at a minimum. They must listen to what others say, think about what has been said, and remember what they want to say when they get the floor. Doing any one of those three things effectively precludes doing the other two. For instance, if people stop to ponder a point, they will miss what someone else is saying. Thus, groups are by nature distracted, and adding software to a group setting introduces yet another demand on limited attention resources.

Groups are Expensive

The cost of a group meeting adds up quickly. A meeting of 12 managers can cost upwards of $600 per hour in salaries alone. Thus, groups are expensive, and the cost of teaching a group to use an application is very much higher than the cost of teaching a single user.

Groups are Time-Constrained

It is not trivial matter to schedule times when everyone in a large group can attend a meeting. Furthermore, it is axiomatic that everyone at a meeting has a number of other pressing activities waiting in the wings. It is therefore not likely that large group meetings will be scheduled solely for the purpose of teaching a group to use a new software package that may make them more productive at some future time. Whatever training the group will experience will probably have to take place in the same session in which the group uses the system to accomplish their goals. Yet, when they meet, their purpose and desire is to accomplish the team goal, and any time taken to learn new software will detract from the limited time available to do productive work.

Groups Are Ad Hoc Users

When people gather in an electronic meeting room, it is often for the first time in many weeks or months (Huber, 1984), and human memory fades as time passes. Thus, any learning the group accomplishes with one use of the interface is quite likely to have faded by the time the group uses the software again. The interface must therefore be designed as if every user were a first-time user.

Interface Implications of Group Constraints

Given the constraints described here, it is critical that user interfaces for group support tools be the epitome of simplicity. Groups of users will not tolerate long training times. If they cannot become productive within a very few minutes of when they sit down to use electronic meeting tools, they will reject the tools as a distracting nuisance. Thus, the interfaces must be visually very plain, and the tools must be almost immediately usable by people who are completely computer illiterate. Training sessions and manuals are out of the question for supporting EMS users.

The need for simplicity in group interface design is complicated by the fact that groups need rich, complex tools to support their work or they cannot derive enough benefit from the EMS to have made it worth the added distraction. Thus, designers of group interfaces find themselves between the proverbial rock and the legendary hard place.

GROUP INTERFACE SOLUTIONS

There are two strategies that have proved quite effective in addressing the constraints on group interfaces.

Repetitively Superfluous Redundancy

A developer must make a group interface very easy to learn and very easy to use in order to gain acceptance in a group environment. Two traditional ways of teaching users—reference manuals and tutorial sessions—are generally unacceptable to groups. Groups meet to get work done, not to learn software. Users of Electronic Meeting Systems have many things on their minds besides using a computer.

Group interface designers can make it easy for users to learn and use group software by giving many redundant cues about how the system works. A group will of course receive verbal instructions at the beginning of a session, but EMS professionals find that some fraction of the group will miss or misunderstand any verbal instruction. In a meeting environment charged with stimuli, three, four, or even five repetitions of verbal instructions are sometimes not sufficient to assure that all users understand what to do. The interface must supply as many cues as possible. For example, a given feature might be accessible from both a menu and a hot key. The users can be alerted to the availability of the hot key by a screen prompt. Further directions might be available under a help key. Judicious use of color can also cue users about what to expect. For instance, all read-only screens might be in blue, whereas all input fields might be in black. Transient screen prompts might be on a reverse video background, whereas permanent screen prompts might be in normal video. Contrasting colors can be used to direct user attention to critical information on the screen. The larger the variety of cues available, the larger will be the percentage of users who can proceed with their work unimpeded by the interface.

Just-In-Time Features

The functionality of a group interface must be immediately obvious to the users. They are already distracted by meeting activities, so their interactions with the computer must not place undue cognitive and perceptual loads. When user groups sit down in front of a visually complex screen, their eyes glaze over and they resist using the system, so screens must be visually simple. Yet, the system they use must be powerful and flexible. One solution to this paradox is to offload the system complexity from the users to a facilitator who controls what features are available to the users. The facilitator would have a full, complex system that could be parceled out to the users as they need it. The users would attend a session with a single, very simple interface with only a rudimentary set of core features. As the session proceeds, the users may ask for additional functionality, which the facilitator could then enable.

Consider the Case of Group Idea Organizing Sessions

The group begins with a large, disorganized set of text from which they must extract the key issues. The sessions might begin with users browsing text in one window and writing issues on a list in another. The screen prompts on the browser would only cue the users about moving through the text with up-arrow, down-arrow, page-up, and page-down. A pull-down menu would offer only the option to exit the session. At some point a user might ask the facilitator whether the system permits searching for key words. At that point the facilitator could set a software switch on the facilitator station, and a text-search feature would be enabled for the users. A prompt would cue them as to which hot key would activate the search, and a search item would then appear on the menu. The facilitator could give short verbal instructions, and then wander around the room to help those who still need it. In this fashion the interface would slowly grow in complexity as the session progressed, but the users would not be overwhelmed by having to sort out all the features at the outset of the session.

The notion of slowly growing interface complexity can be extended to the whole EMS environment. Rather than describing all the tools in an EMS toolkit, the users can be started with a single tool, for example, an electronic brainstorming tool. At the outset one tool is their electronic meeting world. At some later point when they would benefit from measuring group consensus, the group could be introduced to electronic voting tools. When they need to weigh their options, they can be introduced to an alternative evaluation tool, and so on. However, their initial entry to the electronic meeting environment can begin with the plainest, simplest interface of a single tool.

NEW CHALLENGES IN GROUP INTERFACES

Until recently, Electronic Meeting Systems primarily supported face-to-face meetings. Now developers are turning their attention to distributed meeting systems in which participants may not be in the same room or may not even be participating at the same time. In such a setting the complexity of the environment cannot always be shunted to a facilitator. The users will have to manage the system for themselves. Distributed users will not be able to turn to the facilitator to request help or request additional features. Thus, distributed users will have to make more of a commitment learning the technology than do the ad hoc users of the face-to-face facilities. One plausible scenario for easing groups into managing complex group support environments for themselves is to have the group begin their EMS work in a face-to-face facility under the guidance of a facilitator. There they can slowly familiarize themselves with the features and functions of the environment. At some point, when the users feel themselves ready, the facilitator can establish distributed sessions for the participants to run from their own offices. A team leader can take over the software management responsibilities that were previously handled by the facilitator.

There is another problem with distributed meetings that cannot be so easily addressed. In a face-to-face meeting the participants can continuously sense the subtle nonverbal cues that indicate when the group is being productive or when it is spinning its wheels. In face-to-face groups the flow of activity moves smoothly from fully electronic to verbal to a comfortable mix, as the dynamics of the situation demand. In distributed sessions all the subtle cues of group dynamics are lost. It will be an ongoing challenge for designers of group interfaces to find some synthetic interface substitute for these cues or to try to extend meeting dynamics into the distributed meeting. There have been several early attempts at re-creating such cues. Some environments have chat boxes that let participants exchange asides as they might in a face-to-face meeting. Some developers are experimenting with hand-shaped cursors that the distributed users can wave and move around on the screen to direct the attention of other users. However, the issue of distributed meeting dynamics remains largely unresolved and as such remains one of the most interesting and challenging problems for interface designers today.

NEW TECHNOLOGIES

Several interface technologies that have been in the laboratory for decades have recently matured to the point that they hold promise for further improvements to group interfaces. Voice-recognition systems are now available with 30,000 to 40,000 word vocabularies. These systems are not yet user independent, which is to say that each user must train the system to recognize his or her own voice. As such, voice recognition would not be of much use to ad hoc users. However, in face-to-face meetings the facilitator might use voice recognition to control the software or to dictate input when the group is working in a chauffeured mode. In distributed settings, with more long-term users, voice recognition simplifies the interface for distributed users and possibly speeds up input for text-intensive tasks such as brainstorming. The effective input rate (after correcting errors in recognition) for the leading commercial voice-recognition system ranges from about 20 words per minute (WPM) for beginners to about 60 WPM for experienced users who have fully trained their systems. For non-typists this may be an appealing alternative to the keyboard.

Pen-based computers also offer the potential to simplify group interfaces. A pen-based computer interface consists of a digitizer, a pen-like stylus, and an output screen. On early pen-based systems the screen. and digitizer were separate components attached to the computer. More recently the digitizer, screen, and computer have been integrated into a single box about the size of a thick tablet of paper. The digitizer senses the presence of the stylus (e.g., by a magnetic field, pressure sensitivity, or a weak radio signal) and reports its location to the computer at any given moment.

Recent studies have demonstrated that users prefer the pen-based interface over the keyboard and mouse for tasks involving pointing and selecting, as when making menu selections, and for fine-motor position control, as with graphics (Briggs et al., 1992). Pen-based interfaces offer several strategies for software control that can produce simpler dialogs than those possible with keyboard-and-mouse interfaces. For instance, an application can be controlled by means of labeled "buttons" that appear on the screen as needed. The user can tap the button with the stylus, and the software can take the appropriate action. The pen-based interface offers a somewhat simpler interaction than the mouse because the user does not have the perceptual load associated with finding the current cursor position and then moving the cursor into position over the button. With a pen-based interface there is no need for a cursor because the user can go directly to any position on the screen with the stylus. Software control can also be accomplished by means of gesture recognition (Wolf & Morrel-Samuels, 1987). For example, the system can be configured so that text may be deleted simply by scratching it out or inserted by drawing a carat mark.

Handwriting recognition has received much play in the academic and trade press (Schlender, 1991; Tappert, Suen, & Wakahara, 1990). However, it has yet to advance to such a state of maturity that users find it to be an acceptable substitute for the keyboard. A reasonable alternative for pen-based character input might be the virtual keyboard. It is possible to display an image of a keyboard on the screen whenever character input is required. The user can tap letters in with the pen (or with the fingers if the screen is touch sensitive), and the virtual keyboard can disappear when it is not needed. Recent empirical studies at the University of Maryland show that users of a touch-sensitive virtual keyboard comfortably achieve input speeds of 10 to 30 WPM, depending on the size of the virtual keyboard (Sears, Revis, Swatski, Critenden, & Shneiderman, 1991). In contrast to handwriting recognition, the virtual keyboard requires little in the way of computer resources, is quite accurate, and places very low cognitive demands on the user.

CONCLUSIONS

The discipline of group interface design is still in its infancy, and much work still must be done to define its boundaries and issues. As group applications become more and more common, developers will continue to face new interface challenges. New design strategies and new technologies will be required to deal with the special constraints imposed by working in a group.

REFERENCES

Briggs, R., Beck, B., Dennis, A., Carmel, E., R. Nunamaker, J., F. & Pfarrer, R. (1992). Is the pen mightier than the keyboard? In *Proceedings of the Twenty-Fifth Hawaii International Conference on Systems Sciences. Vol III: Information Systems.* Los Alamitos, CA: IEEE Computer Society Press.

Huber, G. P. (1984). Issues in the design of group decision support systems. *MIS Quarterly, 8*(3), 195–204.

Nunamaker, J. F., Dennis, A. R., Valacich, J. S., Vogel, D. R., & George, J. F. (1991). Electronic meeting systems to support group work. *Communications of the ACM, 34*(7), 40–61.

Schlender, B. R. (1991). Hot new Pcs that read your writing. *Fortune,* pp. 113–118.

Sears, A., Revis, D., Swatski, J., Critenden, R., & Shneiderman, B. (1991). *Investigating touch-screen typing: The effect of keyboard size on typing speed* (No. CAR-TR-553, CS-TR-2662). College Park: Center for Automated Research, University of Maryland.

Shneiderman, B. (1987). *Designing the user interface: strategies for effective human–computer interaction.* Reading, MA: Addison-Wesley.

Tappert, C.C., Suen, C., & Wakahara, T. (1990). The state of the art in on-line handwriting recognition. *IEEE Transactions on Pattern Analysis and Machine Intelligence, 12*(8), 787–808.

Wolf, C. G., & Morrel-Samuels, P. (1987). The use of hand-drawn gestures for text editing. *International Journal of Man-Machine Studies, 27,* 91–102.

An Evaluation of Icon Performance Based on User Preferences

Julieta K. Yamakawa
IBM—Austin, TX

Nadalyn Miller
Texas A&M University

R. Dale Huchingson
Texas A&M University

INTRODUCTION

The ultimate goal of user-computer interface design is twofold: to provide easy-to-learn dialogues while reducing the user's short-term memory load. Human-computer dialogue designers seem to have found a simple answer for a complex task. Icons save display space, are aesthetically pleasing, reduce typing errors, reduce fear of computer commands, and, most importantly, eem to reduce ambiguity because a picture is worth a thousand words. "Visually rich, easy to understand screen icons are fast replacing empty command lines and esoteric control keys" (Bartimo, 1986, p. 58). Office metaphors such as filing cabinets, garbage cans, folders, and so on are taking over computer screens.

Symbolic signs or logos have been successfully used in many fields. For example, a variety of symbols have been successfully used on road signs. They conserve sign space and are very practical for international use because they do not depend on the use of a verbal language (Mackett-Stout & Dewar, 1981). Huchingson (1981) explains that symbolic signs for highways have been empirically studied, and it was found that they are more quickly detected and comprehended than word messages. Ells and Dewar (1979), in an experiment to measure comprehension of verbal and symbolic traffic sign messages, have found that signs with symbolic messages could be understood more quickly than those with verbal messages.

Although the use of symbols have been proven to be effective in traffic signs, it is not clearly known how well they represent their intended messages in computer systems. For example, most of the existing icons are used together with a descriptive textual label. This may be because the dialogue designers anticipated the difficulty users would have in successfully guessing the objects they represent (Gittins, 1986). Iconic interfaces alone may not be effective. A study (Kacmar, 1988) indicated that a menu constructed of a mixed format (text and graphics) provides the most accurate means of selection. A similar study was conducted to compare the relative utility of pictures, labels, and the combination of both as a navigational aid for computerized catalog browsing (Egido & Patterson, 1988). The results suggested that pictures plus labels yield superior performance compared to other conditions.

Icons are also used as cue enrichment, and it has become fashionable to use text items mixed with geometric aids as recall aids. Landsdale, Simpson, and Stroud (1987) compared the memorability of these cues with key words used in the same way, but little difference was found between the operation of verbally based systems and visually based ones. Although the underlying metaphor tends to be the same across many systems, their graphical styles vary from very simple to very complex renderings. Although some systems may be utilizing improved screen resolution to present these complex renderings, it was found that simplified graphical renderings were more readily understood than more complex, detailed renderings (Hakiel, 1988). In the same study, it was found that graphical style is correlated with message comprehension. Recognition was found to be more effective when concrete renderings were presented instead of more abstract or highly stylized renderings (Hakiel, 1988).

Mackett-Stout and Dewar (1981) conducted a study on public information signs in terms of legibility distance, comprehension, preference, and glance legibility. The author points out that the importance of specific criteria depends on the purpose of the symbol and where it is used; however, comprehension and presence are essential ingredients in the evaluation of symbols.

One of the major problems in the design of user interfaces is that programmers must accommodate a diversity of users ranging from the guru type to the naive beginner. Each of these users approaches the system with a different conceptual model and different expectations on how to user it (Dudley, 1987). Shneiderman (1987) states that one of the problems with graphical interfaces is that users have to learn the meaning of the components. The icon that is meaningful to the designer may require users as much or more learning than a word. Some icons may be misleading because users understand the analogy but make incorrect conclusions about permissible actions. To match the user's conceptual model it is necessary to establish who the users are, what the goals are in performing the tasks, what information they generate, and what methods they employ when performing the task (Smith, Irby, Kimbal, & Verplank, 1982).

OBJECTIVES

Little information exists as to which icons are best for computer functions. Each software manufacturer develops a plausible set that appears to describe the functions, but the icons are not tested against other icons to determine which is functionally superior.

The first objective was to determine if one of the four candidate icons was highly preferred by a sample. This was done for each of 24 functions. The least preferred icon was also noted so that characteristics could be compared.

The second objective of the study was to determine the validity of user preference in predicting icon recognition. In other words, it was to determine if the most preferred icons by one sample were also the ones most readily grasped by another sample. Icon decoding performance would be measured by the trials (guesses) required to learn an icon for a function.

The third objective was to attempt to abstract from the findings certain general strategies for developing icons. These would include features to use and features to avoid.

METHODOLOGY

Part A

A paper-and-pencil preference survey consisted of a five-page booklet. Each page presented five computer operations and four icons as selection choices per operation. Subjects were also given a blank space in which to draw their own icon in case they did not like any of the ones shown. The survey was administered in a classroom at Texas A&M University. The icons presented are shown in Table 4.1.

Macintosh icons were intentionally left out of the paper-and-pencil survey, and therefore out of Part B of this experiment, because of their widespread familiarity among available subjects. Including these icons may have biased the results, so they were not used.

Subjects.

Forty-two students at a major southwestern university who were familiar with mainframes, IBM, and Macintosh participated in this portion of the study.

Experimental design.

Each subject was presented with the set of 96 icons. A Latin Square research design was used to balance any sequencing effect.

Data analysis.

The number of times an icon was selected as most or least preferred for an operation was tallied. The total number of times that icon was selected for either most or least preferred was converted into a percentage by calculating the ratio of selection frequency over the total number of participants. When two icons for a particular operation fell within five percentage points of each other, they were both included in Part B of the study.

Part B

The second part of this study consisted of presenting the most preferred and least preferred icons to a new set of subjects. The rationale was that those icons identified as "most preferred" would be decoded with fewer mistakes than the "least preferred" icons. Also, given one trial of training with feedback of the correct description, the "most preferred" icons should be grasped more quickly than the "least preferred" ones. Also, given one trial of training with feedback of the correct description, the "most preferred" icons should be grasped more quickly than the "least preferred" ones on the second trial. A total of 51 icons were used. (These icons can be found in Table 4.1.)

The icons were presented on a Macintosh computer (Mac Plus), using a prototype built with Hypercard. One icon and 12 computer operations were presented per screen. Eight of the computer operations used on each screen were extracted from the set of computer operations used in this study, and four were "dummy" operations. Subjects were told to match a computer operation to a given icon. There was only one correct answer per screen. Feedback, via a pop-up window displayed for three quarters of a second, was provided every time a selection was made. If the wrong icon was selected, an error message appeared. Subjects had to keep choosing until the correct match was found. Once the appropriate selection was made, the correct answer message appeared, and the next screen was presented. On the second trial (the next day), subjects were to recall the correct task description from the first trial.

Subjects.

A total of 28 students familiar with MS-DOS, mainframes, and the Macintosh environment participated in this portion of the study.

Experimental design.

The sequence of computer screens was varied among subjects to balance any sequencing effect. The location of the correct answer and the location of the selection choices (computer operations) were also varied for each of the screens. For example, if "Save File" appeared in the upper-left corner as a choice for one icon, it would be in a different position the next time it appeared as a selection.

Data analysis.

The independent variables were the two sets of icons, the most preferred and the least preferred set. The dependent variables were error rates for the first trial and for a second trial (conducted the day after the first trial). The data were analyzed in terms of the average number of guesses required to correctly decode an icon. An analysis of variance was performed for both of the dependent variables to determine if significant differences at a 95% confidence internal existed between the icon sets being studied. The statistical package SAS was used to perform an analysis of variance.

RESULTS AND DISCUSSION

Table 4.1 presents each of the 96 icons studied. The 24 functions or computerations the icons were designed to indicate are given in the first column. The second column lists in rank order of agreement the most preferred of the four icons and, in the next column, the least preferred of the four icons. The last two columns show other candidate icons.

The value obtained in Part A represents the percentage of the sample who selected the icon as the best or worst depicter of the operation and is in the upper-left corner of each cell. When within parentheses, this value represents the worst depictor of the operation. Otherwise, it represents the best depictor. The value at the bottom of each cell represents the mean number of guesses required in Part B of the study for the new sample to correctly decode the icon. To illustrate, the Mail icon represented by an envelope with a document partially out of it was preferred as best by 78%, whereas the other 3 were preferred by 22%. The mean number of guesses to decode it was 1.107. Similarly, the truck that was presented as a letter with wheels was least preferred by 46%. This was the largest percentage when asked which icon they disliked most for the Mail icon. The other three Mail icons were selected as least descriptive of Mail by 54%. The mean number of guesses to decode the truck icon was 1.286.

Note that for 18 of the 24 operations, the least preferred icon was guessed in substantially fewer trials than the least preferred icon. For three functions (Clipboard, Clock, and Graphic Tablet), there was little difference in guesses. For three other operations (Spreadsheet, Message, and Remove) the least preferred icon was guesses in fewer trials.

Several icons presented considerable difficulty in learning in Part B. Those requiring three or more guesses are in need of further study or redesign because the relationship between the icon and the operation is not clear. There were a few instances in which the most or least preferred icons were within 5% of one another for a given operation. When there was no clear-cut choice, both icons were included in Part B of the study. Drawing Tool, Display, and Message were the only ones noted.

Rendering style seemed to play a strong role in object recognition and therefore in influencing subjects in preference selection. As can be seen in Table 4.2, users showed preferences for certain types of icons such as three-dimensional representations with many details and shadings.

Table 4.1. Icon Preferences*

	MOST PREFERRED	LEAST PREFERRED	OTHER	
CLIPBOARD TEMPORARY BUFFER TO STORE CONTENTS OF FILE	91 3.536	(49) 3.536		
REPEAT TO PERFORM THE ACTION REPEATEDLY ASSOCIATED WITH A KEYSTROKE	84 Repeat 1.071	(52) 1.714		R
SCROLL CONTROL TYPE THE ARROW FOR DISPLAY MOVEMENT	79 1.000	(62) 4.643		
MAIL LETS YOU ORGANIZE YOUR MAIL	78 1.107	(46) 1.286		
DRAWING TOOL AN ELECTRONIC TOOL THAT ALLOWS YOU TO DRAW AN OBJECT	70 1.285	(48) 1.536	(45) 1.571	
COPY DUPLICATES A MARKED OBJECT	69 1.241	(93) 3.241		
MAIL OUT SENDS MAIL TO OTHER COMPUTERS	67 1.357	(46) 2.536		
HARD DISK	67 5.250	(46) 9.393		

---

* Special thanks to Hayes Saxon of Texas A&M's Computer Services Center for his suggestions about this table.

Table 4.1. continued

	MOST PREFERRED	LEAST PREFERRED	OTHER	
SPREADSHEET DOCUMENT	66 5.714	(48) 4.178		
WASTEBIN A BUFFER STORAGE AREA READY FOR DISPOSAL	66 1.465	(70) 2.857		
FOLDER ALSO DIRECTORY— CONTAINS OTHER DOCUMENTS	62 3.821	(76) 6.714		
ERASE ERASE PART OF DRAWING	58 1.036	(41) 4.393		
CALENDAR MAY KEEP APPOINTMENT OR JUST DATE	52 1.444	(69) 5.286		
MAIL IN YOU RECEIVED MAIL	51 1.285	(53) 2.464		
A TEXT DOCUMENT	50 1.071	(35) 1.714		
PRINTER AN OBJECT GENERATING A PRINTED REPRESENTATION OF AN OBJECT	50 1.428	(58) 5.286		
MESSAGE SENT BY A COMPUTER TO AN OPERATOR/OR HUMAN TO HUMAN COMMUNICATIONS	48 5.786	(33) 3.464	4.286	

Table 4.1. continued

	MOST PREFERRED	LEAST PREFERRED	OTHER	
PROCESSING THE CURSOR TELLS YOU THAT THE COMPUTER IS PROCESSING AN ACTION	45 2.036	(60) 5.602		
DISPLAY A COMPUTER CRT	45 1.750	42 1.143	(85) 4.357	
DISK DRIVE PROVIDES ACCESS TO DISK DRIVE MANAGEMENT	45 2.500	(73) 9.071		
CLOCK TELLS YOU THE TIME	43 1.000	(57) 1.036		
REMOVE REMOVE THE MARKED OBJECT	42 3.643	(36) 1.679		
GRAPHICS DOCUMENT GENERATES GRAPHICS	37 1.429	(51) 1.500		
USER PROFILE STORES SETTINGS FOR DOCUMENTS, FOLDERS, AND KEYBOARDS	36 3.571	(45) 4.667		

ERROR RATES

The first objective of Part B of the study was to determine the error rate for each icon associated with the most preferred and the least preferred sets. Subjects whose best performance with the icons were considered best in the preference survey. Error rate data suggest that icons in the most preferred set presented fewer errors than icons in the least preferred set. These data were gathered during the first trial in Part B. A pairwise comparison of means was used to analyze the data. The overall results are presented in Table 4.2, which gives the means, standard error, and p-values of the number of guesses. The most preferred set of icons required 1.55 fewer guesses than the least preferred set.

Lowest Error Rates.

The 13 icons with lowest error rates (first quartile) were represented by excellent renderings of concrete objects. The metaphors adopted for most of these icons were found in our daily lives. For example, the icon used for Mail was not a mail tray found in offices, but a mailbox found in cities (see Table 4.1).

Highest Error Rates.

Of the 13 icons with the highest error rates (fourth quartile), only 3 icons were from the most preferred set. Some of the task descriptions in the lower quartile required subjects to have some familiarity with computer tasks or hardware. For example, many subjects have never seen a hard disk or a disk drive and obviously could not recognize its graphic representation. Poor graphic representation seemed to be one of the causes of low performances. Some icons depicted generic objects but with very poor and stylized renderings (see Display, Calendar, and Directory icons in the least preferred set in Table 4.1).

A second objective of this part of the experiment was to determine the validity of user preference in order to assure that user preference was a good indicator of performance. To assess whether the most preferred set from Part A of the experiment presented fewer errors than the least preferred set, a split plot statistical model was used to evaluate the error rates for each set of icons (most and least preferred). The results for the dependent variables' error data (mean number of guesses) indicated that there was a significant difference at the 0.013 level for error rate. The error rate data for the first trial, with their associated means are presented here. Table 4.3 presents the split plot ANOVA for the dependent variable, error rate, or mean number of guesses.

Table 4.3 presents the mean number of guesses averaged on both trials (Day 1 and Day 2), the standard error, and the level of significance.

The least preferred set presented a higher average number of guesses than the most preferred set, indicating that preference is a good predictor of performance. A Spearman rank correlation was performed between each icon's preference rank percentile in Part A and the mean number of guesses in Part B to see if preference is a good predictor of performance in selecting the correct task description. A coefficient of 0.5 (mean number of guesses) was found, indicating that icons showing high fre-

TABLE 4.2. Error Rates—First Trial

ICON SET	TRIAL MEAN	STD ERR MEAN	SIG LEVEL
LEAST PREF	3.783	0.094	0.0001
MOST PREF	2.237	0.094	0.0001

Table 4.3. Error Rate ANOVA Results

SOURCE	DF	SS	F	Pr > F
Subject	27	1294.06	7.65	0.0001
Set	1	960.13	6.62	*0.0000
Icon(set)	47	6819.48	23.16	0.0001
Day	1	471.43	75.26	0.0001
Set*Day	1	99.80	15.93	0.0001

TABLE 4.4. Error Rates—Both Trials

ICON SET	TRIAL MEAN	STD ERR MEAN	SIG LEVEL
LEAST PREF	3.189	0.322	0.0133
MOST PREF	2.018	0.322	0.0133

quency of preference required fewer guesses to match an icon to the correct task description.

One learning trial resulted in improvement for both sets of icons, but it did not bring the two sets to the same level. The icons with fewer errors were from the most preferred group, as would be expected. A comparison of Tables 4.2 and 4.4 shows that the preferred set dropped from 2.2 to 2.0 mean guesses, whereas the least preferred set dropped from 3.8 to 3.2 mean guesses. The least preferred set showed a greater improvement but still required more guesses than the most preferred set.

Preference and Performance: An Evaluation of Factors

Factor 1: Graphic Style.

One essential factor in icon decoding is the recognition of the icon as being a certain object. Rendering style seemed to play a strong role in object recognition and therefore in influencing subjects in preference selection. Subjects showed a preference for the more elaborate, three-dimensional renderings. Figure 4.1 shows examples of two- and three-dimensional icons. Of those shown, the three-dimensional icons B, D, and F were consistently preferred and showed superior performance.

INCOMING MAIL   OUTGOING MAIL   CALENDAR

Figure 4.1. Examples of Two-dimensional and Three-dimensional Icons.

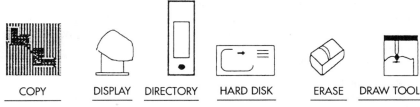

| COPY | DISPLAY | DIRECTORY | HARD DISK | ERASE | DRAW TOOL |

Figure 4.2. Icons with Stylized Renderings.

| PRINTER | | DRAWING TOOL |

Figure 4.3. Icons Depicting Computer-Specific and Generic Objects.

DISK DRIVE   PROCESSING

Figure 4.4. Icons With Unusual Metaphors.

Comprehension of the intended message was harder when icons were poorly rendered. The icons in Figure 4.2 were rated very frequently as least preferred and showed poor performance.

Factor 2: Metaphor.

Another factor in icon preference was the use of familiar objects as metaphors. When presented with icons depicting generic objects and those depicting computer specific objects, subjects preferred the generic. For example, Printer A in Figure 4.3 requires the user to know the exact appearance of that specific printer, whereas Icon B displays a generalized printer familiar to most users. Similarly, Drawing Tools C and D illustrate an icon that is computer specific and one that is familiar to anyone who has used paper and pencil. The familiar icons were preferred in Part A and showed higher performance in Part B than the system-specific ones.

Factor 3: Agreement of Metaphor and Command or Operation.

Another important factor for preference may be the agreement of the metaphor with the command or operation represented. For example, the file drawer was not perceived as analogous to a disk drive. In terms of least preferred, the Disk Drive icon in Figure 4.4 was rated by 76% of the subjects as the poorest representation. The bee was not perceived as analogous to processing and was also rated as least preferred. In each case, recognition of the object may have been simple, but the underlying metaphor was not. These icons also showed poor performance during interactive icon decoding (Part B of this study).

Factor 5: Analogy.

Subjects showed a high preference for icons that did not require the interpretation of an analogy. Clipboard A, shown in Figure 4.5, was rated very highly as most preferred (90.80%). The reason for this high rating may be that users did not have to refer to an underlying analogy to decode the message. Clipboard is a name used by some computer systems to describe a temporary buffer used to store the contents of a file. The word *clipboard* was mentioned in the questionnaire, and subjects selected the object that best depicted the name of the operation.

Message decoding was difficult when obscure analogies were used, and such icons were rated as least preferred. For example, Clipboard B (Figure 4.5) was depicted as a pushpin, and subjects could not associate the analogy with the corresponding task. To understand the analogy, subjects needed to be aware of all the steps involved in the task. Pushpins are used to hold temporary messages on bulletin boards, which is analogous to the buffer. Clipboard, most preferred, showed a high percentage of preference but presented low performance. The discrepancy in preference and performance is probably due to the fact that the word *clipboard* was not used on the screen in Part B of this study, and users did not associate the description of the operation with the word *clipboard*.

Factor 6: Object Discrimination.

A factor that seems to have aided subjects in selecting icons is object discrimination (Figure 4.6). Four of the icons presented for Clock were depicted as follows: a

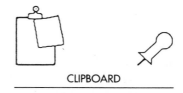

CLIPBOARD

Figure 4.5.   Familiar versus Obscure Analogies.

CLOCK   MAIL

Figure 4.6.   Easily Discriminated Icons (B, F).

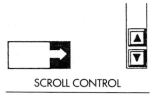

SCROLL CONTROL

Figure 4.7. Icons for Scroll Control

cuckoo clock, a digital watch, an analog wall clock, and an old-fashioned alarm clock. Each clock was well rendered, but the wall clock with numbers (B) was rated as most preferred, whereas the cuckoo clock (C) was rated as least preferred. Clock B can be discriminated faster than the other clocks because it presents clearly and in detail the face of an analog clock. All the other renderings require more time to be discriminated as clocks because they show other distracting details, such as the pendulum and the house shape of the cuckoo clock.

Another example is Mail. Mail E which is very similar to icon F was selected as least preferred. Icon E added humor to the icon, using the envelope as the trailer of a truck. This may actually be a distracting factor in discrimination.

Factor 7: Universality.

Similarity of an icon to those used in other systems seems to have influenced subjects' preferences. Most of the icons used for Scroll Control include arrows in the representation. Icon B, selected as the most preferred with 79.09%, uses a very elegant three-dimensional representation of arrows similar to the icons used by other manufacturers. Icon A was selected as least preferred by 61.90% of the subjects. It is interesting to note that Scroll Control B showed no errors.

Design Guidelines

Within the constraints of this study, the characteristics of icons presenting high performance were subjectively analyzed by the authors, and the following is recommended for icon design. These concepts are illustrated in previous figures and represent the authors' opinions.

Guideline 1: Use associative icons with concrete generic objects and well-rendered, familiar items.

Guideline 2: Use easy-to-depict, familiar objects to represent computer tasks.

Guideline 3: Icons can be very effective when a symbol is used universally across many systems.

Guideline 4: Use action to depict an abstract computer task such as copy and erase (see Figure 4.8).

COPY   ERASE

Figure 4.8.   Icons Depicting Abstract Tasks.

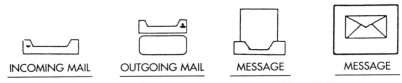

INCOMING MAIL   OUTGOING MAIL   MESSAGE   MESSAGE

Figure 4.9.   Icons using Similar Objects to Depict Different Tasks.

Guideline 5:   Avoid the use of obscure metaphors that require users to have an in-depth knowledge of computer operations to detect the analogy.

Guideline 6:   Avoid the use of mnemonic icons because they are not meaningful for first-time users. (Mnemonic icons simple depict an object having the same name as the computer operation such as Clipboard.)

Guideline 7:   Use objects that are well rendered and not stylized.

Guideline 8:   Avoid the use of computer- or system-specific objects as icons.

Guideline 9:   Avoid the use of similar objects to depict different tasks (see Figure 4.9).

CONCLUSION

In conclusion, the data suggest that user preferences play an important role in the design of icons. The two sets of icons determined by user preferences produced significant differences in performance. A Spearman rank correlation was performed between each icon's preference rank percentile in Part A and the mean number of guesses in Part B to see if preference is a good predictor of performance in selecting the correct task description. We conclude that preference required fewer guesses to match an icon to the correct task description. We conclude that preference is an excellent predictor of comprehension.

A careful inspection of the guesses recorded for the operations on Table 4.1 shows that 18 of the 24 functions had significantly fewer guesses for the preferred versus the least preferred icons. Three had no difference between the mean guesses for the least preferred icon and the most preferred. In three of the operations, the least preferred had fewer guesses. An icon that requires more than three guesses on the average is not recommended; a more effective icon must be designed.

The effectiveness of icon decoding may be attributed largely to rendering style. Icon preferences need to be further researched to collect valuable information that can be used to aid computer-screen designers in building successful user-computer interfaces.

RECOMMENDATIONS FOR FURTHER RESEARCH

A list of possible experiments and/or research questions follows in the form of questions that should be addressed:

1. Can users learn an iconic interface faster than a menu-driven interface with the exact same application?
2. Which, if any, of the iconic characteristics (analogies, metaphors, and graphic styles) are understandable across cultures?
3. Do icons with three-dimensional rendering of icons provide more cues than two-dimensional renderings in a paired-comparison research design?
4. Is learning improvement affected by changing the time elapsed between exposures?
5. Can a classification scheme for iconization of computer operations be determined through experimentation?
6. What interaction effect is there between icons, manipulation technique, and text?
7. Is there a combination of icons, manipulation technique, and text that performs best for learning and understanding across all tasks and applications?

REFERENCES

Bartimo, J. (1986). The new human interface comes of age. *Personal Computing, 10*, 58–65.

Dudley, T. (1987). Report generation using a visual program interface. In *Proceedings of the Second International Federation for Information Processing Conference on Human-Computer Interaction INTERACT '87* (pp. 521–528). Berlin: Elsevier Scientific.

Egido, C., & Patterson, J. (1988). Pictures and category labels as navigational aids for catalog browsing. In *Proceedings of the CHI '88 Conference* (pp. 127–132). Washington, DC: ACM Special Interest Group on Computer Human Interaction.

Ells, J.G., & Dewar, R.E. (1979). Rapid comprehension of verbal and symbolic traffic sign messages, *Human Factors, 21,* 161–169.

Gittins, D. (1986). Icon-based human computer interaction. *International Journal of Man-Machine Studies, 24,* 519–543.

Hakiel, S.R. (1988). *Issues in the design of icons.* Roke Manor, Romsey, Hants, England: Plessey Research Roke Manor, Ltd.

Huchingson, R.D. (1981). *New horizons in human factors.* New York: McGraw-Hill.

Kacmar, C. (1988). *An experimental comparison of text and icon menu item formats.* Unpublished dissertation, Texas A&M University, College Station, TX.

Landsdale, M., Simpson, M., & Stroud, T. (1987). Comparing words and icons as cue enrichers in an information retrieval task. In *Proceedings of the Second International Federation for Information Processing Conference on Human-Computer Interaction INTERACT '87* (pp. 911–916). Berlin: Elsevier Science.

Mackett-Stout, J. & Dewar, R. (1981). *Designing the user interface: Strategies for effective human-computer interaction.* Menlo Park, CA: Addison-Wesley.

Shneiderman, B. (1987). *Designing the user interface: Strategies for effective human computer interaction.* Menlo Park, CA: Addison-Wesley.

Smith, D.C., Irby, C., Kimbal, R., & Verplank, B. (1982). Designing the star user interface. *BYTE, 7,* 242–282.

Part II

Information Presentation

Design Implications of Children's Successes and Failures in Information Retrieval: A Case Analysis

Paul Solomon
University of North Carolina at Chapel Hill

INTRODUCTION

Information systems are often designed for the prototypical user. This design decision rests on an implicit assumption that individual differences can be ignored in favor of some central tendency model of information system user behavior. In contradiction to this assumption, people approach information systems with various states of knowledge, skill, and ability. Some users may be novices, never having experienced the system before. Others may be experts, having been motivated to discover and learn most of the system's features and capabilities. Most users, however, are somewhere in between. They learn enough to make do (Carroll & Rosson, 1987). They forget; they relearn; they learn anew. Thus, the dynamics of people's use of information systems alone create a need for adaptive, intelligent information systems (Solomon, 1992).

Information system designers have an opportunity to move beyond a prototypical approach to software design to develop intelligent information systems that instruct, guide, diagnose, or advise in response to breakdown situations. To produce such intelligence in information systems, designers need to appreciate the range and variation of user behavior. To design information systems that can adapt and guide people with a wide range of knowledge, skills, and abilities toward success, designers need to understand the diversity of demands likely to confront an information system—the terminology that users employ and the control actions they take.

Understanding of the factors that lead to success and failure in the use of information systems is fundamental to the design of intelligent and adaptive systems. Current structured approaches to information system design offer real benefits for the programming task but seem to emphasize design for prototypical users. Thus, techniques that identify factors of success and failure in support of user-based design need to be refined or developed and tested.

Reported here is a research effort designed to test techniques for appreciating the range and variation of user successes and failures and to use that appreciation to move toward information system intelligence and adaptability. The research example is a case study of children's use of an information system designed for adults—an online public access catalog (OPAC)—to identify and select materials in a school library media center (SLMC) (Solomon, 1991, 1993). Thus, the methods, research findings, and their implications for information system design were focused on a system in operation and not a new design.

CHILDREN AND AN OPAC

The OPAC

Online public access catalogs are employed to locate materials in library collections. Fundamental to OPACs are databases containing information about the materials in the library collection. These databases contain an abundance of data, minimally including author, title, and subject entries. Author and title entries are determinate attributes of materials. Subject entries are more perplexing. First, databases supporting OPACs contain standard subject entries drawn from an index language, in this case Library of Congress Subject Headings (LCSH). The content and structure of the index language govern the subject terms that can be assigned to items. Second, an indexer or cataloguer assigns subject terms that try to match the major subjects of an item with those available in the index language. Indexers interpret the items being evaluated and then must interpret the LCSH schedule. Third, users, often unknowingly, have to translate their expressions of subject interest into the subject terms assigned by catalogers from the index language. Users must select subject terms and hope that they match those in the database. This standard of subject indexing leaves the information retrieval task vulnerable in several respects: (a) the index language may be incomplete or out of date, (b) indexers may not consistently apply the index language, or (c) users may apply their own natural language and not the specific descriptors of the index language.

Also fundamental to OPACs are the retrieval mechanisms in operation (in this case keyword match using Boolean operators and b-trees) and the interfaces that allow users to apply the retrieval mechanisms to the databases. For the OPAC under study, the initial interface is simple and straightforward: three selection blocks for subject, title, and author entries.

The Users

The knowledge, skills, and abilities of users are potentially influenced in many ways. A key potential influence for children as users is that their stage of cognitive development may influence adoption of search strategies (Kuhlthau, 1988). For instance, first graders might be able to view an information need from only one point of view at a time; older children might be able to shift to alternate views (e.g., recognizing that if a term does not work for a subject search, it may work in a title search). Furthermore, the constrained character of the human information processing system (e.g., the limited nature of the sensory channels for noting information stimuli) might affect children's abilities to use an OPAC (Siegler, 1986). Children who are learning to use an information system might be unable to shift to alternate search strategies (e.g., subject to title shift) because their mental resources are focused on learning the basic flow of the software.

The status of children's knowledge in subject areas especially as reflected in their vocabularies and the character of their concepts and categories may limit or enhance their abilities to use an OPAC (Brown, 1990). First graders who are experts on dinosaurs or trains are able to readily come up with alternate terms; sixth graders who have been assigned a topic that they have little knowledge of (e.g., Greek gods) have little basis for proposing alternative terms. The character of mental models or procedural models of information system operation may transfer to OPAC use (Singley & Anderson, 1989). Experiences with Nintendo, a computer in the classroom or at home, or some manual activity may give rise to expectations about how other systems work that may help or hinder a child employing an OPAC. Finally, communicative competence and conversational style may influence ability to communicate with a computer-based information system (McTear, 1985). For instance, children may have difficulty assuming the telegraphic style of the subject term required in the OPAC.

Methodology

If a user is to gain access to pertinent materials in a bibliographic (or other) database, the supporting information system must either anticipate the variety of terms employed by users or present its users with tools for comprehending the variety of terms present in the database. Also, the next query to be encountered by an information system is uncertain and, therefore, unpredictable. Use of an OPAC, as other information systems, is complex and at times subtle (Bates, 1986). It is by understanding these factors of variety, uncertainty, and complexity that intelligence can begin to be built into information systems. In turn, to understand the variety, uncertainty, and complexity that underlie human use of information systems, there is a need to emphasize the full richness of natural settings of information system use and not limit it initially by employing an artificial or laboratory setting. Thus, a case study of children's natural use of an OPAC was selected to test these ideas for gaining the understanding necessary to begin to add intelligence to an OPAC.

Part and parcel of the case study approach is the use of multiple methods for understanding the rich interactions of social (and by extension) technological systems (Goetz & LeCompte, 1984). Methods employed in this research included observation, interviews, collection of protocols, and document analysis. In the course of the research, methods often became integrated. For instance, interviews became central to the observations. The initial strategy for data collection was to emphasize observations to gain a baseline of data. The idea was to compare these baseline data with data collected in later stages of the research, when the researcher was more involved in the OPAC transaction, through questioning about actions taken or not taken by children.

In this research, within minutes of starting observations the researcher was involved. Children in a school are encouraged to ask for help when something does not seem quite correct to them. They quickly made full use of the new resource available to them (the researcher at the OPAC). Thus, the researcher was forced into understanding the OPAC transaction, the character of children's information needs, the nature of children's actions at the OPAC, and their rationale for taking control actions at the OPAC. This requirement of interaction of the observer with the user in order to observe had the remarkable benefit of frequently providing answers to questions without having to ask them.

As the research progressed the need for asking children about their action or inaction increased. Yet, it was found that special interviews with children were problematic. Although questioning a child during an OPAC session was accepted, later follow-ups were either seen as an invasion of privacy or greeted by memory loss. Thus, it was necessary to ask questions while the information was fresh in the child's mind and the observer's role was an interested partner not interrogator.

Essential to the case study process is the joint development of a record of observations, interviews, protocols, and documentation and analysis of that record. The basic record included handwritten notes made during the course of observation or interviews and recordings of conversations between or among children and the observer. To minimize the effect of decay of memory and confusion among observation sessions, this basic record was transcribed and then expanded with observer comments, interpretations, and analysis before another observation session took place. This transcription process made use of a computer-based text management system named askSam (askSam Systems, 1991). Expansion of the basic record was for the purpose of pointing out emerging patterns of behavior, as well as for suggesting the need for new or varied questioning approaches during subsequent observations or questions for the media specialist, reading teacher, or classroom teacher.

A fundamental technique for data analysis was the development of a categorization scheme for use in coding the expanded record and other data to facilitate retrieval and analysis (Tesch, 1990). Although preliminary codes were constructed prior to the beginning of the research, codes representing, for instance, strategies, sources of breakdowns, and user intentions were not physically added to the textbase until after an initial period when the coding structure was refined to conform with children's actual patterns of behavior at the OPAC. At the end of the research all coding assignments were reviewed by the researcher and finally by independent reviewers. Codes were used to sort the text base as well as retrieve related information from the text base.

Summary of Research Findings

Two major interests in the analysis of children using an OPAC were understanding the characteristics of success and failure. These two different sides of the same coin give complementary perspectives for design: Fix the broken, but not at the expense of what works.

Success

Success was viewed from the child's eyes as the production of a satisfactory list of materials in the library collection. Success is achieved when a child sits down at the OPAC, enters a term or terms, perhaps through several moves, and receives a list of materials. Fifty-eight percent of the observed transactions were of this sort. There were two other situations of success: the instances in which children knew they were in trouble and sought adult assistance and in which two or more children worked cooperatively to solve an OPAC problem. Both of these situations (adult and cooperative assistance) were viewed as successes when the children involved completed their OPAC transaction satisfactorily. The success rate reached 66% (of the 857 OPAC transactions observed) with the addition of these two contributors.

The next question was what aspects of children's action at the OPAC resulted in success. The assistance strategies already mentioned (adult and cooperative) were one source. They accounted for about 8% of the observed OPAC transactions. Two other sources were the use of common terms (41%) and OPAC control strategies (17%). The common term success factor refers to children's use of terms that were also LCSH. Most of these common terms reflect the fact that children's interests in animals, sports, and the like result in their use of simple concrete terms that are also LCSH (e.g., cats, dogs, horses, baseball). That is, the match between children's search terms and LCSH is high for concrete concepts (e.g., dogs) and low for more abstract concepts having synonyms and closely related terms (e.g., weapons). Terms selected as descriptors for these abstract complex concepts often do not correspond to general usage (e.g., arms and armor for weapons). Given that children's interests and the curricular demands in an elementary school result in a circumscribed set of search terms, tools for identifying and applying alternate terms need to be built into the OPAC software to allow local specification and adaptation of terminological needs.

Strategies refer to the variety of controlling actions that children took to overcome initially unsatisfactory OPAC retrieval. These children succeeded because they realized that their previous move was unsuccessful and that they needed to take some follow-up action to try to recover. The control actions that children took ranged from shifts in focus (e.g., subject to title, title to subject), to shifts in search-term relations (e.g., broader, narrower, or related terms), to the use of system features (e.g., truncation, instructions), among others.

The understanding of children's natural strategies for information retrieval at the OPAC provided by this research suggests ways that an OPAC or other information system for children could be designed to intelligently respond to search failures. For instance, a shift from a subject search to a title search for a term such as *weapons* satisfied children's search requirements because the term *weapons* is not an LCSH, but it was included in the titles of some number of items. When the subject search term employed in an initial move fails, an OPAC for children could be designed to automatically test the possibility of retrieval given a focus shift to title. If the focus shift did lead to retrieval, the alternative set of items would be offered to the child. If the shift did not lead to retrieval, additional alternate strategies could be either tried by the information system or offered to children for their consideration and possible action.

Breakdowns

Thirty-four percent of the transactions ended in breakdown. In thinking about how children control the OPAC, especially dynamically over the period of a school year, it became apparent that there was movement or development in children's capabilities. First graders and others who were new to the OPAC initially had a great deal of difficulty with basic skills including reading, spelling, keyboarding, and a sense of the steps required to make the OPAC work. This incapacity was short-lived. Children were able to proceed beyond the level of a novice to make the system work for them in most situations. A few children reached the level of OPAC expert and fully understood not only OPAC operational strategies but the conditional nuances of their usage. As evidence of their expertise, these experts were able to help others solve their OPAC problems.

As children approach an OPAC independently for the first time, they bring the sets of skills, rules, and knowledge that they have been taught or discovered on their own. Children's experience, including any orienting activities, helps them form expectations about what tasks an OPAC supports, what actions are required to operate the OPAC, and what functions an OPAC performs. Children use these mental resources to take action; the result is another experience that may reinforce expectations, cause expectations to be revised, give rise to new ones, or have no apparent influence.

This insight of dynamic change, coupled with the specific situations of breakdown or failure in OPAC use, led to the further understanding of what children were developing in terms of OPAC capability. On one level there were fundamental skills (locating letters on the keyboard) that moved from being a time-consuming diversion from the rest of the OPAC task to automatic activities that children no longer needed to think about. This is the skill level. Next there was the development of a sensitivity to the conditional requirements of the OPAC. For instance, use of a plural search term usually results in greater retrieval than use of a singular term because LCSH are generally plural (e.g. fishes). This is the *rule level*. Finally, there was the ability to transfer knowledge from one setting to action at the OPAC. The use of analogy or metaphor to come up with alternative search terms is one example. This is the *knowledge level*.

Fundamental Skills

Initially children make errors in spelling or key entry, forget the next key to press, forget where they are in searching, and so on. A curious thing happens, however: they quickly begin to automate the basic sensory and motor skills required to operate the OPAC. This skill development and automation became evident even in first graders. Children who had completed a hands-on orientation provided to first graders were able to return later in the day and perform searches not yet in an automatic way but by "playing back" the script of their earlier, supported sessions. This playback behavior was evident in their conversations with classmates, in their talking to themselves, and in their verbal protocols.

By the following week many of these first graders could race through the procedural aspects of their searches, seemingly without thought. The hands-on experience seemed to provide the basis for rapid skill development, whereas the demonstration approach used with older children who had experienced the OPAC in the previous school year had less of an impact possibly because some of the older children were not motivated to listen or attend.

It also became apparent in observing the behavior of older children, particularly in the patterns of their breakdowns over time, that automation at the skill level had also taken place but at what seemed a somewhat slower rate. The keyboard, which was a major challenge for most children at the beginning of the school year, became only a minor hindrance by the end of the year. Although children at all grade levels had not become 10-finger typists, they did not need to spend minutes looking for individual letters on the keyboard but had developed a sense of where the individual letters were located. Also, the frequency of procedural errors, such as not recalling the key to press to enter a search request (ENTER) or to obtain a document summary (F4), greatly diminished over the school year.

In summary, breakdowns at the fundamental skill level were categorized into three divisions: OPAC system skill, Reading skill, Spelling/Keyboarding skills. Together these skill-level sources of breakdown accounted for about 50% of the breakdowns. Design amelioration of breakdowns at the skill level offers a substantial source of improvement in children's OPAC success. A tutor, other learning aids, and system response to action or inaction would reduce breakdowns due to a lack of system skills. A voice synthesis feature would help overcome breakdowns due to reading inadequacies. A spell checker or the entry of search terms through a touch screen or "point and shoot" interface option would remove spelling/keyboarding as a source of breakdown and offer the potential of a 14% improvement in the OPAC success rate by itself.

Procedural Rules (Conditions)

Beyond the skill level of control, children need to acquire rules to mediate their operation of the OPAC. These rules pertain to a variety of situations, including the insertion of spaces in query statements and the use of plural words as search terms. To acquire rules children must either be informed or notice a pattern in the process of attending to errors. When rules are not understood, breakdown occurs. In this research situation, breakdowns resulted from a lack of knowledge or misapplication of knowledge of rules of syntax (no space after a search term or set of terms, no more than one space between search terms, and no punctuation in search statements), query term form (use the plural form of nouns, do not use the interrogative form), and search focus (evaluate focus of search: subject, title, author).

Rules provide another level of user control over action at the OPAC. Rules may not be subject to automation by children because often they represent cues and associations that require variable input depending on the situation. That is, they provide mechanisms for choice and recovery during an OPAC search session. Rules that were commonly acquired by children as part of their OPAC experiences included:

1. Plural search terms work better than singular ones
2. If you get a TERM(S) NOT FOUND message, check the spelling of the search term
3. If you get a QUERY ERROR message, check for extra spaces between words or a space or spaces at the beginning or end of the query
4. If use of a given subject search term does not result in retrieval, try a synonym
5. If a subject search term does not work, try the term in a title search.

Understanding these rules is basic to supplementing the OPAC interface with suggestions for follow-up user actions or intelligent prompting of user action.

In summary, breakdowns at the rule level were of the following types: syntax, query form, and focus. Overall breakdowns at the rule level accounted for about 32% of the breakdowns. Many of the breakdowns generated at the rule level can be avoided by design changes. For instance, syntax problems can be easily eliminated by modifying the software to ignore punctuation and extra spaces in parsing or evaluating the query. This simple programming modification would result in a 3% improvement in the overall success rate. Query form problems could be mitigated by a display of word forms in use (e.g., an alphabetic list of spelling variants) when use of an initial search term results in no retrieval. Focus breakdowns could be reduced by automatic testing of a failed query in one focus (e.g., subject) against the others (author and title).

Knowledge-Based Interactions

Children use their experiences and the knowledge they gain from them to enable action in new or different situations. When children were introduced to the OPAC, or even later when they encountered breakdowns in OPAC use, they were presented with the opportunity to use this knowledge and experience base to suggest actions. Some children walked away from the opportunity, others followed an incorrect hunch, and others moved correctly. The latter two cases presented an occasion for learning that led to establishing skills or discerning rules.

Ultimately, success at the OPAC rests on the application of knowledge about the world: experience in determining controlling actions (strategies), understanding of facts and relationships among entities (organization of knowledge), and understanding of the conditions in which controlling actions and knowledge come together (knowing when the application of a strategy in a particular knowledge domain is appropriate). These knowledge-based interactions are problematic because of the considerable differences in people's experiences, knowledge, and abilities to apply knowledge and experience. Three types of breakdown that fall in this realm involve the interaction of conditional, processing, and declarative knowledge.

With the lack of *conditional* knowledge breakdown, children entered a search term that retrieved nothing, very few idiosyncratic items that were retrieved because the search term happened to be part of a multiword term (e.g., fish is part of the LCSH tropical fish, the LCSH in use was fishes), or irrelevant items because the term entered is a homonym of the real information interest (e.g., Wales for whales). In each case the children who suffered this kind of breakdown took the result as truth and moved on. In each case they had no sense that further controlling action was needed or possible, let alone desirable.

Breakdowns of the first type, in which nothing is retrieved, offer a signal that could be exploited in information system design efforts. At a minimum, alternate term strategies could be suggested. The identification of frequently used search terms that are not LCSH suggests the need for local tools in the OPAC to allow the construction of appropriate mappings between children's search terms and LCSH in use. The second type of mismatch, serendipitous retrieval, is difficult to overcome electronically. If term relations were built into the database, children could be offered the opportunity to view and select alternate subject search terms. A similar mechanism could apply in the third type of breakdown, incorrect homonyms, if the homonym relations were encoded in the database.

Some children who knew that they needed to take some action were unable to produce actions or strategies to recover either from their use of words as search terms that were not LCSH or from their use of words that were too general or too specific. Although they had developed mental models of sufficient detail to succeed with queries using search terms that matched LCSH, they lacked a scheme for moving beyond a breakdown. They had neither rules nor insights to move them forward. They had not acquired the necessary *processing* knowledge by training, induction, or transfer from other experiences.

The question for information system designers is how support could be built into the system either to encourage users to consider processing alternatives or to have the system provide better error recovery. At a minimum, an information system could offer some strategy hints: If the retrieval set is large, a narrower term or qualifying term approach could be suggested. If the retrieval set is small or nonexistent, related term or broader term approaches could be offered.

Some children understand that there are actions that overcome breakdowns. Still, these children do not have the *content* knowledge to generate follow-up moves. That is, although they might have a sense that procedures exist (e.g., follow up a failed initial move with another term), they do not have the knowledge required to make the procedure work.

The character of the knowledge requirement varies considerably and reflects the varying interests and demands of children of different ages and grades. For instance, a first grader entered A B C as her subject search term. Her query failed because A B C is not a LCSH. The child tried to think of another word but could not produce an alternate word like the subject heading in use: *alphabet*. At the other extreme, a sixth grader entered *Spartan* as her subject search term, followed by *Spartans*, followed by *Athens*. Given her state of knowledge, she could not generate a broader LCSH that would have given her information about Sparta (i.e., *Grecian History*).

Information system support in this situation is more problematic and potentially more costly than in any other encountered because it would have to be independently developed. Use of a machine-readable version of LCSH would result in much extraneous information. A focus on the curriculum and children's interests would suggest the need for authoring aides to develop information access tools.

Conditional, processing, and content knowledge breakdowns account for some 45% of all breakdowns observed during children's OPAC sessions. To overcome these breakdowns, children need help in evaluating queries, learning and using strategies, and identifying and using appropriate subject headings. Substantial improvement here depends on the availability of knowledge tools ranging from those appropriate to a particular setting (e.g., airplanes or black history) or potentially enhanced or supplementary databases (e.g., a thesaurus to cue the user to options and alternatives). A major point here is that analysis of these breakdowns maps the kinds of knowledge required.

Table 5.1 summarizes this discussion of the skill, rule, and knowledge breakdowns observed in children's use of an online public access catalog for information retrieval. This framework and examples of breakdown within the framework help focus design attention on key requirements for use of an OPAC.

Dynamics of Children's OPAC Behavior

Two points need to be made in closing the discussion of control of action at skill, rule, and knowledge levels. First, there is interaction among the three levels. Skill-based behavior at the OPAC has slots at which rules or knowledge and reasoning may be called into play. The three levels of action ultimately work together to enable children to succeed or fail at the OPAC.

Second, what is knowledge-based action during initiation of OPAC use may shift

Table 5.1. Summary of Breakdowns in OPAC Use

	User Requirements	Occurrence	Design Implications
Skills			
System	Sense of system purpose, scope, and products.	Mostly first grade with some in second, third and fifth. Conflict: Keystrokes conflict with software in computer lab.	Provide learning aids (e.g., tutor), context-sensitive help (user initiated), and system response to action or inaction.
Reading	Ability to read basic words.	First graders for titles; all grades for at least some document summaries.	User selected voice synthesis.
Spelling/Keyboarding	Ability to locate keys, accurately press keys, spell, and review term entry.	Most prevalent source of breakdown; found at all grades.	Spell checker, possible entry of terms through "point and shoot" interface.
Rules			
Syntax	Knowledge of form requirements: Avoid space at end of query, more than one space within query or punctuation.	All grades. Conflict: Use of punctuation is emphasized in classroom, but causes breakdown at the OPAC.	Ignore punctuation and extra spaces in "parsing" a query.
Query Form	Well-formed queries (e.g., use nouns, and plural form).	All grades, but more frequent in upper grades and less in second.	Display of word forms in use. Ignore terms not in use.
Focus	Evaluate focus of query: subject, title, or author.	All grades, but occurrence low in first and fourth.	Follow failed subject query with test on author and title.
Knowledge			
Conditional	Understand the need to monitor OPAC response and take action.	Starts low in first grade and increases. Most prevalent following spelling.	Displays of subject headings in use and local authoring tools for term relations.
Processing	Understand that follow-up action is the user's responsibility.	Low in lower grades to high in upper grades.	Offer strategy opportunities.
Content	Content knowledge within the subject domain of interest.	Uniform across all grades; character varies with grade.	Information access tools tailored to the curriculum and children' interests.

eventually to the rule or skill level. When children started to use the OPAC, they had to struggle and think about every step. Soon much of this action became automated at the skill level and children were able to focus mental resources on other aspects of the search problem.

DISCUSSION

It is remarkable to see even the smallest of first graders achieve some success in information retrieval despite an information system that makes no particular accommodation for children. This achievement takes time, and the observed children had moments of both success and failure as they used the OPAC. Even those few children who came to understand the subtleties of information retrieval using the OPAC (e.g., the index functions of subject headings and call numbers) suffered breakdowns on occasion. In fact, their skill and expertise seemed to cause them to fail at times because they had so completely automated some OPAC operations that they sometimes neglected to perform the detailed steps of the information retrieval process.

Thus, the information system support needs of individual users vary over time. An individual may begin as a novice, reach some intermediate level of competence, or even become an expert. For some information retrieval tasks, the children succeeded easily. For others, they struggled or failed. Understanding changes in the information retrieval behavior of individual children over time gives a designer one view of the conditions that an information system must operate under.

Another view is provided by analysis of other patterns of behavior. Particularly evident in this research was the variation in strategy use and forms of breakdown across grade levels (one through six). For instance, breakdowns due to system skills and reading skills were most prevalent among first graders. Spelling and keyboarding breakdowns were widespread in all grades. Query-form breakdowns tended to occur more frequently at the higher grades. These grade-level patterns of breakdown give a designer another view of the variety of demands likely to be put on the information system. Patterns of term use and information needs give a designer other perspectives on information system requirements. Simple, concrete terms need only minimal design attention, whereas complex, abstract terms provide real design challenges that might be handled most quickly and economically by providing authoring tools to allow local option. Together the several views give designers of information retrieval systems information needed to combat the problems of variety, uncertainty, and complexity endemic to OPACs and other information retrieval systems.

CONCLUSION

It has been the intent of this presentation of a case study of children's use of an online public access catalog to demonstrate the potential links between methods for investigating information systems in operational settings, the need for understanding the range and variation of user behavior as applied to information systems, the factors underlying success and failure in information system use, and the development of information systems that can intelligently and adaptively respond to user problems or breakdowns. Gathering information about range and variation or success and failure in either operating or projected information systems is a time-consuming, labor-intensive task. However, such an approach offers insights into user needs and task requirements that may not otherwise be obtainable.

There is evidence in this research that children learn some basic sets of features that are required to use the information system and ignore others that are not self-evident or required. Thus, there is little point in adding features without likelihood of their use. The critical challenge, then, is to design tools and mechanisms into an information system so that they are naturally applied as appropriate and do not themselves become sources of breakdown. The design opportunity is to use what is known about user successes and failures to develop robust information systems that do not simply say "TERM(S) NOT FOUND" or "QUERY ERROR" but offer guidance toward success.

In this context care must be taken to maintain those aspects of the existing system or situation (for a projected system) that make the information system work for the user, while attempting to overcome factors that lead to breakdown or system failure. At the same time, the idea that a single, inflexible, and unresponsive information system can meet the needs of its users is one that we need to move beyond. If we systematically listen to our users and appreciate the information-seeking situations in which they participate, we can make this move and develop information systems that empower their users.

REFERENCES

askSam Systems. (1991). *askSam* [Computer program]. Perry, FL: askSam Systems.

Bates, M.J. (1986). Subject access in online catalogs: A design model. *Journal of the American Society for Information Science, 37*(6), 357–376.

Brown, A.L. (1990). Domain specific principles affect learning and transfer in children. *Cognitive Science, 14*(1), 107–133.

Carroll, J.M., & Rosson, M.B. (1987). Paradox of the active user. In J.M. Carroll (Ed.), *Interfacing thought: Cognitive aspects of human-computer interaction* (pp. 80–111). Cambridge, MA: MIT Press.

Goetz, J.P., & LeCompte, M.D. (1984). *Ethnography and qualitative design in educational research.* Orlando: Academic Press.

Kuhlthau, C.C. (1988). Meeting the information needs of children and young adults: Basing library media programs on developmental states. *Journal of Youth Services in Libraries, 1*(1), 51–57.

McTear, M. (1985). Breakdown and repair in naturally occurring conversation and human-computer dialogue. In G.N. Gilbert & C. Heath (Eds.), *Social action and artificial intelligence* (pp. 104–123). Hants, UK: Gower.

Siegler, R.S. (1986). *Children's thinking.* Englewood Cliffs, NJ: Prentice-Hall.

Singley, M.K., & Anderson, J.R. (1989). *The transfer of cognitive skill.* Cambridge, MA: Harvard University Press.

Solomon, P. (1991). *Information systems for children: Explorations in information access and interface usability for an online catalog in an elementary school library* (Doctoral Dissertation, University of Maryland, 1991). (University Microfilms No. 91-33166).

Solomon, P. (1992). On the dynamics of information system use. *Proceedings of the 55th Annual Meeting of the American Society for Information Science, 29,* 162–170.

Solomon, P. (1993). Children's information retrieval behavior: A case analysis of an OPAC. *Journal of the American Society for Information Science, 44*(5), 245–264.

Tesch, R. (1990). *Qualitative research: Analysis types and software tools.* Philadelphia: Falmer Press.

Assessing the Value of Information in a Decision Support System Context: A Simulation Study

Ahmer S. Karim
University of San Diego

INTRODUCTION

Information value is not uniquely defined but instead depends on the type of decision supported by the information (Ahituv & Neumann, 1986). As information systems are primarily developed to support decisions, it is imperative that designers review what is known about human decision-making processes before designing computer-based decision aids. This chapter presents a simulation study to explore the value of information for decision makers in a decision support system (DSS) environment. The research is developed from the premise that designers of computer-based decision aids can directly or indirectly influence the value of these systems by paying careful considerations to *what information* is captured in these systems, the *level and detail* of the information provided, its *intrinsic value* to the decision maker, and its *impact* on the decision making environment.

Research has shown that decision makers are involved in a cost/benefit tradeoff while making decisions (Payne, 1982). The benefits may include the probability of making a correct decision, the speed of making the decision, and its justifiability. Similarly, costs might include the resources utilized in acquiring information or the resources spent in processing information (e.g., decision time or cognitive effort). Information systems can be designed to help balance the cost/benefit tradeoff under situations, for example, when decisions have to be made under a less than perfect information environment, whereby all the relevant information is not present (partial information completeness) as it may be inaccessible or too costly, and when these situations are presented to the decision maker under different information load (overload) situations. By understanding how performance is affected, powerful computer-based decision aids can be designed to guide or restrict the decision making process in order to make effective and efficient decisions.

This chapter presents a simulation study to evaluate the benefits of increased levels of information completeness on the performance, based on an effort/accuracy tradeoff, of a hypothetical decision maker and the resulting implications for designing effective computer-based decision aids. Accuracy and effort have been regarded as common means for measuring effectiveness and efficiency while selecting among information strategies (Beach & Mitchell, 1978; Johnson, 1979; Johnson & Payne, 1985). Typically, *decision accuracy* has been defined in terms of maximization of expected value (EV) or the degree of improvement in EV over a random choice, whereas *effort* has been defined as a function of the total/average decision time or total/average number of cognitive operations.

Information load or information quantity will be measured by the number of alternatives, the number of attributes, and the number of distinction levels for the attributes in a particular task. As the number of alternatives, attributes, and/or number of levels increase, the level of information load increases. Similarly, information completeness will be measured by the number of rank-ordered information dimensions presented in a given task from the finite set of all possible relevant rank-ordered information dimensions for that task. If set A consists of n possible relevant information dimensions rank-ordered from the most to least important, then the information completeness factor will be gauged by determining how many information dimensions (from $1 \ldots n$ possible dimensions) are included in the particular task. The value of information, therefore, can be gauged by the decision makers' attempt to maximize expected value while minimizing cognitive effort under task situations in which the level of information provided is controlled.

By focusing on the relationship between effort/accuracy and information completeness, designers and researchers involved with computer-based decision aids will be able to develop a better understanding of the information processes involved through these systems. The findings, for example, can enable designers to take measures to save valuable resources that go into acquiring, storing, and processing information. This, in turn, can directly or indirectly influence the value of these systems for the decision makers.

This chapter is divided into two major sections. The first part presents a survey of decision making and information processing literature, the implications of utilizing simulation methodology in decision making research, and the impact of the value of information on the decision making process. The last section focuses on the proposed study, provides a detailed description of the simulation methodology, and presents the findings of the study.

SURVEY OF LITERATURE

Compensatory and Noncompensatory Models

In order to facilitate the decision making task, decision makers utilize various strategies, decision rules, and/or heuristics. The two major types of strategies described in the decision making literature are compensatory and noncompensatory models. A compensatory strategy uses all the available information related to the decision task, with the advantages of one dimension being traded against the advantages of another dimension (Klayman, 1982). Noncompensatory models, on the contrary, are indicated by the interactive use of informational cues in which a low score on one dimension is not compensated for by a high score on another (Billings & Marcus, 1983). Noncompensatory strategies involve the use of simplifying rules to reduce the complexity of the decision problem.

Measures of Efficiency and Effectiveness

Accuracy and effort have been regarded as common means for measuring effectiveness and efficiency while selecting among information strategies (Johnson & Payne, 1985). Typically, *decision accuracy* has been defined in terms of maximization of expected value (EV) or the degree of improvement in EV over a random choice. Similarly, *effort* has been defined as a function of the cognitive resources utilized to complete a given task. Total/average decision time or total/average number of cognitive operations are typical measures of effort. Johnson and Payne (1985) measured effort by gauging components of basic cognitive operations, called elementary information processes (EIPs), utilized under different decision strategies.

Process Tracing Approaches

Information search strategies and decision making studies have utilized several techniques for studying the decision making process. Process tracing looks at what information was utilized and the order in which it was utilized to form a judgment. The two major types of process tracing techniques are verbal protocol analysis and information boards. Verbal protocol analysis requires the decision maker to think aloud while actually making decisions, whereas information boards require participants to explicitly search information about available alternatives and usually require a choice among available alternatives. Evaluation of a subject's pattern of information search can provide valuable insights toward discriminating among alternative models of decision making. Information search studies have utilized information boards or verbal protocol analysis, and these experiments have involved both human subjects and computer simulation programs.

Simulation Studies in Decision Making Research

Simulation experiments have been utilized in various studies in decision making research. Kleinmuntz and Schkade's (1990) study, for example, proposed a theory-based approach for research on information displays in computer-supported decision making. In their work the authors point out that simulation allows a variety of decision strategies to be investigated over many variations in task features and requires the researcher to specify the task features and decision strategies in great detail, which can help to uncover hidden assumptions and gaps in knowledge (Kleinmuntz & Schkade, 1990). Similarly, Klayman (1982) used computer simulation to investigate how decision makers modify their strategies in response to task complexity. The study found that simulations can be very useful in generating, testing, and modifying hypotheses about human decision strategies and can also be a source of hypotheses about how decision behavior is likely to be affected by changes in task characteristics. Simulation experiments can be a powerful mechanism for looking at decision making behavior and understanding the information processes involved in different environments.

Decision Making and the Value of Information

In the decision making and information system context, the value of information can be considered from several different perspectives. Information value is not uniquely defined but depends on the type of decision supported by the information (Ahituv & Neuman, 1986). Ahituv and Neumann (1986) define the value of information from three perspectives: normative, realistic, and subjective. The normative value is calculated for highly structured situations in which all the factors are known and quantifiable; the realistic value of information is derived from measuring actual performance achieved under different information sets; finally, subjective value results from individuals' subjective assessment of various information alternatives. How decision makers perceive the value of information can significantly affect the impact information systems have on an organizational setting. Uecker, Schepanski, and Shin (1985) suggest that individuals may perceive the value of information as positive, even when it is not. As designers of computer-based decision aids it is important to measure the value of information relative to the decision making process before it is incorporated in the system.

SIMULATION STUDY

This chapter presents a simulation study to evaluate the performance of a hypothetical decision maker as the degree of information completeness is varied with a information search strategy and two different levels of evaluation measures. The results will provide valuable insights toward designing effective and efficient computer-based decision aids. In order to effectively address this problem, it is important to understand the different components of the simulation model, how the performance of the decision maker will be measured, and how the results will be evaluated and analyzed. The following sections concentrate on these components.

Decision Task Characteristics

This study focuses on multicriteria decisions in which all the relevant information will be known or can be obtained for each decision task (deterministic), and in which each alternative can be evaluated individually and the alternative set can be rank-ordered according to these evaluations (enumerated). In addition, the mutual preferential independence condition will be satisfied. In terms of task size, task situations that have been utilized in previous studies and that have been found to be cognitively demanding for the decision makers (Johnson & Payne, 1985; Klayman, 1982; Payne, 1982) will be utilized. Based on this criteria, a 6 x 6 task size was selected.

In terms of the number of levels, once again the emphasis was on levels that would be cognitively demanding for the decision maker. Due to an absence of research on information load or task complexity as a function of the number of levels, the following two levels were selected: two-level, and continuous. The two-level and continuous scales were selected to represent extreme points for the number of distinction levels. Finally, another important issue that needed to be considered was whether to allow dominance to exist among the feasible alternative set. With varying levels of information completeness, adding or removing attributes could result in dominance surfacing or disappearing from the alternative set. In order to avoid such inconsistencies and to limit the confounding effect on the analysis, this model will allow dominance to exist.

Decision Strategies

This study utilizes the elimination by aspect strategy. In this study, the elimination by aspect strategy was selected for several reasons. First, among the different strategies, elimination by aspectis a widely used strategy in performing decision tasks. Second, this study incorporates a strategy based on a more satisficing approach (noncompensatory).

Information Completeness

As a majority of decision making occurs in a less than perfect information environment, decision makers are routinely making decisions with only a subset of all the available information. This phenomenon may be attributed to a cost/benefit tradeoff with which a decision maker is routinely involved. Decision makers have to weigh the benefits of making a correct decision, the speed of making the decision, and its justifiability against the cost of information acquisition and expenditure of time and cognitive effort (Payne, 1982). The cost/benefit analysis is heavily dependent on the individual decision maker and the specific domain. Hence, for a given decision task, the decision maker may have access to all or a majority of relevant information dimensions (high degree of information completeness) or only a few of the relevant information dimensions (low degree of information completeness). For the purpose of this study, the level of information completeness will be designated by m:n. As an example, suppose there are 10 possible relevant information dimensions (set A= a1....a10), and all the relevant dimensions are completely rank-ordered (a1 > a2 >... a10). Then a completeness level of 2:10 implies that the task is utilizing the top 2 out of the 10 information dimension for that particular task.

MEASURES OF ACCURACY AND EFFORT

In this proposed study, the dependent variables are the effectiveness (accuracy) and efficiency (effort) measures of performance. The dependent variables are evaluated by two measures of effort (computational and executive) and two measures of accuracy (relative optimal, and relative random). Based on the flow diagram for the strategy (see Appendix A1), the overall effort can be broken down into two categories: computational processes (Check, Calculate, Store, Recall, Scan, and Count operations), and executive processes (Next, Branch, and Loop operations). By breaking basic cognitive operations into components, called Elementary Information Processes (EIPs), the total expenditure of effort can easily be measured in a simulation study. For example, in applying the additive strategy, each time a decision maker CHECKs a value, STOREs a sum, or CALCULATEs a value, and so on, the program will automatically increment a computational processes variable. Similarly, each time an appropriate NEXT item is selected, or a BRANCHing takes place, based on the outcome of a decision, an executive processes variable is likewise incremented. By systematically capturing each of the elementary information processes, an assessment of the total cognitive operations can be made by following the normative model of the strategy.

In order to measure effectiveness, two different performance measures are utilized. These measures gauge performance relative to the optimal choice and a random choice. The performance measures are similar to the one utilized by Johnson and Payne (1985). The primary difference is that these measures emphasize practical gain.

$$\text{Relative Optimal Performance} = \frac{\text{Voptimal choice - Vstrategy choice}}{\text{Voptimal choice}}$$

$$\text{Relative Random Performance} = \frac{\text{Vstrategy choice - Evrandom choice}}{\text{Evrandom choice}}$$

where:

V = $\neg$ wi vi(xi)

xi = evaluation attributes (x1, x2, ... xn)

wi = weight associated with attribute xi

$vi(xi)$ = value of attribute x for a given alternative based on the attribute scale

EV = $\neg$ Vi / m

V_i =   value of the alternative $(1 \dots m)$
m =   total number of alternatives in the alternative set

Relative Optimal is bounded with a value of +1.00 (worst) and 0.00 (best).

Relative Random is bounded with a value of +M (more is better) and -1.00 (worst), where +M represents a very large positive number.

The benchmark of optimal and random have important implications, especially from an IS/DSS design perspective. Effectiveness of decisions are commonly measured in terms of the optimal (emphasizing an exhaustive approach). Findings of this study not only emphasize the tradeoff in terms of the added effort needed to reach this goal but also the deterioration from the optimal as a different subset of information completeness is provided. The ultimate goal of computer-based decision aids should be to enable the decision maker to reach this optimal. The closer the system can take the decision maker to the optimal (without sacrificing too much efficiency), the more effective it will be. Similarly, the random benchmark highlights an approach whereby alternatives may be selected without any type of analysis. A computer-based decision aid is not of much use if it cannot at least perform better than an alternative selected randomly, without any evaluation.

ANALYSIS OF RESULTS

In this study, the analysis focues on the following two components while utilizing the elimination by aspects strategy: (a) two matrix task sizes—$6 \times 6 \times 2$ and $6 \times 6 \times$ Con; and (b) information completeness factors (constituting an exhaustive set)—6:6, 5:6, 4:6, 3:6, 2:6, 1:6. For each combination (e.g., elimination by aspects strategy with 6 alternative, 6 attribute, continuous scale with 4 out of the 6 attributes), 5,000 randomly generated problems, utilizing uniform distribution, are generated using the same random seed. By utilizing the same random seed, variance among the simulation runs can be reduced. Johnson and Payne's (1985) work, which utilized 200 trials for 36 treatments, found that while the large number of trials ensures stable estimates, it also provides overwhelming statistical significance for many effects.

There are 12 different combinations from these components, which are divided into Table 6.1 and 6.2. Table 6.1 highlights the first 6 cases of discrete (two-level) values in a 6x6 decision task, whereas Table 6.2 exemplifies the other 6 cases of continuous values in a 6x6 task. The division of the results into two tables, with 6 cases each, is based on how the task matrices and their associated values are generated. Because the evaluation measures are the key components in determining the range of values allowed for the task, the division of the 12 possible combinations into 6 cases each ensures that the same matrix is applied for the different information search strategy + information completeness level combinations. It should be noted, however, that the random seed, which has a 16-bit cycle, ensures that the possibility of the same matrix being repeated over the 5,000 runs is substantially reduced. Before looking at the data in the two tables, it is important to note some common features across the tables. These common attributes can greatly facilitate the readability and interpretation of the data provided in the tables.

Tables 6.1 and 6.2 represent a specific task; for example, Table 6.1 contains the data from 6×6 tasks with binary (two-levels) evaluation measures. In addition, each table presents the elimination by aspects strategy along with the exhaustive set of levels of information completeness (this information is captured in the first column of the tables). The abbreviation EBA designates elimination by aspects strategy. The m:n notation is used for the levels of information completeness. As an example, EBA_4:6 specifies a decision maker employing an elimination by aspects strategy with the top four attributes from the set of six possible attributes in the task. The second and third columns capture the two cognitive effort measures utilized in this study—computational and executive. These are designated with the abbreviations COMP_EFFORT and EXEC_EFFORT. All the values posted under this column are averaged over the 5,000 runs. The fourth column, TOT_EFFORT, sums the computational and executive cognitive effort values from the second and third columns. The fifth and sixth columns capture the two accuracy measures (REL_OPTIMAL is the percentage of deterioration of the choice selected relative to the optimal choice, and REL_RANDOM is the percentage of improvement of the choice selected relative to a choice selected at random). Once again, these choices are averaged over the 5,000 runs.

The weights for the different attributes are presented at the bottom of each table. The notation WT #1.....WT #n is used to designate the weights for the 1..n attributes in a decision task. The attribute weights are rank-ordered from highest to lowest. The weights follow a linear distribution with a very small slope. The small slope, as mentioned earlier, ensures that all the attributes have significance to the task and reduces the possibility of only a single attribute analysis occurring in the decision making process. Hence, the difference between the highest weight and the lowest weight is very small (.0016666 for the two 6×6 cases).

Finally, in addition to the attribute weights, each table also presents three types of information that can provide important insights about the magnitude of differences within the elimination by aspects strategy and information level combinations. These are the overall improvement or deterioration, based on 5,000 runs, among the three benchmarks: optimal choice, random choice, and worst choice. If we look at these benchmarks on a continuum scale, the following type of information can help improve our interpretation and understanding of the results: (a) what is the percentage of deterioration in the decision when moving from an optimal to a random decision, (b) what is the percentage of deterioration in the decision when moving from an optimal to a worst decision, and (c) what is the percentage of deterioration in the decision when moving from a random to worst decision. These measures are designated with the notations OPT-TO-RAND, OPT-TO-WORST, and RAND-TO-WORST, respectively, and are presented at the bottom of the table. The following section highlights some of the important findings in terms of the relationship between effort/accuracy and information completeness.

In looking at the data from the elimination by aspects strategy with two levels, the first thing that should be pointed out is that the cutoff criteria in order for the alternative to pass on a particular attribute was set at 1 (pass) and 0 (signifies that the alternative failed on that attribute and is eliminated from the feasible set). Moreover, another important point that needs to be considered before looking at the data is the percentage of improvement or deterioration among the benchmark points of optimal, random, and worst choice. For this scenario (Table 6.1 only), the percentage of deterioration in the decision when moving from an optimal to random decision is 32.2% (OPT-TO-RAND), the percentage of deterioration in the decision when moving from an optimal to worst decision is 63.8% (OPT-TO-WORST), and the percentage of deterioration in the decision when moving from a random to worst decision is 47.5% (RAND-TO-WORST).

In utilizing the elimination by aspects strategy, when only one attribute was provided, it resulted in only approximately 23% deterioration in decision from the optimal choice and about 14% improvement in decision over an alternative selected at random. Moreover, providing all the attributes while utilizing this strategy resulted in only about 11% deterioration in decision over the optimal and approximately 33% improvement in the relative random performance.

Another important aspect that needs to be considered in terms of the cognitive effort measures (computational and executive) is the effect on the measures as the number of attributes is increased. In the computational effort case, going from one attribute to two adds approximately 12 units, two attributes to three about 5 units, and three attributes to four adds only 2 units. The increase with additional attributes is marginal, incrementing four attributes to five attributes adds only .40 of a unit and five attributes to six only contributes about .06 of a unit. The same phenomenon is duplicated in the execu-

Table 6.1. 6 × 6 Task Size—Discrete Scale (2 Levels)
5,000 Runs—Weights Linearly Distributed (Small Shops)

	COMP_ EFFORT	EXEC_ EFFORT	TOT_ EFFORT	REL_ OPTIMAL	REL_ RANDOM
EBA_6:6	41.03	36.81	77.84	0.1120	0.3329
EBA_5:6	40.97	37.70	77.67	0.1112	0.3341
EBA_4:6	40.57	36.18	76.75	0.1159	0.3268
EBA_3:6	38.97	34.42	73.39	0.1240	0.3137
EBA_2:6	33.87	29.79	64.66	0.1566	0.2640
EBA_1:6	22.06	19.80	41.86	0.2322	0.1424

WEIGHTS:
WT#1 = 0.1674999, WT#2 = 0.1671666, WT#3 = 0.1668333, WT#4 = 0.166500, WT#5 = 0.1661667, and
WT#6 = 0.1658333 TOTAL = 0.9999998

OPT-TO-RAND: 33.2%
OPT-TO-WORST: 63.8%
RAND-TO-WORST: 47.5%

**Table 6.2. 6 × 6 Task Size—Continuous Scale
5,000 Runs—Weights Linearly Distributed (Small Shops)**

	COMP_ EFFORT	EXEC_ EFFORT	TOT_ EFFORT	REL_ OPTIMAL	REL_ RANDOM
EBA_6:6	41.33	37.02	78.35	0.1120	0.3329
EBA_5:6	41.20	36.85	78.05	0.1112	0.3341
EBA_4:6	40.67	36.24	76.91	0.1159	0.3268
EBA_3:6	38.91	34.38	73.29	0.1240	0.3137
EBA_2:6	33.76	29.70	63.46	0.1566	0.2640
EBA_1:6	22.01	19.78	41.79	0.2322	0.1424

WEIGHTS:
WT#1 = 0.1674999, WT#2 = 0.1671666, WT#3 = 0.1668333, WT#4 = 0.166500, WT#5 = 0.1661667, and WT#6 = 0.1658333
TOTAL = 0.9999998

OPT-TO-RAND: 22.60%
OPT-TO-WORST: 45.50%
RAND-TO-WORST: 30.20%

tive effort measure, adding the first two attributes results in 10 and 5 units increase, respectively. Additional attributes, once again, provide only a marginal increase in effort.

This behavior becomes more interesting and less unusual as the effect at the different levels are analyzed in terms of the accuracy measures. A 22 unit increase in total effort, going from one attribute to two, provides approximately 7% improvement in relative optimal performance and about 12% improvement in relative random performance. Another 10 units of cognitive effort, going from two attributes to three, provides about 4% and 5% improvement in relative optimal and relative random performances, respectively. Once again, with marginal increase in effort as the number of attributes increase, the effect on the relative optimal and relative random performances is trivial. These performances even deteriorate slightly as we move from five attributes to six. These results overwhelmingly emphasize the unique characteristic of utilizing the elimination by aspects strategy with different levels of information completeness. The data show that even though the decision maker may have access to more information, the nature of the strategy, under the given environment, allows the decision maker to select an alternative by analyzing, in most cases, three attributes or less. There seems to be very limited evaluation taking place, as is apparent from the effort and accuracy measures, beyond the first three attributes. There is a very obvious threshold level emerging while utilizing the elimination by aspects strategy, which suggests that added information, beyond a certain level, may provide only a marginal improvement, no improvement, or may even worsen the decision.

The primary difference between Table 6.1 and 6.2 is the number of levels for the evaluation measures. Table 6.1 used a two-level (binary) evaluation measure, Table 6.2, on the contrary, presents the other extreme—findings based on a continuous evaluation measure for the decision task. As was the case with the first table, the findings are presented first within and then across strategies. Before considering the data, it is important to once again emphasize some of the statistics about the percentage of improvement or deterioration among the benchmark points of optimal, random, and worst choice. In Table 6.2, the percentage of deterioration in the decision when moving from an optimal to random decision is 22.6% (OPT-TO-RAND), the percentage of deterioration in the decision when moving from an optimal to worst decision is 45.5% (OPT-TO-WORST), and the percentage of deterioration in the decision when moving from a random to worst decision is 30.20% (RAND-TO-WORST). Notice that there is anywhere from a 10% to 20% difference in these numbers from the previous scenario (Table 6.1) with two levels. It is very important to account for these differences while comparing the two tables.

Before looking at the data from the elimination by aspects strategy with continuous levels, the cutoff criteria in order for the alternative to pass on a particular attribute needs to be considered. In the continuous case, in which an interval between 0 and 1 was utilized to generate the values, the cutoff was set at 0.50. Values that are equal or greater to 0.50 passed, and values less than 0.50 failed; the alternative was eliminated from the feasible set.

When the elimination by aspects strategy was utilized with only one attribute, the deterioration from the optimal choice was approximately 17%, and the improvement in decision over an alternative selected at random was around 8%. Moreover, providing all the attributes while utilizing this strategy resulted in only about 10% deterioration in decision over the optimal and approximately 17% improvement in the relative random performance. In terms of the amount of cognitive effort utilized in applying this strategy with different levels of information completeness, several important characteristics are highlighted. Interestingly, the cognitive effort expended in utilizing the elimination by aspects strategy with continuous levels for the evaluation measure (Table 6.2) is almost the same as the effort expended with two-levels for the evaluation measure in the same strategy (Table 6.1).

Another important aspect that needs to be considered, in terms of the cognitive effort measures (computational and executive), is the effect on the measures as the number of attributes is increased. In the computational effort case, going from one attribute to two adds approximately 10 units, two attributes to three about 5 units, and three attributes to four adds about 2 units. The increase with additional attributes is marginal, incrementing four attributes to five adds only .61 of a unit and five attributes to six only contributes about .17 of a unit. The same phenomenon is duplicated in the executive effort measure, adding the first two attributes results in 12 and 6 units increase, respectively. Additional attributes, once again, provide only a marginal increase in effort. These findings are almost identical with the two-level case (Table 6.1).

This behavior, once again, becomes more interesting and less unusual as the effect at the different levels are analyzed in terms of the accuracy measures. A 22 unit increase in total effort, going from one attribute to two, provides approximately 4% improvement in relative optimal performance and about 5% improvement in relative random performance. Another 10 units of cognitive effort, going from two attributes to three, provides about 2% and 2.5% improvement in relative optimal and relative random performances, respectively. Once again, with marginal increase in effort as the number of attributes increase, the effect on the relative optimal and relative random performances is trivial. These results once again emphasize the unique characteristic of utilizing the elimination by aspects strategy with different levels of information completeness. The data show that even though the decision maker may have access to more information, the nature of the strategy, under the given environment, allows the decision maker to select an alternative by analyzing, in most cases, less than four attributes. Here again, as found in Table 6.1, there seems to be very limited evaluation taking place beyond the first three attributes. There is a very obvious threshold level emerging while utilizing the elimination by aspects strategy. Adding information beyond this level provides only a marginal improvement in the decision.

DISCUSSION

This chapter presented a simulation study to explore the concept of the value of information for decision makers in a DSS context. The value of information was based on the performance of a hypothetical decision maker, involved in an effort/accuracy trade-off, under different task situations. The evaluation of the two phases will enable researchers to gain some general insights on this relationship and to formulate specific hypotheses for further research. Some of these general issues, mentioned earlier, follow:

- What constitutes the set of all relevant information attributes for a particular task?
- Can a subset of relevant information attributes provide the same value as a complete set?
- What criteria should we employ to include or exclude a particular information attribute?
- What is the marginal benefit of including additional attributes on the decision maker's performance?
- Can we take measures to save valuable resources that go into acquiring, storing, and processing information?
- What is the value of the information for decision makers under different strategies and its impact on the decision making environment?

A general understanding of the effort/accuracy and information completeness relationship provides the stepping stone for developing specific hypotheses from an information system perspective.

Consider a situation, for example, in which decision makers in an organization utilize a computer-based decision aid to perform several decision tasks in a particular domain (e.g., accounting, finance, or marketing). Moreover, these tasks may be repeated on a daily, weekly, or monthly basis over a year. The tradeoff between the amount of effort expended and accuracy desired, and its relationship with information completeness, can be very valuable from the design perspective. For example, due to the nature of a task and its overall relevance in the decision making environment, decision makers may have to derive an approximate assessment of the amount of effort and level of accuracy that should be needed in performing that task (from a practical perspective, this would be a very realistic scenario as decision makers may be constrained by time and resources or company policies and objectives). Under this scenario, it would be very important from the design perspective to know whether we can determine, for example, the level of information completeness needed under different strategies and task sizes to achieve the desired effort/accuracy balance.

Moreover, under similar conditions, as presented earlier, decision makers may be forced to work with specific levels of information completeness (due to acquisition costs or cognitive constraints). Under this context, it would be important to find out whether there is a best strategy suited for the level of accuracy and effort desired by the decision maker. Furthermore, decision makers working under different information completeness environments may be attaining the desired level of accuracy with the complete set as well as a subset of information; whereby the marginal benefit of utilizing additional attributes is only contributing to an increase in effort, and the effect on the level of accuracy is marginal or nonexistent.

As researchers and designers of computer-based decision aids, we have to be careful in assuming that the introduction of a computer-based system in a decision making environment would result in positive value for the decision makers. Careful consideration has to be given to the information that is captured, the level and detail of the information provided, its intrinsic value to the decision maker, and its impact on the decision making environment. It is conceivable, for a given task in a given environment, that there is a point at which the marginal value of adding an extra dimension is zero or close to it. Findings of this study can help designers take measures to save valuable resources that go into acquiring the extra dimensions, storing the dimensions, and processing them.

By understanding how performance can be affected, valuable insights can be gained about designing effective decision aids that can guide or restrict the decision making process. For example, by identifying the limitations of the decision maker under an information overload situation or the potential of the decision maker to make effective decisions with a subset of information, a DSS can be designed to force decision makers to employ certain strategies under specific situations (system restrictiveness) or suggest application of strategies for different choice tasks (decisional guidance).

CONCLUSION

This proposed research uses the simulation approach to focus on the relationship between effort/accuracy and the benefits of increased levels of information completeness. The findings have important implications for designing effective computer-based decision aids in terms of what information needs to be captured in these systems, the level and detail of the information provided, its intrinsic value to the decision maker, and its impact on the decision making environment. Guidelines can be developed by designers to not only save valuable resources that go into acquiring and storing information, but can also indirectly or directly influence the decision maker's information processes.

REFERENCES

Ahituv, N., & Neumann S. (1986). *Principles of information systems for management.* Dubuque, IA: W.C. Brown.

Beach, L.R., & Mitchell, T.R. (1978). A contingency model for the selection of decision strategies. *Academy of Management Review, 3,* 339–449.

Billings, R.S., & Marcus, S.A. (1983). Measures of compensatory and noncompensatory models of decision behavior: Process tracing versus policy capturing. *Organizational Behavior and Human Performance, 31,* 331–352.

Johnson, E.J. (1979). Deciding how to decide: The effort of making a decision. Working Paper, University of Chicago.

Johnson, E.J., & Payne, J.W. (1985). Effort and accuracy in choice. *Management Science, 31*(4), 395–414.

Klayman, J. (1982). *Simulation of six decision strategies: Comparisons of search patterns, processing characteristics, and response to task complexity* (Working Paper). Chicago: Center for Decision Research, University of Chicago.

Kleinmuntz, D.N., & Schkade, D.A. (1990). *Cognitive processes and information displays in computer-supported decision making: Implications for research* (Working Paper). Chicago: Center for Decision Research, University of Chicago, 1990.

Payne, J.W. (1982). Contingent decision behavior. *Psychological Bulletin, 92,* 382–402.

Uecker, W., Schepanski, A., & Shin, J. (1985). Toward a positive theory of information evaluation: Relevant tests of competing models in a principal-agency setting. *The Accounting Review, 60*(3), pp. 430–457.

APPENDIX A

EBA Strategy Flow Diagram

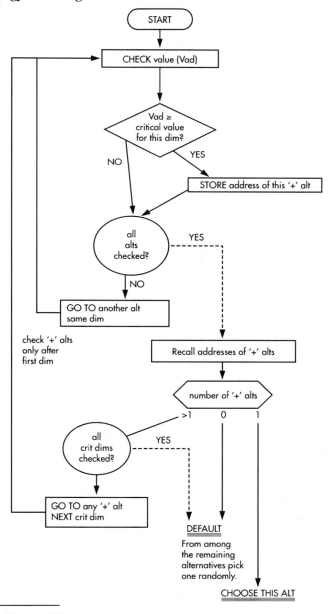

Source: Klayman 1982

Cognitive Maps for Communication: Specifying Functionality and Usability

Dov Te'eni
David G. Schwartz
Richard J. Boland, Jr.
Case Western Reserve University

INTRODUCTION

The objective of this research is to enhance collaboration by promoting richer forms of communication. By richer communication we do not just mean a richer medium but rather a richer content of communication. Daft and Lengel (1984) define richness as a media characteristic. For example, face-to-face communication is richer than a written memo because of nonverbal gestures. In contrast, our objective is to enrich the content of communication by providing the capability to communicate decisions in their context. Richer communication, however, will result in higher complexity that may render the communication unusable. Hence, functionality and usability must be studied together.

Context is what gives meaning to communication (Givon, 1989; Levinson, 1983). For us, context is a complex layering of description that is developed over time as a decision maker develops an understanding of a situation and shares it with others. Context is not just numbers and relevant facts but also beliefs, preferences, and the web of ideas, conditions, and understandings that provide the rationale for a position. Recent work has attempted to use information technology to provide a context for critiquing decision making. Fischer et al. (1991) advocated systems that critique individual decision making, and Sengupta and Te'eni (1990) described the effects of sharing underlying policies in a group decision-making environment. In this research, the decision maker is actively in control of creating and modifying the representations of context. We begin, therefore, with the identification of those contextual characteristics deemed significant by decision makers. We assume that a large portion of what decision makers need for their own decision making is also necessary for communication to others. However, added context may result in additional complexity that may build rather than break barriers to effective communication. Therefore, a suitable structure should be imposed on communication for coordinated decision making (Leatherwood, Dilla, & Boland, 1990). Cognitive maps provide such a structure.

Cognitive Maps (CM) are structured representations of decisions depicted in graphical format (Eden, 1988; Huff, 1990). Our thesis is that CMs can be used as an interactive communication aid in the context of distributed decision making. This chapter reports on an ongoing project to determine the functionality and usability of CMs for communication. To simplify the presentation, we begin with functionality and then proceed to usability. We take a human-factors approach to developing CMs for communication that includes four iterative steps: (a) describe a model of actual decision making in a collaborative context, (b) compare the model to normative theories of decision making in order to define human limitations in this context, (c) apply this knowledge together with usability aspects of communication to the design of CM, and (d) test for usability.

DECISION AND COMMUNICATION AIDS: FUNCTIONALITY

Simon's (1981) theory of bounded rationality provides an excellent framework for our discussion. Simon views decision making as an iterative process of gathering information, modeling the situation in question and devising possible actions, and choosing an action. Complex decisions usually require substantial data gathering and take time. Thus, there is a need to organize information and use it subsequently in the right context. Information gathering both shapes and is shaped by the decision maker's model of the situation being confronted. The model may include descriptions of factors that seem relevant to the situation, relationships between the factors, alternative scenarios for these factors and relationships, and a view of these factors in terms of the decision maker's value system (i.e., utility function). Individual decision makers use their models to choose an action in light of their value system. Moreover, they may use their models in different ways to choose an action. Indeed, Payne (1982) has suggested that decision behavior is contingent on a variety of factors such as decision complexity and presentation format.

In distributed decision making, the individuals act as described earlier but additionally must communicate with each other in order to coordinate decisions. They may communicate isolated pieces of information, parts of their respective models, and their choice of action. The receiver uses the incoming information in his or her own thought processes but to do so must often infer from the communication what the sender meant and accordingly assimilate it into the receiver's own models (Krauss & Fussell, 1990).

The theory of bounded rationality assumes that only limited cognitive resources are used to gather information and create models, and that, once a model exists, attention must shift between different parts of the model. In comparison to normative theories of decision making, this descriptive theory may be suboptimal in several ways. First, the current decision is made independently of many other important issues that may affect it (i.e., the models are relatively narrow in scope). Second, decision making does not usually include detailed calculations of conditional probabilities that are necessary to compute an optimal decision. Third, future scenarios are ignored or not weighted appropriately. Finally, decisions are not made in light of a comprehensive utility function leading to local optimization (Simon, 1979).

This has led several researchers to recommend that people devote more effort to make more comprehensive decisions. Janis and Mann (1977) recommend more intensive information processing and processing of more information. This is because people tend to be inaccurate, overlook important details, and are too narrow in their scope of information search. Janis and Mann require decision makers to consider a wider range of alternatives and values, reexamine assumptions and consequences, and carefully calculate all costs and benefits. While striving for a better analysis of information in all aspects of decision making, Janis and Mann do not stress the dynamics of shifting between aspects of decisions that follows because of limited cognitive resources. A more dynamic approach is taken, independently, by both Schon (1983) and Rasmussen (1986). Both argue the need to reflect on decision making from different perspectives or different levels of understanding in relation to what the decision maker is trying to accomplish. Rasmussen (1986) describes these levels as a hierarchy of why, what, and how decisions are made. Clearly, one level of understanding affects other levels. Indeed, people shift back and forth from one level to another in order to converge to a final decision.

The previous discussion suggests that any structure for communicating information among decision makers should (a) include the elements of the decision maker's simplified model, (b) show how the decision maker uses the model (assuming that decision making is contingent), (c) trigger a critical examination of the model's adequacy, and (d) facilitate easy shifts between different levels of understanding. The next section extends the current use of CMs to fulfill these criteria.

COGNITIVE MAPS AS DECISION AND COMMUNICATION AIDS

In this section we review work on the use of CMs as a decision aid, extend their functionality, and reexamine them as communication aids rather than decision aids. The literature abounds with different and varied uses of CMs, which, depending on the quantitative aspects used, are referred to as cause maps, influence diagrams, or belief nets. The seminal examples of Axelrod (1979) introduce mapping as a valuable tool in understanding the decisions of politics. Ramaprasad and Stubbart (1987) encode maps as matrices in order to perform quantitative analysis using matrix algebra to extract the logic used by decision makers and also apply a similar technique to elucidate biases in decision making (Stubbart and Ramaprasad, 1987). Cropper, Eden, and Ackerman (1990) use CM software to structure accounts of events in a way that identified areas of corroboration and conflicts in different accounts. Recent uses of CMs include organizing knowledge in the areas of systems analysis (Montazemi & Conrath, 1989), expert knowledge (Montazemi & Chan, 1990), knowledge elicitation (Schwartz, 1991), and medical technology assessment (Shachter, Eddy, & Hasselblad, 1990). One thing held in common by each of these cases is that the CMs are created by outside observers and, at best, presented to the subject for feedback and confirmation. These uses are quite significant, and our purpose is not to suggest that the use of CMs as a research tool should be abandoned. Rather, we wish to take a well understood, robust representation model and mold it into a tool for enriching communication in a distributed decision-making environment.

Standard CMs convey a limited amount of information in their nodes and arcs. Common practice is to label a node with the name of a factor used in the decision. As the value associated with this factor changes, a related change is expected in any node that is directly connected ahead of the current node. Although the direction of this change is indicated as being positive or negative, the extent of change is not specified. Thus, given a relationship of PRICE → VOLUME, all we know is that in the eyes of the decision maker, a rise in PRICE will lead to a drop in VOLUME.

Standard CMs aid decision making in several ways. First, they facilitate a systematic and balanced analysis of factors. The factors most directly affecting the final objectives tend to be placed near these objectives and thus receive closer scrutiny (Owen, 1978). Second, CMs provide an effective way of examining the relationships between factors. CMs have been compared with road maps that direct attention to possible routes between towns on a map, thereby encouraging reflection over identified and unidentified relationships (Smithin, 1980).

In the CMs described previously, the decision maker cannot convey any preference for the value of, or changes in the value of, PRICE and VOLUME. He or she cannot indicate that there are certain assumptions underlying the contention that there is a relationship between PRICE and VOLUME. There is no indication that this relationship is linear or nonlinear. In fact, based solely on the cognitive map one could not even conclude whether a 5% rise in PRICE will lead to a 5% drop in VOLUME or to an 80% drop in VOLUME.

The importance and feasibility of representing the nature of the relationship between factors has been noted by several researchers. Keeny (1987) demonstrates how to construct attribute scales in CMs, but the resulting scales are usually not comprehensive. Stubbart and Ramaprasad (1987) state that the significance of a relationship can be measured in terms of the number of times the relationship is mentioned by the subject. They further argue that in evaluating a relationship that was described by their subject on three occasions as positive and on two occasions as negative, the cognitive map should indicate the net value of one negative relationship. It is questionable whether this approach is appropriate when using a cognitive map to understand a decision rationale. The fact that two concepts relate positively on some occasions and negatively on others can give us insight into the specifics of a decision and should not be aggregated away.

Three plausible solutions for representing changing relationships between two factors are (a) a note added to a set of undirected relationships indicating how the relationship changes, (b) multiple maps for different situations, or (c) alternative decision paths on a single map. An additional text note or graphic depiction of a relationship is feasible if the relationship is positive in one situation and negative in another or if it is curvilinear. If there are drastic differences between the rationale for a decision under two sets of very different circumstances, it is reasonable to draw two separate maps. Alternatively, one can plot alternative paths on a single map when there is little or no overlap between the paths or when the alternative paths occasionally converge into one (analogous to different routes on a road map).

Showing alternative decision paths is also important for communication purposes. The issue of contingent decision making complicates the communication between decision makers. Explicit reference to alternative decision paths can avoid such confusion. Without the ability to represent multiple decision plans, a decision maker is faced with the choice of either diluting the actual complexity of the decision process to fit into a single decision model or use alternative means of communication other than CMs. Discarding certain decision paths, such as short cuts, and communicating the common and usually more comprehensive path may confuse rather than clarify communication when the discarded paths are indeed used. It will also lead to an incorrect understanding of the sender's logic. The existence of decision paths in a map that could "short-circuit" a standard decision rationale corresponds to the notion of asymmetry in influence diagrams (Call & Miller, 1990).

TESTING FOR FEASIBILITY: EDITORIAL JUDGMENT OF A MANUSCRIPT

An experiment was designed to test the feasibility of using CMs to communicate between decision makers. As there have been no reports of using CMs for communication purposes, we set out to observe whether CMs can and will be used, and if so, how. Our target population for the computerized system were experts in their domain fields but not necessarily experienced with CMs. We assumed, therefore, that we would need to help our subjects in constructing their CMs. Furthermore, we wanted to test the feasibility of CMs in the context of a complex task. It would not be worthwhile to construct and exchange maps for trivial tasks.

The domain chosen for the experiment was that of the decision of an Associate Editor in evaluating a manuscript. We worked with three experienced associate editors of leading MIS journals. A realistic scenario was constructed that included a full-blown manuscript and a set of realistic reviews. The task of the Associate Editor was to integrate the reviews with his or her own evaluation and reach a decision as to the disposition of the manuscript. Possible decisions include:

1. Accept the submission with no revisions
2. Accept the submission conditional to revisions being made

3. Suggest the author revise and resubmit the paper
4. Reject the paper completely.

After the Associate Editor forms an opinion, he or she had to reach a joint decision with another Associate Editor on what to do with the manuscript.

We began with unstructured interviews with each of three associate editors and created a different map for each of them. The three resulting maps can be seen in Figures 7.1a, 7.1b, and 7.1c. In additional sessions we let the subjects edit the maps until they were satisfied that the maps reflected their decision strategies.

As expected, the maps generated were very different. In particular, note the drastically different structure of Figure 7.1c compared with Figures 7.1a and 7.1b. This difference in structure dramatically demonstrates the reason for questioning the feasibility of using CMs as a means of communication. Furthermore, note in Figure 7.1b the thick links on the lefthand corner. These were indicated to be decision paths of first choice, or as the subject put it—"short cuts." A similar decision path is indicated in Figure 7.1c.

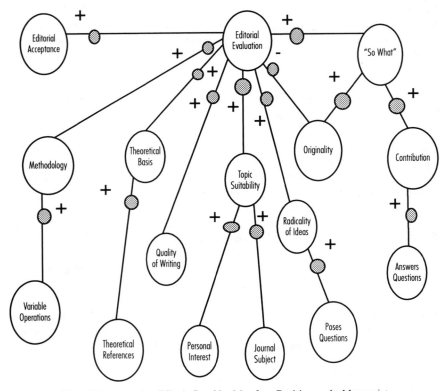

Figure 7.1a. Associate Editor's Cognitive Map for a Decision on the Manuscript.

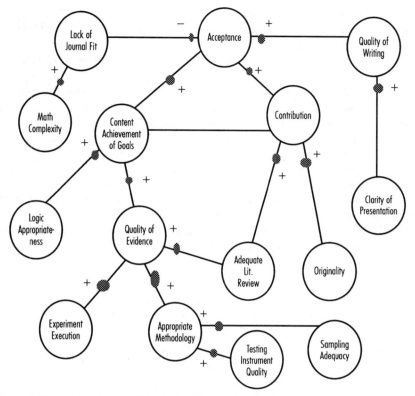

Figure 7.1b. Associate Editor's Cognitive Map for a Decision on the Manuscript.

Following confirmation and acceptance of each map by its owner, the participants were each asked to perform three tasks:

1. Evaluate a new journal submission using their own map
2. Read, understand, and explain a colleague's map
3. Reach a joint decision with a colleague referring to both of their maps.

Although each participant performed the first task well, during this stage there was considerable modification to the original maps based on forgotten or misused factors. For example, in using his original map to evaluate a papers, Participant A indicated that a new factor raised by this particular paper had to be taken into account and should be added to the map. This indicates the need for dynamic modification of maps if they are to be used by the decision maker himself. It further raises a question as to the accuracy and completeness of maps produced solely on the basis of interviews and protocol analysis by external researchers.

Once the maps had been dynamically modified through a series of meetings, the maps were traded by the participants. Participant A was given map C, Participant C had map B, and Participant B received map A. Each participant was asked to express his or her understanding, acceptance, and ability to use his or her counterpart's map in evaluating a journal submission. Here the results were mixed, with conflicting use of factor labels causing some confusion. Indication was given that a one line description of each factor on the map would be enough for them to understand the relationships between the factors as expressed by the map owner. Because all three work in the same domain, a simple reconciliation that one person's "writing quality" is another's "language usage" was enough clarification. In addition to confusion surrounding the terminology used, there were significant questions raised by the participants as to the preferences and assumptions of the map author in applying the relationships.

The third task, reaching a joint decision with a colleague referring to both of their maps, allowed each decision maker to clarify the others' preferences and assumptions. Having a map before them during conversation allowed easy reference to points of agreement and points of contention in the decision rationale. After identifying the

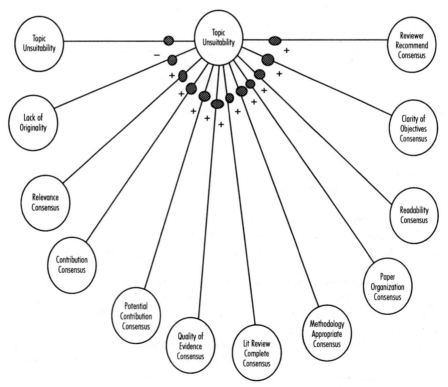

Figure 7.1c. Associate Editor's Cognitive Map for a Decision on the Manuscript.

points of disagreement between the two decision maker, the map was not used to reconcile the disagreement over value judgments. The map was useful in identifying the point of contention between the decision makers but not in resolving the problem once identified. However, once identified, the disagreement was easily addressed by direct negotiation in reference to the overall structure of the map. Thus, we identified dialogue at several levels, in which the focal point shifted from one level to another. As experienced decision makers, the participants moved from one perspective to another even though the tool did not readily support such shifts. In fact, as indicated earlier, when the tool did not support a certain perspective, the tool was discarded. This point is developed later.

These initial observations indicate that CMs are a feasible and apparently effective means of communication between decision makers. Nevertheless, from the observation of the users and their own comments, CMs seem incomplete. There would seem to be considerable benefit in explicitly representing the preferences and assumptions underlying a decision rationale. Not only does the inclusion of preference and assumption create a representation that can communicate a comprehensive decision rationale to a colleague, it also fosters relevant and insightful dialogue in resolving conflict surrounding a joint decision. The issues of explicit preferences and assumptions are also developed later.

INTERACTIVE COGNITIVE MAPS: MORE FUNCTIONALITY

Interactive (computerized) CMs that support dynamic shifts in user's attention by dynamically presenting alternative parts of decision context offer new opportunities to complement human sub-optimality in decision making. The two most important aspects of additional context are preferences and assumptions, which represent different levels of understanding in the decision maker's simplified model of the problem situation.

Preferences

In our definition of functionality we included the decision maker's values (preferences) as part of his or her simplified model. It is useful to distinguish between preferences for action (intermediary factors that are controllable) and preferences for outcomes (factors that represent the final objectives). The importance of preference of action and preference of outcome is discussed by Radford (1990), who refers to them as strategic and tactical analysis, respectively. Phillips (1990) includes preference as one of the aspects of "exercising discretion," considering it a key component of the human interaction that must be supported by a group decision support system. In an attempt to provide guidelines for selecting a decision support method, Cropper (1990) suggests that a representation of preference is required to give a decision model "analytic potential" so that it may be used for semiformal bargaining between those that share the model.

Perhaps the most convincing argument for the representation of preference is a pragmatic one: Whether the desired cooperative strategy is Axelrod's (1984) golden rule of "unconditional cooperation," unconditional confrontation, or something in between, one cannot develop any cooperation-based strategy without having some indication of the desires, expectations, and preferences of the parties involved.

Interestingly, many of the reasons for including preferences in knowledge-based systems (see Bradshaw & Boose, 1990) are relevant to our goal of enriching communication: (a) unique tradeoffs for a given situation can be addressed, (b) the impact of a particular piece of evidence on a decision can be evaluated, (c) the value of obtaining additional information can be ascertained, (d) the value of being able to control an uncertain variable can be determined, and (e) risk attitude and time preferences can be explicitly taken into account.

In presenting the PRICE → VOLUME relationship described earlier, nothing is expressed regarding the decision maker's preference of action or outcome. Does the decision maker want the price to drop in order to increase volume? Does the decision maker want the price to remain constant so that volume is unchanged? Would the decision maker prefer a rise in price thus lowering sales volume? Each of these scenarios are possible given different circumstances, and there is potential benefit in being able to communicate these preferences between decision makers. This issue is treated by first looking into implicit versus explicit preferences and offering a graphical solution.

In constructing a cognitive map, much attention is given to the meaning associated with the concepts or nodes of the map. A decision maker may express a relationship between LOAN-APPROVAL, DISPOSABLE-INCOME, and PROPERTY-MARKETABILITY in a mortgage decision as:

DISPOSABLE-INCOME → LOAN-APPROVAL ← PROPERTY-MARKETABILITY

indicating that a high or increased disposable income will increase the chances of a loan approval, and a high or increased level of property marketability will increase the chances of a loan approval. Inherent in the LOAN-APPROVAL node is the knowledge that our preferred decision is to approve the loan. Based on that, we have inherent preferences that trickle down to the nodes below. We clearly prefer a high DISPOSABLE-INCOME because our preferred decision is LOAN-APPROVAL, and there is a positive relationship between the two. An inherent preference may suffice in cases such as this in which the preferred decision is both binary (YES/NO) and well known. The following scenario does not present such clear preferences.

With an implicit preference of maximizing PROFIT, we can trickle down a preference of INCREASED VOLUME and INCREASED PRODUCT-FUNCTIONALITY due to the signs of the cause-effect relationships. Yet, following that same argument, a preference to maximize PROFIT implies a preference of INCREASED MARGIN and DECREASED PRODUCTION-COST, which implies a preference of *DECREASED* PRODUCT-FUNCTIONALITY! There is a tradeoff regarding

PRODUCT-FUNCTIONALITY (the number of features a product offers) in this representation. On the one hand, a more robust product will increase sales volume, but on the other hand it will cost more to produce. Trying to interpret the decision maker's preferences based on the implicit meanings of nodes and the sign of relationships will lead to a conflict and perhaps a complete misinterpretation of the decision maker's thought process.

By augmenting the graphical map representation with a color scheme we can positively indicate preferences. Given the discrete nature of the relationships between nodes on a map (i.e., positive, negative, none), and the resulting necessity that nodes or factors be described in terms of values that can *INCREASE, DECREASE,* or *REMAIN STABLE,* a simple three-level color scheme can be used to represent preferred changes in nodal values. Thus, the relationship with a color scheme of green—preferred INCREASE, red—preferred DECREASE, and yellow—preferred STABILITY would indicate that the decision maker wants to increase profits by increasing volume and product functionality while maintaining the current levels of production cost and margin. This "reading" could open the door to a useful discussion on ways to increase product functionality without increasing production costs. Facilitating this kind of communication between decision makers is one of our primary goals. Much work has been done in analyzing the effectiveness of color in user interface and visual communication (Shneiderman, 1987) that can justify the choice of a color scheme. The simplicity of this approach lends itself to quick acceptance by a decision maker required to draw his or her own cognitive map and intuitive understanding by a colleague reading a map.

Underlying Assumptions

Providing a facility for explicitly stating the assumptions underlying the factors and relationships and then accessing them during the decision-making process makes CMs more effective in both individual and interpersonal decision-making processes. A factor can be linked to an assumption annotation. This annotation most commonly takes the form of a textual note, but is not limited to that. For example, assumptions can also be graphs that show relationships between scaled factors or data matrices that describe associations between factors, probability functions, and preference functions.

The ability to travel from a decision to a map that explains the decision, and from a factor or a relationship in a map to an underlying assumption, is essentially our way of supporting the necessary shifts in levels of abstraction (i.e., levels of understanding), as we identified them earlier. We take a hypermedia approach (Landow, 1990; Meyerowitz, 1986) in facilitating these shifts so that users can travel between levels of abstraction. Note, however, that in the proposed structure the direction of links is all important. If a decision is *linked to* a map, we mean that the map explains the decision.

USABILITY

Usability problems in using CMs arise as soon as the CMs are used without restriction to support complex (realistic) problems. The complexity of CMs may render them unusable in both individual processes and a fortiori in interpersonal processes. Primarily, it is a problem of trying to overload a map with too much information for it to be processed effectively. If we wish to avoid the unbridled expansion of maps to 200 factor monstrosities such as those encountered in previous reports (e.g., Cropper et al., 1990; Eden, Jones, & Sims, 1979), without resorting to arbitrary aggregation, we must formalize the usage of the tool. The techniques of Data Flow Diagrams (DeMarco, 1979; Gane & Sarson, 1977), which have proven themselves with over a decade of practical application, suggest that around seven bubbles is a good rule of thumb. Intuitive guidelines from the CM literature suggest a much higher number—around 25 (Cropper et al., 1990)—but this high number was derived from expert decision analysts as opposed to end users. We therefore limited the number of factors in a map to 10. Furthermore, we adopt DeMarco's (1979) hierarchical decomposition, that is, bubble explosion, in order to cover detail that is lost.

Rigid limitations, however, are inappropriate because the map's complexity is affected by personal and environmental factors, for example, experience with the problem situation. In order to manage complexity dynamically, groups of factors on a map can be combined and hidden under one encompassing factor. When a group of factors are identified for "combination" into one, the encompassing factor appears in their place and is indicated by an asterisk. At any point in time the encompassing factor can be "expanded" to recreate the original factor set. In addition to facilitating the combination and expansion of factors, any individual factor can be linked to a separate map. These facilities are especially useful to control the level of complexity in communication by adapting the structure to, say, experience. These ideas have been used extensively in communication (e.g., Campbell, 1991). It also enables the sender to begin with a set of general concepts and gradually go into the details of each concept (LaDuc, 1991).

The same principle of hiding and unhiding greater levels of detail holds true for all information in the decision maker's model that is stored in the computerized system. This includes decisions, preferences, general maps, expanded maps, direct assumptions on factors and relationships, and underlying assumptions to the direct assumption. For example, having the assumptions "hidden" at a level below that of the map allows the user to control his or her map development and study by working at different levels of abstraction. The user can choose to study a map on its own, leaving the assumptions hidden, or display the assumptions underlying one or more factors and relationships.

These usability issues are primarily aimed at managing complexity; they are cognitive oriented. However, our limited testing indicate powerful emotive issues that will have to be studied. Foremost is the issue of trust and security. Several users in a business environment have insisted on using a "hiding" facility (as described previously) for concealing information before transmission. Others have indicated that an exchange of maps enhances mutual trust, which leads to an even greater level of information sharing and reliance. As one user put it, "Without trust, there is no use for maps." A plan to study these issues is now under way.

CONCLUSIONS AND FUTURE DIRECTION OF RESEARCH

Based on a model of actual decision making in a collaborative setting, we defined the functionality necessary for supporting communication between decision makers. Using these requirements we adapted standard CMs to include several new elements and, most importantly, redesigned CMs to be interactive. In particular, the augmented CMs for communication have been defined to represent preferences, assumptions, and multiple decision paths. Moreover, the interactive CMs have been designed to include the layering of context to provide multiple levels of communication richness. Furthermore, usability guidelines for the maps have been defined to ensure that the maps are used effectively by decision makers to both analyze and communicate their decision rationales.

A computer-based collaborative environment has been implemented to bring the functionality of CMs for communication to the desktop of decision makers. We are currently testing the use of the tool in a corporate setting among managers who must present joint decisions to common problems. The initial test stage requires that the decision makers use the tool to create their own CMs and share these maps with their colleagues.

There are a number of areas that we are examining to determine the effect of using CMs for communication as they have been defined and to gain insight into ways to modify and improve their representational capability and usage guidelines. Future research will focus on the areas in which changes are expected to appear in the performance of cooperating decision makers. Areas of investigation include:

- Increased clarity of decision rationales
- Levels of confidence in one's own decisions
- Higher levels of confidence in colleagues decisions
- The ability to modify and update decision rationales
- The ability to identify problems in decision rationales
- Increased levels of decision consistency over time.

Hopefully, gaining knowledge about these issues will move us a step closer to putting effective cognitive tools where they belong——in the hands of the decision maker.

REFERENCES

Axelrod, R. (1979). *Structure of decision*. Princeton, NJ: Princeton University Press.
Axelrod, R. (1984). *The evolution of cooperation*. New York: Basic Books.

Bradshaw, J.M., & Boose, J.H. (1990). Decision analysis techniques for knowledge acquisition: Combining information and preferences using Aquinas and Axotl. *International Journal of Man-Machine Studies, 32,* 121–186.

Call, H.J., & Miller, W.A. (1990). A comparison of approaches and implementations for automating decision analysis reliability. *Engineering and System Safety, 30,* 115–162.

Campbell, K.S. (1991). Structural cohesion in technical texts. *Journal of Technical Writing and Communication, 21*(3), 221.

Cropper, S. (1990). Variety, formality, and style: Choosing amongst decision-support methods. In C. Eden & J. Radford (Eds.), *Tackling strategic problems* (pp. 92–98). Beverly Hills: Sage.

Cropper, S., Eden, C., & Ackerman, F. (1990). Keeping sense of accounts using computer-based cognitive maps. *Social Science Computer Review, 8*(3), 345–367.

Daft, R.L., & Lengel, R.H. (1984). Information richness: A new approach to managerial behavior and organization design. *Research in Organizational Behavior, 6,* 191–233.

DeMarco, T. (1979). *Structured analysis and system specification.* New York: Yourdon Press.

Eden, C. (1988). Cognitive mapping. *European Journal of Operational Research, 13,* 1–13.

Eden, C., Jones, C., & Sims, D. (1979). *Thinking in organizations,* New York: Macmillan.

Fischer, G., Gruding, J., Lemke, A. McCall, J., Ostwald, J., & Shipmand, F. (1991). *Supporting asynchronous collaborative design with integrated knowledge-based design environments.* Boulder: Department of Computer Science, University of Colorado.

Gane, C., & Sarson, T. (1977). *Structured systems analysis: Tools and techniques for improved systems technologies.* New York: Prentice Hall.

Givon, T. (1989). *Mind, code and context: Essays in pragmatics.* Hillsdale, NJ: Erlbaum.

Huff, A. (1990). *Mapping Strategic Thought,* Chichester, England: Wiley.

Janis, I.L., & Mann, L. (1977). *Decision making.* New York: Free Press.

Keeny, R.L. (1987). Value-driven expert systems for decision support. In J. Mumpower (Ed.), *Expert judgment and expert systems* (pp. 155-171). Berlin: Springer-Verlag.

Krauss, R.M., & Fussell, S.R. (1990). Mutual knowledge and communicative effectiveness. In J. Galegher, R.E. Kraut, & C. Edigo (Eds.), *Intellectual teamwork: Social and technological foundations of cooperative work* (pp. 111–145). Hillsdale, NJ: Erlbaum.

LaDuc, L. (1991). Infusing practical wisdom into persuasive performance. *Journal of Technical Writing and Communication, 21*(3), 160.

Landow, G.P. (1990). Hypertext and collaborative work: The example of intermedia. In J. Galegher, R. E. Kraut, & C. Edigo (Eds.), *Intellectual teamwork: Social and technological foundations of cooperative work* (pp. 407–428). Hillsdale, NJ: Erlbaum.

Leatherwood, M.L., Dilla, W.M., & Boland, R.J. (1990, July). *Network communication facilities and user perceptions of task and social environments.* Paper presented at the IFIP 8.3 Working Conference on Decision Support Systems, Budapest.

Levinson, S.C. (1983). *Pragmatics.* Cambridge, England: Cambridge University Press.

Meyerowitz, N. (1986). *Intermedia: The architecture and construction of an object-oriented hypermedia system and applications framework.* Paper presented at OOPSLA '86, Portland, Ore.

Montazemi, A.R., & Conrath, D.W. (1989). The use of cognitive mapping for information requirements analysis. *MIS Quarterly, 13,* 45–53.

Montazemi, A.R., & Chan, L. (1990). An analysis of the structure of expert knowledge. *European Journal of Operational Research, 45,* 275–292.

Owen, D. L. (1978). The use of influence diagrams in structuring complex decision problems. In R.A. Howard & J.E. Matheson (Eds.), *Readings on the principles and applications of decision analysis* (vol. II, pp. 763–771). Menlo Park, CA: Strategic Decision Group.

Payne, J.W. (1982). Contingent decision behavior. *Psychological Bulletin, 92,* 382–402.

Phillips, L.D. (1990). Decision analysis for group decision support. In C. Eden & J. Radford (Eds.), *Tackling strategic problems* (pp. 142–150). Beverly Hills: Sage.

Radford, J. (1990). The analysis and resolution of decision situations with interacting participants. In C. Eden & J. Radford (Eds.), *Tackling strategic problems* (pp. 68–77). Beverly Hills: Sage.

Ramaprasad, A., & Stubbart, C. (1987). *Q-analysis of cognitive maps.* Southern Illinois University, Department of Management, Cabondale, Illinois.

Rasmussen, J. (1986). *Information processing and human-machine interaction: An approach to cognitive engineering,* New York: North-Holland.

Schon, D.A. (1983). *The reflective practitioner: How professionals think in action.* New York: Basic Books.

Schwartz, D.G. (1991). *Cognitive mapping as a knowledge engineering tool.* Pittsburg: Center for Automation and Intelligent Systems Research, Case Western Reserve University.

Sengupta, K., & Te'eni, D. (1990). *Cognitive feedback in group decision support systems* (Working Paper No. 90-06). Pittsburg: Department of Management Information and Decision Systems, Case Western Reserve University.

Shachter, R.D., Eddy, D.M., & Hasselblad, V. (1990). An influence diagram approach to medical technology assessment. In R.M. Oliver and J.Q. Smith (Eds.), *Influence diagrams, belief nets and decision analysis* (pp. 321–350). Chichester, England: Wiley.

Shneiderman, B. (1987). *Designing the user interface: Strategies for effective human-computer interaction.* Reading, MA: Addison-Wesley.

Simon, H.A. (1979). *Models of thought.* New Haven, CT: Yale University Press.

Simon, H.A. (1981). *The sciences of the artificial* (2nd ed.). San Francisco: Jossey-Bass.

Smithin, T. (1980, December). Maps of the mind: New pathways to decision making. *Business Horizons,* pp. 24–28.

Stubbart, C., & Ramaprasad, A. (1987). *A strategist's cognitive map of the steel industry: A case study of Mr. David Roderick* (Chairman, US Steel). Amherst: University of Massachusetts, Department of Management.

Part III

System / User Communication

Assessing the Use of an SQL Minimal Manual in Self-Instruction*

Ronald A. Guillemette
SoftDoc

Minnie Yi-Miin Yen
University of Alaska–Anchorage

INTRODUCTION

A major problem with many computer software user manuals is *usability*. Novice or infrequent users of a software product or system often find it difficult to access, understand, and apply relevant information needed to achieve software-related behavioral objectives (Guillemette, 1989a). Typical problems include: the need to recall and synthesize fragmented information in performing a task; steep learning requirements involving abstract concepts before the introduction of meaningful, concrete tasks; incomplete information for error diagnosis, recovery, and prevention; and incompatibilities between and within the documentation and the software.

The importance of usable documentation for novice users of the software is underscored by the limited availability of human assistance while the learning tasks are actually performed. That is, the user manual is a key interface when software problems occur. An unusable manual adversely affects learning performance and attitudes and may ultimately contribute to software disuse or misuse (Guillemette, 1989b).

---

* Portions of an earlier version of this article were discussed at the 1991 Decision Sciences Institute National Conference (Yen et al., 1990). The authors wish to thank Lisa Ann Brown for her participation in the study.

One explanation for a mismatch between the novice user and software documentation is the frequent failure to include representative reader input in the editorial review process (Guillemette, 1988). An implicit assumption is made that the reviewer, who may have technical expertise in the use of design of the software or may be an experienced technical writer, can effectively serve as a user surrogate. However, an expert software user can subconsciously compensate for knowledge gaps in the material. Moreover, the novice user might find it difficult to apply even well-written material to the task at hand.

The chapter focuses on the subjective evaluation of a minimal manual by a college student without prior exposure to SQL (Structured Query Language). SQL is emerging as the de facto standard language for interacting with relational databases (ANSI, 1986). The student recorded observations during the process of learning SQL through a minimal manual designed for an educational version of a microcomputer relational database product. A minimal manual is designed to lessen the magnitude of the learning effort required to accomplish realistic tasks and to encourage an active learning style (Carroll, Smith-Kerker, Ford, & Mazur, 1986). The chapter discusses the minimal manual concept, examines the student's experience in using the minimal manual, draws conclusions regarding the use of the minimal manual in instructional practice, and identifies directions for further study of the minimalist design concept in education and training.

THE MINIMAL MANUAL: CONCEPT AND BACKGROUND

The software user develops a mental model of a system or product based on prior knowledge and experience, interaction with the software, and oral and written communications of system personnel, documenters, and other users (Norman, 1983). In early stages this mental model is simplistic, erroneous, unstable, and incomplete; initial hypotheses guiding novice user interaction with the software are frequently based on knowledge of and experiences with other software. The mental model evolves as hypotheses are rejected and revised through user interaction with the system. The system designer can influence development of the user's mental model by providing a "natural" context (that is, compatible with prior knowledge, abilities, and skills) for user learning and action through the interface. Similarly, the documenter may use graphic representations, analogies, and concrete examples to facilitate user learning.

Minimalist manual design is based on three fundamental principles: (a) to limit the amount of material presented, (b) to focus on real users and tasks, and (c) to support error recognition and recovery. A reduced amount of information lowers cognitive load in learning or executing a realistic task and minimizes the need of the user to engage in coping activities, such as scanning the text to find task-relevant information. Explicit consideration of target user task requirements lowers the cognitive effort of the user in attempting to link task characteristics to abstract concepts or unrelated examples. Frequent system interaction during learning allows the user to test and revise his or her conceptualizations at an early stage, limits the risk of needing to unlearn and relearn the material, and provides an opportunity to obtain user confidence in and commitment to the system early in the learning process. Effective learning requires that errors be diagnosed and corrected as soon as possible; this process is facilitated through error messages understandable in the context of system interaction and through preventive and corrective guidance in the documentation.

The minimal manual is composed of loosely coupled, self-contained, function-oriented modules or topics; the number of topics is restricted to coverage of core software functions, which are determined through observations and analyses of task behaviors.

Each topic is only a few pages long and contains three types of information: "read-only," which provides background and explanation; "instructional," which states learning tasks to be performed by the user; and "recovery," which indicates what to do if something goes wrong. The user is not required to learn multiple methods to achieve a particular result or infrequently used, specialized system option. The user is encouraged to work at his or her own pace and to experiment with the system; a series of "ON YOUR OWN" exercises is provided at the end of each topic.

Empirical data to date have revealed favorable performance and learning effects for the minimalist manual approach relative to standard, commercial manuals. Moreover, these effects continue when users are transferred to advanced chapters in standard manuals (Carroll, 1984, 1985, 1990; Carroll et al., 1986; Carroll, Smith-Kerker, Ford, & Mazur, 1987–88).

THE CURRENT STUDY

The lead author had composed an SQL minimal manual that was designed to run with a limited educational version of a relational database product (Guillemette, 1990). (See Table 8.1 for a listing of topics.) Because the authors were familiar with SQL, a decision was made to have a student without prior knowledge of SQL test the effectiveness of the minimal manual. The student was instructed to learn the relational package using the manual, not the instructor, as the primary learning interface.

The student was asked to record her observations in a diary (Meister, 1985) guided by a problem categorization scheme analogous to one used in a previous microcomputer learning study (Mantei & Haskell, 1983). All but one of the categories, summarized in Table 8.2, were qualitative in nature, the exception being self-reported time intervals in reading topic chapters and in completing "ON YOU OWN" exercises, respectively.

RESULTS

The student reported efficient learning achievement in using the system through the guidance of the manual and rated the quality of the manual as excellent. She felt that the minimal manual approach, with its emphasis on short length and modular arrange-

Table 8.1.   SQL Minimal Manual Table of Contents

TOPIC	TITLE
1	What is This Thing All About?
	• Understanding This Manual
	• Getting Started: The Sample SQL Session
2	Retrieving Something Stored: The Basic SQL Query
3	Storing, Retrieving, and Modifying Queries & Commands
4	Using Numeric Columns in Arithmetic Expressions
5	Summarizing Column Data: Aggregate Expressions
6	Rearranging Query Results by Column Values: ORDER BY
7	Summarizing Rows with Common Column Values: GROUP BY
8	Choosing Rows from Tables by Column Values: WHERE Clause
9	Choosing Groups of Rows from Tables: HAVING Clause
10	Combining Data From Related Tables: The JOIN
11	Changing Table Data: Adding, Deleting, and Modifying Rows

Adapted from *SQL: A Minimal Manual,* by R.A. Guillemette, 1990, unpublished manuscript. Reprinted by permission of author.

Table 8.2.   Minimal Manual Evaluation Criteria for Student Diary

- Completeness
- User Orientation
- Clarity
- Accuracy
- Organization and Level
- Vocabulary
- Timeliness of Problem Resolution
- Quality
- Time to Complete Task

ment of chapters, is preferable to standard approaches in the development of software-oriented manuals.

Table 8.3 presents a classification of text-related problems derived from the student's comments (Brown, 1990). Perhaps the most significant problem (deviations of observed from documented results) is more directly attributed to the software itself: Use of the software often leads to the generation of lost data clusters, the presence of which can adversely affect the reliability of query results. Although this potential problem was explicitly addressed in Topic 1, the student did not remember the warning as she worked through the manual. This incident provides a good example of how user testing of a minimal manual can provide a basis for assessing the usability of the software product itself.

Table 8.3.   A Classification of Self-Reported User Problems

- Minor Formatting Inconsistencies
- Improvements Needed on the Use of Typographic Cues
- Additional Emphasis Necessary on Syntactic Issues (Brackets, Commas, Quotation Marks, Hyphens)
- Occasional Readability Problems
- Variations Between Documented and Observed Results
- Need for Listings and Graphical Overviews of Example Databases
- Additional, More Varied Examples Required to Motivate the User and to Provide a Basis for Increased User Confidence
- More Narrative and Progression of Examples Necessary for Complex Topics (Compound Conditions and Joins)
- Need for Greater Accessibility of Error-Related Information and Vocabulary Definitions

User testing can also yield insights on usability of the interface. For instance, the author enclosed all character strings used in examples with single, ending quotation marks. The student initially failed to notice that the quotation marks were the same and invalidly applied English language conventions of double or balanced quotation marks. Whereas the author did not anticipate this problem and thus alert the user to it, a more natural interface would allow the user to substitute semantically equivalent punctuation.

DISCUSSION

Many software manuals have significant usability problems, such as variances of documented from actual procedures, uses of undocumented features in examples, omissions of installation details, and incomplete error listings. The instructor may find that considerable energy must be expended to compensate for such problems (Guillemette, 1989). This study shows that learnability problems can surface even with relatively well-written texts, and that user studies provide informative feedback to the author. (Novice user feedback is being used to drive revision and enhancement of the SQL minimal manual; Guillemette, 1990.)

Qualitative data generated during this study suggest that the minimal manual approach can be an effective instructional alternative for novice learning of core software functions; this approach has potential benefits of increasing instructional flexibility to deal with user problems on an individualized basis and of allocating additional training time to the discussion of more advanced aspects of software use. Users also find that they can access and learn aspects of software use in a more manageable, flexible manner than that needed for standard manuals.

Potential problems with the minimalist design approach include feasibility concerns in conducting user studies and deviations from reader expectations. A number of users should be involved in order to allow more reliable detection of general learning problems (versus user-specific difficulties and preferences); however, it is difficult to recruit a sufficiently large base of representative users in a timely fashion. Another concern is the considerable time and effort required to develop and validate learning achievement measures.

User comments in this study also revealed some discomfort with the lack of exhibits and other supplementary features that are routinely included in standard manuals but intentionally omitted from minimal manuals. This reaction is analogous to the resistance of some end users to prototyping (Guillemette, 1987). They feel that minimalist design of systems and products implies that professional development standards are being short-shrifted, and that there are long-term tradeoffs with software quality and functionality.

There is reason to believe that a minimal manual may benefit from the inclusion of certain exhibits and advance organizers, for example, a hardcopy listing of database structures and a graphical overview of relationships among database tables. Whereas the manual encouraged the user to obtain database descriptions through the interface, the user repeatedly had to suspend her activities to retrieve the same listings. Moreover, the user had to synthesize her own overview of table relationships using a piecemeal table structure listing.

FUTURE WORK

Additional user feedback is being obtained for the SQL manual; future plans include formal testing of the revised manual's comparable effectiveness using objective and subjective learning measures.

REFERENCES

American National Standard Institute (ANSI). (1986). (ANSI X3). New York: Author.

Brown, L.A. (1990). *Journal of experiences using [Vendor] SQL Query.* Unpublished project diary, University of Alaska-Anchorage, Business Computer Information Systems Department.

Carroll, J.M. (1984). Minimalist training. *DATAMATION, 30*(18), 125ff.

Carroll, J.M. (1985). Minimalist design for active users. In B. Shackel (Ed.), *Human–computer interaction-INTERACT'84,* (pp. 39–44). Amsterdam: Elsevier Science.

Carroll, J.M. (1990). *The Nurnberg Funner: Designing minimalist instruction for practical computer skill.* Cambridge, MA: MIT Press.

Carroll, J.M., Smith-Kerker, P.L., Ford, J.R., & Mazur, S.A. (1986). *The minimal manual.* Yorktown Heights, NY: User Interface Institute, IBM Thomas J. Watson Research Center.

Carroll, J.M., Smith-Kerker, P.L., Ford, J.R., & Mazur, S.A. (1987–88). The minimal manual. *Human–Computer Interaction, 3,* 123–153.

Guillemette, R.A. (1987). Prototyping: An alternate method for developing documentation. *Technical Communication, 34*(3), 135–141.

Guillemette, R.A. (1988). Readability assessments of college data processing texts. *INTERFACE (The Computer Educational Quarterly), 10*(3), 30–36.

Guillemette, R.A. (1989a). The cloze procedure: An assessment of the undertstandability of data processing texts. *Information & Management, 17,* 143–155.

Guillemette, R.A. (1989b). Usability in computer documentation design: Conceptual and methodological considerations. *IEEE Transactions on Professional Communication, 32*(4), 217–229.

Guillemette, R.A. (1990). *SQL: A minimal manual.* Unpublished manuscript.

Mantei, M.M., & Haskell, N. (1983). Autobiography of a first-time discretionary microcomputer user. In A. Janda (Ed.), *Human factors in computing systems,* (pp. 286–290). New York: Association for Computing Machinery.

Meister, D. (1985). *Behavioral analysis and measurement methods.* New York: Wiley.

Norman, D.A. (1983). Some observations on mental models. In D. Gentner and A.L. Stevens (Eds.) *Mental Models,* (pp. 7–14). Hillsdale, NJ: Erlbaum.

Yen, M., Guillemette, R.A., & Brown, L.A. (1991) Minimalist design of instructional materials: Diary of a college student learning SQL. In *Proceedings of the 1991 Decision Sciences Institute Annual Meeting,* [Abstract], (p. 711). Atlanta, GA: Decision Sciences Institute, S. Melnyk (coordinator).

Part IV
The Analyst

The Impact of Production Emphasis on Programmer Productivity

Raghava G. Gowda
University of Dayton

Donald R. Chand
Bentley College

INTRODUCTION

In the book *Peopleware*, Tom DeMarco and Timothy Lister (1987) described one senior manager's view of management as "Management is kicking a - -." They go on to make the observation that "even if kicking people in the backside did boost their short term productivity, it might not be useful in the long run." Management is a complex thing, and any simple definition of management, how so ever generic it may be, is incorrect and misleading. However, the issue here is not what management is but rather whether management pressure increases software development productivity.

This chapter reports on our findings on the relationship between production emphasis and programmer productivity. This relationship was measured as part of a four-year study conducted in a large data processing organization to investigate the impact of both group factors and individual factors on programmer productivity. Programmer productivity was modeled as a function of IC, GC, and LB, where IC represents the individual characteristics of the software developers, GC represents the Group Cohesiveness of the project team, and LB represents the leader behavior of the project leader.

Individual characteristics were measured in terms of years of college education, training, and months of experience in a language at the site. Group cohesiveness was measured in terms of person-to-group attraction, person-to-person attraction, and person-to-leader attraction. Leader behavior was measured in terms of production emphasis, which is the application of pressure for productive output.

Empirical studies in the area of programmer productivity have established that there are significant differences among the individual productivity of programmers (Benbasat & Vessey, 1980; Brooks, 1982). In addition, it has been shown that high-order software tools such as fourth-generation languages and advanced programming environment such as windows, language-sensitive compilers, and automatic test generators increase programmer productivity (DeMarco & Lister, 1987). An exploratory study was initiated to assess the impact of group cohesiveness and manager/leader behavior on programmer productivity. This chapter describes the overall research study and reports our findings on the relationship of production emphasis on programming productivity.

THE RESEARCH MODEL

The analysis of the productivity literature led us to the conceptualization of the programmer productivity model described in Figure 9.1. The conceptualization of this model is described in Gowda (1988). It shows the factors that impact programmer productivity. The independent variables selected in this exploratory study were individual characteristics, group cohesiveness, and leader behavior. The reasons for their selection are: (a) It has been shown that individual characteristics affect programmer productivity and, therefore, they must be accounted for in any research involving software productivity; (b) the concept of group cohesiveness has been studied in fields such as military, sports, and the classroom, and although the results are inconclusive, one cannot rule out the impact of cohesiveness on productivity; and (c) the leader behavior was included because the impact of production emphasis by the project leader on the productivity of the programmer is an important issue, but apparently no study dealing with this issue has been reported in the open literature. The dependent variable for this study was individual programmer productivity.

For the production emphasis portion of this study, the null and alternate hypotheses formulated were:

HO: There is no relationship between production emphasis and programmer productivity.
H1:   There is a demonstrable relationship between production emphasis and programmer productivity.

The operationalization and measurement of the dependent and independent variables in the research model are discussed next.

Measurement of Programmer Productivity

Three surrogate metrics—the actual lines of code (LOC), the executable lines of code (ELOC), and the Halstead's effort (E)—were used to measure productivity of pro-

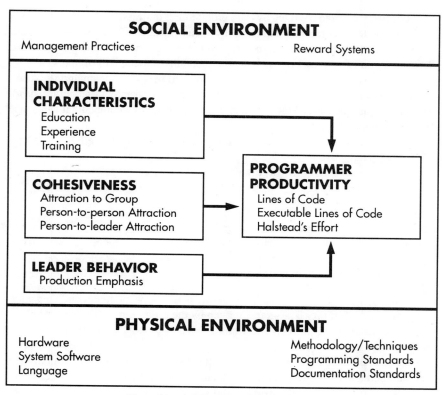

SOCIAL ENVIRONMENT

Management Practices   Reward Systems

INDIVIDUAL CHARACTERISTICS
Education
Experience
Training

COHESIVENESS
Attraction to Group
Person-to-person Attraction
Person-to-leader Attraction

LEADER BEHAVIOR
Production Emphasis

PROGRAMMER PRODUCTIVITY
Lines of Code
Executable Lines of Code
Halstead's Effort

PHYSICAL ENVIRONMENT

Hardware   Methodology/Techniques
System Software   Programming Standards
Language   Documentation Standards

Figure 9.1.   Programmer Productivity Model

grammers. Thus, LOC, ELOC, and E are the dependent variables.

Weekly time reports on the programmers/analysts working on 12 new development projects were collected from 1984 to 1987. The amount of time spent by each member of the team in various phases of the project was derived from the time data. In addition, source listings of all the projects were examined for size and complexity with a code analyzer developed for this study. The average size of the projects was approximately 20,000 LOC. Productivity of each programmer was determined from the time data and source codes.

To measure programmer productivity, the total amount of time spent by the programmers on particular projects was obtained from the weekly time reports. For each project, the project leader provided the details of all the development work performed by each member of the team. Source listings of all programs were kept in a library. All the programs developed by the members during the time period were analyzed for code complexity. The list of programs supplied by the project leaders was compared with the library listing to ensure that all the programs developed during the time period were included in the analysis.

The list of programs written by each programmer during the time period was verified both by the programmer and respective project leader. The listings of programs were manually inspected, and the total number of lines of code were noted. Productivity in LOC was derived by dividing total lines by number of hours.

Executable lines of code (ELOC) was computed by adding command verbs such as *add, multiply,* and so on. This list is a subset of total operators used in Halstead's software science metrics. ELOC productivity was derived by dividing total verbs in all programs by total hours spent.

The following formula was used to measure Halstead's (1977) effort:

$$\text{Effort } E = \frac{n1 N2 (N1 + N2) \log(n1 + n2)}{2(n2)}$$

where,   n1 = number of unique operators
           n2 = number of unique operand
           N1 = total number of operators
           N2 = total number of operand

Effort was calculated for each program written by a programmer and then added to get the total effort for all programs written by the programmer. To express productivity in terms of effort, the total effort was divided by the total number of hours spent by the programmer in developing these programs. Two hundred and forty programs consisting of 330,566 lines of code were written by all the participating programmers. One hundred and ninety-three programs totaling 249,126 lines were analyzed by the COBOL analyzer for ELOC operator and operand counts. Some of the programs were analyzed manually because they belonged to separate divisions of the organization where the COBOL analyzer could not be implemented. For three programmers (20 programs totaling 36,407 lines), LOC was the only productivity measure that could be obtained. Halstead counts and ELOC were computed for 260,464 lines out of 294,159 lines.

Measurement of Production Emphasis of Leadership

The production emphasis of leadership was operationalized using Stogdill's (1972) definition of applying pressure for productive output. The Leader Behavior Description Questionnaire (LBDQ), developed and validated for reliability by Stogdill (1963) at the Bureau of Business Research of Ohio State University, measures 12 dimensions of leader behavior and is widely used in group dynamics research.

Although the entire LBDQ questionnaire was administered, the average scores of the following 10 questions, which are designed to measure production emphasis, were used in this study:

8. Encourages overtime work
18. Stresses being ahead of competing groups
28. Needles members for greater effort
38. Keeps the work moving at a rapid pace
48. Pushes for increased production
58. Asks the members to work harder
68. Permits the members to take it easy in their work
78. Drives hard when there is a job to be done
88. Urges the group to beat its previous record
98. Keeps the group working up to capacity

The Research Site

The information systems division of a large corporation located in a metropolitan city in the United States participated in the research, gave its consent to carry out the questionnaire survey, and allowed all project-related documentation and source code to be accessed. This division of the corporation employs around 250 people, of which about 125 are programmers, analysts, and project leaders who develop and maintain software. During the course of this study, the procedures and facilities for the software development teams were uniform. The following aspects of the organization made it an acceptable research site:

1. All the programs were written in the COBOL language.
2. All the teams were working on business applications required to support the operation and management of the division and the corporation.
3. Each project was headed by a project leader. The number of programmers working on a project varied from 3 to 10.
4. All teams worked with the same hardware and software configuration.
5. The policies for training, promotion, and rewards of personnel were consistent throughout the division.
6. All programmers and project leaders were required to submit a time report each week. This report contains the hours spent on activities within various phases of the systems development life cycle.
7. The division enforces standards in the systems development process, from requirements analysis through implementation and support phases. The phases and various activities performed are listed in the Systems Development Process Standards and Guidelines Manual. The major functions, the personnel responsible for these functions, and the evaluation criteria are also addressed in this manual.
8. A software package called Project Planning and Control System (PPC) was employed by the division to process the weekly time reports of the employees. It generates many summary reports for various levels of management.

DATA ANALYSIS

Means and Scatter Plots

The summary of the dependent variables matrix (Table 9.1) shows that there is a wide variation in productivity with all three measures, especially with the Halstead's effort measure. The individual programmer productivity in LOC has a mean of 6.5 with a standard deviation of 4.1; the individual programmer productivity mean for ELOC is 1.6 and standard deviation is 1.04. In both cases the ratios of standard deviation to mean (coefficient of variation) are 62% and 64%, respectively. E has a mean of 10,569 with standard deviation 13,224 and a coefficient of variation of 1.25. Thus, the means analysis clearly shows wide variations in the productivity of individual programmers in this experiment.

Correlation Analysis

The Pearson correlation analysis (Table 9.2) was run to examine the relationship between the productivity measures and the production emphasis. The negative values of the coefficients implies that production emphasis is negatively related with pro-

Table 9.1. Summary of Dependent Variables

	N	MEAN	STAND DEV	MIN VALUE	MAX VALUE	COEFF VAR
Lines of code (LOCAR)	41	6.54	0.41	17.24	0.62	
Executable Lines of Code (ELOCAR)	38	1.63	1.04	0.13	4.72	0.64
Halstead's Effort (EFFOTAR)	38	10568.95	13224.77	312.39	56747.49	1.25

Table 9.2. Correlation Analysis

	Lines of Code (LOCAR)	Executable Lines of Code (ELOCAR)	Halstead's Effort (EFFOTAR)
Production Emphasis by Leader (PRODEPH)	− 0.372[a]	− 0.336[a]	− .256[b]

[a] Significant at the 0.05 level.
[b] Has a significance level of 0.1204.

grammer productivity, and this correlation is at a confidence level of 95% for LOCAR and ELOCAR and 88% for EFFOTAR.

Regression Analysis

A comprehensive multiple regression analysis was carried out. The meaning of the variables that follow and all the regression results are described in Gowda (1988). The independent variables are the production behavior of the leader, three individual characteristics of the programmers, and three items that measure cohesiveness of the group:

Dependent Variables:
LOCAR: Productivity in LOC
ELOCAR: Productivity in ELOC
EFFOTAR: Productivity in E

Independent Variables:
Cohesive measures
ATG: Person-to-group attraction
PPATN: Person-to-person attraction
PLATN: Person-to-leader attraction

Individual Characteristics:
TRGMTHS: Months of training both within and outside the organization (1 month = 20 days)
COLYRS: Years of college education
COBEXP: Months of COBOL experience at the research site

Leader Behavior:
PRODEPH: Production emphasis

Interaction Terms:
PLX: Interaction term obtained by multiplying the two factors, PLATN and ATG.
PPX: Interaction term obtained by multiplying the two factors, PPATN and ATG.

The fitted models are:

1. LOCAR = 45.85 - 5.98 ATG - 8.50 PPATN - 0.59 PLATN + 0.17 TRGMTHS - 0.73 COLYRS - 0.01 COBEXP - 4.11 PRODEPH + 0.05 PLX + 2.22 PPX

    $F = 1.64$ P-value = 0.15 $R2 = 0.32$

2. ELOCAR = 13.34 - 1.74 ATG - 2.15 PPATN - 0.73 PLATN + 0.05 TRGMTHS - 0.16 COLYRS + 0.001 COBEXP - 1.02 PRODEPH + 0.17 PLX + 0.47 PPX

   F = 1.47 P-value = 0.21 R2 = 0.32

3. EFFOTAR = 236760.25 - 45536.60 ATG - 114801.00 PPATN + 49479.12 PLATN + 83.62 TRGMTHS - 1765.48 COLYRS + 44.67 COBEXP - 13017.50 PRODEPH - 13265.10 PLX + 29588.88 PPX

   F = 1.81 P-value = 0.11 R2 = 0.37

The model of EFFOTAR is the best among the three models because it accounts for 37% of the variations in the dependent variables and has a P-value of 0.11. Although none of these model is significant at the desired confidence level of 95%, it should be noted that in all of the models the independent variable, PRODEPH, has a negative coefficient, which suggests that production emphasis by the leader may be counterproductive.

FINDINGS

The correlation analysis shows a negative relationship between production emphasis by leader and programmer productivity. The correlations were significant with LOC and ELOC at the 0.05 level and had a level of significance of 0.1204 with the E measure.

There are two potential reasons for the negative correlation between production emphasis and programmer productivity. Either the application of pressure affected productivity adversely, or production pressure was applied by the leader because the group contained significant number of poor performers. In any case, this study established a negative relationship between production emphasis and programmer productivity.

The results of the regression model are not significant at the 95% confidence level. However, it should be noted that in all the models the independent variable, PRODEPH, has a negative coefficient. This suggests that production emphasis by the leader may be counterproductive.

Limitations of this Study

Sample size is a limitation of this study. At the beginning of the research there were 80 programmers and project leaders participating in the study. After a year or so, 25 of them moved to a different location; therefore, although time data were collected during that period, they could not be used in the research. At the time of the analysis the data for 55 programmers and project leaders were available. Nine of these were project leaders who were excluded from the study in order to avoid mixing leaders and subordinates. Five observations had to be omitted because they indicated extremely high productivity, possibly due to the fact that a particular group of programmers were enhancing an existing system and were also developing new programs. The programmers may have treated the enhancements as new programs. The final data set contained 41 observations.

Programmer productivity measures is an area of controversy. However, most studies use surrogate measures such as lines of code or Halstead's metrics. We found that although Halstead's effort accounts for both the complexity and length of programs, it takes a considerable amount of time to arrive at the productivity measure. Productivity is also a function of the complexity of the task. Further research efforts may be directed toward arriving at a suitable metric that will combine project factors with code complexity and size. Such a measure should be simple enough so that it could be implemented in the industry with ease and accuracy.

CONCLUSION

This study validated the earlier findings that the productivity of the individual programmer varies widely. This was established in a work environment in which the programming language, compiler, machine, motivation, and reward systems were same. In addition, it found a negative correlation between production pressure and programmer productivity. The correlations between production emphasis were significant with LOC and ELOC at the 0.05 level and had a level of significance of 0.1204 with the E measure.

Although the causal relationship between production pressure and programmer productivity has not been formally established, this exploratory study has established a clear hypothesis that emphasis by the project leader adversely affects programmer productivity. In addition, this study has provided a comprehensive model for studying programmer productivity and the means for operationalizing and measuring factors that affect productivity.

REFERENCES

Benbasat, I. & Vessey, I. (1980). Programmer and analyst time/cost estimation. *MIS Quarterly,* 4(2), 31–63.

Brooks, F.P. (1982). *The mythical man-month.* Reading, MA: Addison-Wesley.

DeMarco, T., & Lister T. (1987). *Peopleware.* New York: Dorset House.

Gowda, R.G. (1988). *Impact of group cohesiveness on programmer productivity.* Unpublished doctoral dissertation, Georgia State University, Atlanta.

Halstead, M.H. (1977). *Elements of software science.* New York: Elsevier North-Holland.

Shen, V.Y., & Dunsmore, H.E. (1981). *Analyzing COBOL programs via software science* (Tech. Rep. No. CSD-TR-348). West Lafayette, IN: Purdue University, Department of Computer Sciences.

Stogdill, R.M. (1963). *Manual for the Leader Behavior Description Questionnaire-Form XII* (Tech. Rep). Columbus: Ohio State University, Bureau of Business Research.

Stogdill, R.M. (1972). Group productivity, drive and cohesiveness. *Organizational Behavior and Human Performance, 8*, 26–42.

Groupware, Teamwork, and Performance: Establishing the Links

Peter Docherty
Institute for Management of Innovation and Technology
Stockholm School of Economics

A.B. (Rami) Shani
James Sena
College of Business
California Polytechnic State University

INTRODUCTION

Pressures of global competition are forcing vendors to position their products to meet changes in the needs and interests of their customers. Of special interest as a vehicle for our research proposal is the exponential growth of computer-driven network communication. The utilization of computer-based networks parallel the explosion of interest and involvement of businesses that occurred following the introduction of the personal computer over a decade ago. Concomitant with the growth in electronic networks is an information technology explosion. Specialized software is being designed to capitalize on the network technology, namely, "groupware." Groupware is the subject of rapidly increased attention from the research community, reflected in numerous articles and conferences—at least one a week during the fall of 1991. There has been research on the use of groupware in confined laboratory sessions at universities and industry test environments (Bostrom, 1990). However, no literature can be found on the effect of groupware on team performance and/or organizational productivity.

Telecommunication network systems using microcomputers, terminals, processors, mainframes, and software are being implemented at an unprecedented rate (Docherty, 1992; Shani & Sena, 1993). New organizational forms and processes are emerging to cope with environmental and technological forces and trends. The business team performance and productivity are directly affected by these changes.

Much has been written about groupware—a collection of electronic tools—under an increasing variety of names: CSGW (Computer-Supported Group Work), CSCW (Computer-Supported Cooperative Work), CAT (Computer-Augmented Teamwork), flexible interactive technologies for multiperson tasks, workgroup computing, GDSS (Group decision support systems), EMS (Electronic Meeting Systems), CWSS (Collaborative Work Support Systems), or TWS (Team Work Systems). The multiple meaning of groupware and the complex management dynamics remain a source of managerial challenge and business confusion.

A review of published material reveals that most studies focus on the technical side of groupware. A few exceptions have recently been documented. Vogel, Nunamaker, Martz, Grohowski & McGoff (1989), in studying the assimilation of information technologies, focused on three major clusters of variables within the organizational and environmental context—group, technology, and task. Surprisingly, team performance was not one of the major variables. Applegate (1991) articulated a comprehensive framework with 11 clusters of group dimensions and variables but did not include technology as one of the major clusters. Bair (1991) offered an integrative five-layer multidisciplinary model for unit analysis. A major emphasis was not placed on the team level. In his speculation on future directions of groupware, Johansen et al. (1991) argue that groupware can assist teams in implementing quality improvement methods. They did not explore the potential effect of groupware on team performance and organizational productivity. Overall, few conceptual maps that can guide groupware technology system analysis can be found in the literature. With the exceptions listed earlier, very few have attempted to dissect, define, typologize, characterize, and categorize groupware and its effect on team performance and organizational productivity.

This chapter presents a sociotechnical system-based concept and a framework for the examination of the effect of groupware on teamwork and performance. Special emphasis is placed on business team functioning. A set of research propositions are advanced and discussed based on the study of groupware utilization at the London Air Traffic Control Center Operation and the Bakeroo Line in the London Underground Control Center.

GROUPWARE: SOME KEY FEATURES

Those involved in research and development on information technology or whose livelihood is bound up in some way with the diffusion and utilization of the set or cluster of technologies labeled as information technology (IT) often maintain that IT is very distinctive. It has been called an "enabling" technology that supports and opens opportunities for many (or all) types of businesses, functions, tasks, and activities in organizations. Processes, structures, and products can be maintained and enhanced with its aid.

What are the key features of IT in this context? Certain aspects of IT are shared with other technologies. For example, IT provides an infrastructure for the storage and distribution of one of the key resources in the organization—information. Technical developments have vastly increased the degrees of freedom available to decision makers in designing organizations, reducing the costs involved, and increasing robustness and flexibility.

The technical developments have also radically improved the "storage capabilities" of the technology. ISDN, optical discs, and database technology allow for the storage of vast amounts of information in whatever form and wherever required by the user. These storage and distribution facilities have sometimes been termed the organizational memory and nervous system. Combined with the inclusion of network capabilities such as client-server, SQL server, and shared resources capabilities, groups can access data across heterogeneous platforms in a uniform manner.

A distinctive feature of some of the newer IT facilities is the transparency component. The software in front-end products presented to end users adds an invisible dimension: The software embodies the models that are used to manipulate data. These models themselves may often be "intransparent" or nonaccessible to the users. The manipulations or transformations carried out within the frameworks of these models support different production and decision processes in organizations. The components in the models can formalize both procedural and declarative knowledge from specific domains encompassing both database and knowledge-based systems. The models may be designed to include information on organizational goals and most important form the viewpoint of dynamic efficiency and learning. The models and systems can be designed to provide feedback on the outcomes of actions taken by the users.

These features of the technology can assume different states or values on a number of properties of the systems involved. These include such properties as:

- system complexity—including the number of components and the strength and character of the couplings between them
- system integration—a special aspect of complexity
- system flexibility—the ease with which it can be altered to meet new demands from its users and the environment
- computing power—key technical performance values
- robustness to breakdowns and breaches of security and privacy
- costs, key economic performance values
- "user friendliness"—key cognitive and sociopsychological properties affecting the end users.

The systems are designed to support a number of generic functions in the organization. These include: communication, coordination, collaboration, decision making, and learning.

TEAM PERFORMANCE AND GROUPWARE:
A SOCIOTECHNICAL SYSTEM PERSPECTIVE

At the most basic level the sociotechnical systems perspective considers every organization to be made up of a social subsystem (the people) using tools, techniques, and knowledge (the technical subsystem) to produce a product or service valued by the environmental subsystem (i.e., Herbst, 1974; Trist, 1982). The degree to which the technical and social subsystems are designed with respect to each other and the environmental subsystem determines how successful and competitive the organization will be (Cherns, 1987; Pasmore,1988; Pava, 1986). Thus, although every organization is perceived as a sociotechnical system, not every organization is designed using sociotechnical systems design principles, methods, processes, and philosophy (Gerwin & Kolodny, 1992; Shani & Elliott, 1989). The economic results of organizations designed according to sociotechnical system design principles are significantly better than comparable organizations of conventional design (Hanna, 1988; Pasmore & Gurley, 1991; Stebbins & Shani, 1989; Eijnatten, 1992).

From the STS point of view, the primary work systems in an organization are teams (Davis, 1983). Team and individual decision-making activities are viewed as complex activities that are required to complete the process of transforming an intake into an output. Team performance is perceived as an outcome of the causal relationships among:

- The Team Business Environment subsystem (or the "team context" that is composed of the nature of the industry, the nature of the organization, the level of technological complexity and sophistication, organization structure and, key organizational processes)
- The Team Technological subsystem (the nature of the hardware, computing, telecommunications and audiovisual equipment, etc.)
- The Team Task subsystem (i.e., the nature of tasks, routine vs. nonroutine tasks, the nature of task interrelationships, the nature of task design, etc.).

The team task subsystem is viewed as a system of activities plus the human and physical resources required to perform the activities. As such, the team task subsystem can be examined in terms of differential task environments—teams within an organization face environments that are different from those of others; differential levels of uncertainty—teams face two types or levels of uncertainty; boundary transaction uncertainty—uncertainty over what, where, or when inputs and outputs cross a team's boundary; conversion uncertainty—uncertainty over how to alter the form, shape, location, or meaning of raw materials; and technically required cooperation—cooperation that is required when, for a given technology or production time, any or all the group's products cannot be produced by a single individual because of limits in individual capacities to perform the necessary conversion or boundary transaction activities.

Many team dynamic elements might influence the effectiveness of work teams:

level of team cohesion, team norms concerning performance, stage of team development, technically proficient team members, reward system that promotes cooperative behavior, training, support and resources required to accomplish the team tasks, degree of team's task stability, degree of interdependency between team members to accomplish the team tasks, to mention a few. The proposed Team Review and Design Framework is presented in Figure 10.1. The framework is used to illustrate and examine our case study. As can be seen, team performance is illustrated as an outcome that is influenced by how well the critical factors are balanced (or fit) with one another.

Starting from the social/activity cluster, the first level—the business activity/environment for the team—is made up of elements and forces in the marketplace in which the team and the organization competes, the business strategy elements that spell out h ow the team and the organization plans to compete in the industry and the characteristics of the firm (i.e., technological complexity, structure, reward systems, control systems, information systems, decision-making processes, the management of human resources, organizational culture), and the elements that have to do with the characteristics of the team members. The second level—the team task design elements—is concerned with the nature of tasks (i.e., routine vs. nonroutine tasks), task interrelationships, task environment, and task design.

The third level in the model is the generic behaviors of the teams, such as communication and decision making. It are these generic behaviors or activities that are the object of technological support, especially in the context of groupware. In this respect groupware is similar to office automation systems. IT applications in other areas such as decision support systems and production systems are more clearly linked to the team tasks.

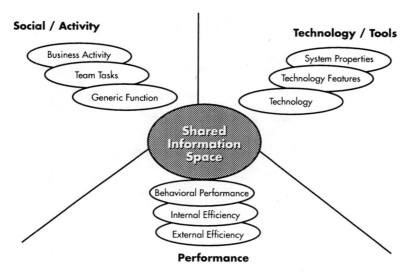

Figure 10.1.   Team Review and Design Perspective.

The second cluster—team technology/tools—is made up of elements of the technology and tools (both hardware and software) utilized by the team. The functional features of these applications that are important for team performance have been indicated earlier, for example, the provision of infrastructure, memory, models, and feedback. Similar key properties of the systems have also been broached.

The matching between levels and sectors (sociology and technology) determine the level of performance—the third cluster. The CSCW and groupware literature reflects a total dearth of interest and evidence regarding benefits and performance of the systems. At best there is a footnote on the difficulties associated with the area. Otherwise the proponents content themselves with the bland statement that the benefits are so patently obvious that a more stringent and scholarly effort to establish the character and extent of the benefits would be a wasteful use of scarce research and development (R&D) resources.

The cited patently obvious benefits are exclusively related to behavioral performance, such as the generation of text (the more, the better, and the quicker, the better). Here the similarity with the earlier reasoning on office automation is positively embarrassing. The team's internal and external efficiency are hardly ever broached. This is also related to the fact that the applications are often used by ad hoc constellations of individuals in an organization that has no real tasks or business goals. Our issue can boil down to: Does teamware have any relevance for teams? Figure 10.2 summarizes our proposed schema for the assessment of the potential contribution of groupware to improved performance in teams. One of the basic definitions of groupware and CSCW

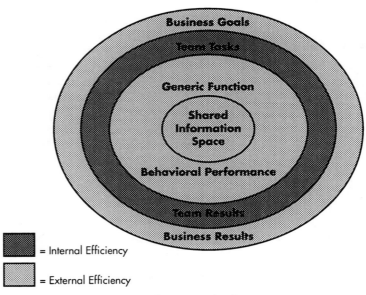

Figure 10.2. Groupware and Performance.

is that the applications provide a shared information space for multiple participants engaged in a common task. Starting from this, we work in our analysis from the general to the specific and from the micro to the macro (team to organization).

The literature, as noted, is mainly composed of two-dimensional frameworks. The main focus, which is understandable, is the relation between the social and the technical spheres as they are presented in Figure 10.1. This also relates the activity in question to the tool that will be used to facilitate its execution. The more established field for the application of sociotechnical systems theory has been the manufacturing setting. In that context the production entails the manipulation of materials. Kern and Schuman (1980) in their studies of the impact of technology on individuals and their competencies classify production processes according to whether they involve the processing of materials, information, or relationships. Here we are principally interested in technologies manipulating information, although this may have consequences for materials and relationships. The potential impact of the technical support on performance affects the terms or dimensions in which the technology is meaningfully described. Teamwork, computer support, and performance must be described in dimensions that allow the identification of meaningful links between the three areas. The natural development process will entail the description of the teamwork situation in terms of a number of subtasks and generic functions, together with the definition of a number of key performance indicators related to the teams goals. The third step is to establish the features of the technical support that are most relevant to the tasks and the performance variables. The features or dimensions in which the technology is defined will not, in the first instance, be technical characteristics but reflect its relations to the business, the organization, and the individual user. This is best understood by providing real-life illustrations of the dimensions.

The task features may be described both in terms of subtasks that are specific for the individual case and in more general functions. Thus, the main tasks of the traffic control team in a city underground train service can be defined as: train schedule revision, provision of station service information, train reallocation, and staff reallocation. Examples of more generalized tasks that may be included in these tasks, are: planning, decision making, coordination, monitoring, evaluation, problem solving, and conflict solving.

The team tasks must be performed efficiently and effectively. When examining performance it is useful to focus on two dimensions: change in and focus on the environment (see figure 10.3). The change dimension refers to an important aspect of the conditions prevailing when the team is performing. Is it designed to perform under static or stable conditions? (This is the usual point of departure in static Western production systems, e.g., in "Fordism" in the manufacturing industry.) Or is it designed to perform under changing and turbulent conditions (for example, characterizing "Toyotism" in the manufacturing industry) (Bjorkman, Berggren & Hollander, 1991)? This turbulence and change is not reserved in this context for world recessions or the like but may simply entail the inclusion of nonroutine activities in the team task, for example, problem solving in contingencies or development work (Koicke, 1989).

		Change Dimension	
		Static	Dynamic
Focus	Internal Effectiveness	Productivity Rationalization	Individual and Organizational Learning
	External Effectiveness	Improved Utility to Customers Improved Quality	Adaptability

Figure 10.3.   Change and Efficiency in Team Work Context.

The second dimension is that of the focus on internal efficiency in an organization's use and development of its resources and on external efficiency in its relations with its environment. Figure 10.3 shows examples of performance aspects in the different subfields broached here.

In the team situation it is important to be aware of the specific motivations and rewards, tasks/functions, and performance associated with the team. We must know what it is that the computer support is supposed to be providing, reinforcing, or enhancing. Technical features of the computer support as they may be expected to affect performance have been the object of considerable study by both social and computer scientists. We feel that the most appropriate ways of describing important system features have mainly emerged in the fields of cognitive and developmental psychology. We present a list of features based mainly on the work of the research groups under the German developmental psychologist Volpert (1988) and the Swiss cognitive psychologist Ulrich (1987).

The research points identify the following features of computer support as important:

- Transparency: The users should be able to "see" and understand the internal processes of the software—to create a personal, internal model to facilitate their learning and their control of the system. They should be able to understand what the system is doing at any given time and why.
- Structurability: The users should be provided with leeway to develop their personal style for carrying out the task. Ulrich (1988) refers to the differential and flexible nature of work in this context, referring to "open" procedure and autonomy of interaction speeds. Corbett (1989) refers to the freedom to trade off requirements and resource limits by shifting operating strategies, without losing the software support. For example, is a "valid" circumvention of the system possible? Other variations on this theme specified by Volpert (1988) are scope for action, autonomy in time, and freedom from regulation hindrances.
- Reliability: This covers such aspects as robustness, or 100% functionality under varying conditions of use; consistency use, that the system reacts in the same way to the same user inputs; and tolerance, which refers to the system's flexibility to allow inter-

rupted or intermittent use or variations in the mode or form for inputting data.
- Integration: This refers to the integration of the various subtasks in the team's work via different applications into a single system.
- Competence support: This covers such aspects as compatibility of the skills required by the system and those already possessed by the users; fallibility, insuring that the users' tacit knowledge and skills have not been designed out of the system; feedback from the system on the efficacy of action taken by the users; and error reversibility, including the forwarding of information so that the likely consequences of particular operations may be assessed by the users.
- Cognitive ergonomics: This focuses on information load and the ability to perceive and understand it correctly. A term that applies here and to the system structure as a whole is "complexity."

A fundamental axiom of sociotechnical system thinking is that whatever decisions are made about or within any one of the organizational subsystems, they should meet the demands of the remaining others. Any decision about work design should meet the demands of the technical, social, and environmental subsystems. Similarly, a strategic decision to increase the market share of a specific product requires not only understanding of the industry, competition, customers' demand, and marketing know-how, but the technological ability to increase production, the trained people to do the work, and the team design to support it.

A strategic decision to utilize groupware as a means of conducting team business needs to incorporate a careful assessment and a matching process of the overall team business environment in concert with the nature of the team task. Cultural and quality issues may impact the selection and use of the most appropriate groupware technology. It may be that a redesign of a company's organizational structure and processes could be warranted to achieve full utilization of the new systems' potential (Chamran, 1991).

THE COMPLEXITY OF THE PHENOMENON:
AN ILLUSTRATION

The sociotechnical-based concepts and framework advanced in this chapter raises many theoretical questions about the potential causal relationship between groupware and team performance. The following three propositions are posed to exemplify the complexity of the phenomenon. Their discussion—based on the Bakeroo Line in the London Underground Control Center and the London Air Traffic Control Center studies—could serve to illuminate both the potential embedded in the utilization of a sociotechnical system-based framework and potential direction for future research.

Proposition 1.   Sociotechnical system design principles must be integrated in the design of groupware systems for collaborative work situations for the systems to be optimally utilized.

We noted earlier in this chapter that whereas every organization is perceived as a sociotechnical system, not every organization is designed according to sociotechnical design principles. At a general level one can find agreement among organization design experts. Regardless of the specific design principles that guided the design of the organization, the technology utilized by the firm must be "compatible" with the existing organizational configurations in order for the technology to be utilized to its potential.

Organization design principles using sociotechnical system concepts have been developed and examined via experimentation over the last 40 years by Emery and Trist (1972), Cherns (1976), Cummings (1978), Davis (1983), Pasmore (1988), and Taylor (1990), among others. Pasmore (1988) grouped the design principles into six broad design objectives: utilizing social and technical resources effectively, development of commitment and energy, maximizing cooperative efforts, developing human abilities, innovation, and awareness of external environment.

Sociotechnical system theorists have been advocating the need to study how technology can be developed and designed to support the kinds of systems that organizations try to develop (i.e., Pasmore, 1988; Shani & Elliott, 1989; Taylor, 1990). The same holds true for the design of groupware technology. The integration of groupware technology into an existing organization requires a major alignment of the two systems. Both the London Air Traffic Control Center (LATCC) and the London Underground Bakeroo Line Control Center (LUBLCC) cases illustrate that we have yet to design a technological system to support an existing system.

The LATCC recently underwent a major attempt to incorporate new groupware technologies for air traffic control (Docherty, 1992; Harper, Hughes, & Shapiro, 1991). The Air Traffic Control (ATC) organization is a complex system that was created to guide, advise, and control aircraft traffic. The system has evolved into an elaborated "rules of the air" and "procedural control" based on a network of airways between hubs. A key feature of the system is the requirement that each pilot submit flight plans before departure to the air traffic control authorities. The air traffic controllers' comparison of these plans is intended to secure safety in the same airspace.

This basic feature—enhanced significantly by innovative radio communications, radar, data processes software, and hardware computer technology—is at the nucleus of the ATC organization. The need to safely secure the airspace resulted in a highly regulated work environment that is worldwide and encompasses multiple ATC organizations. Prior to the introduction of the new groupware technology—labeled RD3—the ATC work organization was based on air traffic control teams that utilized a "mediator" system. Variable data such as wind speed, weather, and departure time were all fed into the computer, and "Flight Progress Strip" and estimated arrival time of the aircraft were provided to the team working in the specific lending strip. The computer printout provided the team with additional information such as desired destination and path, imminent arrival, and speed. The computer was designed to process radar data and present the relevant information on the radar screens. The team could request screen displays for a variety of data combinations. It is important to note that the computer was not programmed to function as an "expert system," that is, to make decisions. The "mediator" system also included the complete station design such as the location of furniture and radar screens.

One major feature of the technological system in ATC organizations is that the pace of technological change remains incremental and piecemeal (Hughes, Shapiro, Sharrock, & Anderson, 1988). Management decision to implement the RD3 system—a system that was initially designed and reported to have worked well in another organization with different work organization—was due the perceived advantages of the system, including providing combinations of flight data processing and radar data processing; changing the type and source of information available to controllers; enhancing team performance; and, because it will use the existing furniture, using the existing system as a backup.

Initially, the expectations for an improved work environment, better information, higher quality of information, improved team work efficiency, and expediting task control were high (Hughes et al., 1988). The results were disappointing. The technological design of the RD3 was not as compatible with the technological designs of the other technical components of the system as was initially anticipated. The RD3 was too structured and did not provide individuals with leeway to develop and utilize their own personal style for working together and carrying out the team task. It did not meet the criteria of structurability, and the RD3 was perceived by the teams as unreliable and untrustworthy due to perceived technological shortcomings. In sum, the RD3 was not designed according to the same design principles that the LATCC organization was, nor was it compatible with the work organization that was in place. The impact of these findings resulted in the decision not to use the RD3 system (Harper et al., 1991).

Proposition 2.   To the extent that the key features of groupware technology (such as transparency, structurability, reliability) "fit" the key features of the team tasks (such as routine and nonroutine tasks, interrelationship, task environment), the team's efficiency is likely to increase.

The holistic nature of the sociotechnical system-based framework proposed in this chapter provides a unique opportunity to investigate the potential causal relationship between key features of the groupware technology, key features of the team tasks, and the team's efficiency. A variety of variables were identified in the proposed framework under each of these factors. It is beyond the scope of this chapter to explore each one of the potential causal relationships. The overriding performance criterion—efficiency—in both the air traffic control and the Bakeroo underground line cases is safety: the avoidance of accidents and "close calls."

At the Bakeroo Line the team tasks included both routine and nonroutine dimensions. Repetitive tasks, such as monitoring the semicircular console, were coupled with nonrepetitive tasks such as infrequent communication with the drivers, the public address on the status of the incoming trains, observation of the close-circuit television, and communication with other team members. The groupware technology that was adopted for the team at the control room was based on its perceived potential to support and enhance cooperative group work. The Bakeroo Line Control Room houses a team—composed of the line controller, Divisional Information Assistants (DIA), and signal men—that oversees and controls the operation of the line. The controller and the DIA sit together at a semicircular console facing a tiled, real-time, hard-line display showing the traffic movement along the Bakeroo Line. The console includes touch-screen telephones, a radio system for contact with the drivers, the public address system keys, and close-circuit television monitors and controls for viewing platforms. Three signal assistants sit at a similar console next to the other console sharing the same display of the line, same audio and video channels of the communication system, and various keypads and monitors (Heath, Luff & Kingdom, 1991).

The team members' ability to be able to see and understand the internal processes of the software and to create a personal, internal model to facilitate their learning and their control of the system meets the first groupware technology feature of "transparency." However, a careful examination of the nature of work reveals the absence of "open" procedures and autonomy of interaction. The team members had very little leeway to develop personal style for carrying out the task. Furthermore, the technology and physical layout of the two consoles side by side were not congruent with the structurability requirement (the second groupware technology key feature). The simplistic discussion of the prior two examples illustrates the complexity of the phenomenon. The intricate potential causal relationships between the key groupware technology features, the variety of team tasks, and team efficiency calls for the need of intense future study.

Proposition 3.   To the extent that groupware technology promotes individuals understanding of the situation, it is likely to lead to improved individual competence and well-being.

The issue of individual knowledge, skills, and competence seems to be at the center of groupware technology (Applegate, 1991; Gallupe et al., 1992; Lyytinen & Ngwenyama, 1992; Vogel & Nunamaker, 1990). A key tenet of sociotechnical system design principles is the commitment to the development and utilization of human abilities (Cummings, 1986; Pasmore, 1988). The interplay between human and technological developments can foster synergistic effects (Nyhan, 1991). Technological designers seldom focus on the effect their development might have on the individuals that will have to make the technology work. Many times the technological designs work against establishing an environment in which self-learning is nurtured.

Competence and self-learning are critical to the successful utilization of groupware technology. Groupware technology can help foster the establishment of a work situation that enables individuals to actively learn. At the Air Traffic Control Center, the RD3 groupware technology seems to have worked against individual's energy to increase competence. Among other things, the teams complained about the difficulty of accessing information displays, the irrelevance of some of the information provided, problems with the data processing, unreliability of the software, lack of understanding of the software, and the software's confusing layout. The experiences at the Underground Control Room—the collaborative-based technology—were similar. Although the technology was designed to support collaborative work, the informal work practices and procedures, whereby team members systematically communicated information and coordinated a disparate collection of tasks and activities, was not enhanced. The new technology had to be redesigned to better accommodate the need to foster collaborative work as well as nurture a work situation leading to the improvement of individual competence.

CONCLUSIONS

We proposed three propositions that lie at the heart of any successful groupware development. Because the obvious objective of groupware is to facilitate group teamwork and decision making it would seem that: (a) sociotechnical design principles or some similar organizational analysis and design platform would be incorporated/integrated into the groupware. Our two example systems indicate that this is not happening. (b) A team's efficiency will increase given that the groupware's key features are commensurate with the features of the team tasks. Because of the intricacy in assessing such efficiency gains, the cursory treatment in this chapter indicates that explicit considerations were given in both studies to match the groupware features to the team tasks. And (c) an individual's understanding of the groupware would increase one's competence and well-being. In both studies this did not appear to be the case. Our analysis, we believe, merits further study of the potential introduction of a sociotechnical system-based framework for the study of the groupware phenomena.

REFERENCES

Applegate L.M. (1991). Technology support for cooperative work: A framework for studying introduction and assimilation in organizations. *Journal of Organizational Computing, 1*(1), 11–40.

Bair, I. (1991). A layered model of organizations: Communication processes and performance. *Journal of Organizational Computing, 1*(2), 187–204.

Bjorkman, T., Berggren, C., & Hollander E. (1991). *Är de oslagbara? (Are they invincible?),* Stockholm, Sweden: IMIT Publications.

Bostrom, R. (1990, October). Keynote presentation at *Human Factors in Information Systems Symposium,* Norman, OK.

Chamran, R. (1991). How networks reshape organizations—for results. *Harvard Business Review,* pp. 104–114.

Cherns, A.B. (1976). The principles of sociotechnical design. *Human Relations, 29*(8), 783–792.

Cherns, A.B. (1987). The principles of sociotechnical design revisited. *Human Relations, 40*(3), 153–161.

Cummings, T.G. (1978). Sociotechnical experimentation: A review of sixteen studies. In W.A. Pasmore & J.J. Sherwood (Eds.), *Sociotechnical systems: A sourcebook.* La Jolla, CA: University Associates; pp. 259–270.

Cummings, T.G. (1986). A concluding note: Future directions of sociotechnical theory and research. *The Journal of Applied Behavioral Science, 22*(3), 355–360.

Davis, L.E. (1983). Workers and technology: The necessary joint basis for organizational effectiveness. *National Productivity Review, 3*(1), 7–14.

Docherty, P. (1992). *CSCW: A promise soon to be Realized.* Stockholm: Teldok Publications.

Eijnatten, M.F. (1992). *An anthology of the sociotechnical system design paradigm.* Eindhoven, Netherlands: Eindhoven University of Technology Press.

Emery, F.E., & Trist, E.L. (1972). *Towards a social ecology.* New York: Plenum Press.

Gallupe, R.B., Dennis, A.R., Cooper, W.A., Valacich, J.S., Bastianutti, L., & Nunamaker, J.F. (1992). Electronic brainstorming and group size. *Academy of Management Journal, 35*(2), 350–369.

Gerwin, D., & Kolodny H. (1992). *Management of advanced manufacturing technology.* New York: Wiley.

Hanna, D. (1988). *Designing organizations for high performance.* Reading, MA: Addison-Wesley.

Harper R.R., Hughes J.A., & Shapiro D.Z. (1991). Harmonious working and CSCW: Computer technology and air traffic control. In B.L. Robinson & K. Schmidt (Eds.), *Proceedings of the 2nd European Conference on Computer-Support Cooperative Work* (pp. 225–234). Amsterdam: Kluwer Academic Press.

Heath C., Luff P., & Kingdom, U. (1991). Collaborative activity and technological design: Task coordination in London Underground Control Room. In B.L. Robinson & K. Schmidt (Eds.), *Proceedings of the 2nd European Conference on Computer-Support Cooperative Work* (pp. 65–80). Amsterdam: Kluwer Academic Press.

Herbst, P. (1974). *Sociotechnical design: Strategies in multidisciplinary research.* London: Tavistock Publications.

Hughes J.A., Shapiro, D.Z., Sharrock, W.W., & Anderson, R. (1988). *The automation of air traffic control* (Final Rep.).

Johansen, R., Sibbet, D., Benson, S., Martin, A., Mitman, R., & Saffo, P. (1991). *Leading business teams.* Reading, MA: Addison-Wesley.

Kern, H. & Schumann, M. (1980). Realization and the Behavior Workers-Conceptual Ideas & Hypotheses for New Research. *Economics and Industrial Democracy, 1*(4).

Koicke, K. (1989). *Human resource development on the shipping floor in contemporary Japan.* Stockholm: Arbetslivscentrum.

Lyytinen, K.J., & Ngwenyama, O.K. (1992). What does computer support for cooperative work mean? *Accounting, Management & Information Technology, 2*(1), 19–37.

Nyhan, B. (1991). *Developing people's ability to learn: A european perspective on self-learning competency and technological change.* Brussels: European Inter University Press.

Pasmore, W.A. (1988). *Designing effective organizations: The sociotechnical systems perspective.* New York: Wiley.

Pasmore, W.A., & Gurley, K. (1991). Enhancing R&D across functional areas. In R.H. Kilman (Ed.), *Making organizations competitive* (pp. 368-396). San Francisco: Jossey-Bass.

Pava, C.H. (1986). Redesigning sociotechnical system design: Concepts and methods for the 1990s. *Journal of Applied Behavioral Science, 22*(3), 201–221.

Sena, J., & Shani, A.B. (1995). Organizational implications of local network systems: A sociotechnical system perspective. In J. Carey (Ed.), *Human factors in information systems,* (Vol. 3, pp. 313–334). Norwood, NJ: Ablex.

Shani, A.B. & Elliott, O. (1989). Sociotechnical system design in transition. In W. Sikes, A. Drexler, & J. Grant (Eds.), *The emerging practice of organization development* (pp. 187–198), La Jolla, CA: University Associates.

Shani, A.B., & Sena, J. (1993). ITs and structural change: The case of local area network implementation, *Journal of Information Technology, 8,* 34–42.

Stebbins, M. & Shani, A.B. (1989). Winter, Moving away from the "Mafia" model of organization design. *Organizational Dynamics,* pp. 18–30.

Taylor, J. (1990, August). *Two decades of sociotechnical systems in north america.* Paper presented at the annual Academy of Management Conference, San Francisco, CA.

Trist, E.L. (1982). Sociotechnical systems perspective. In A.H. Van de Ven & W.F. Joyce (Eds.), *Perspectives on organization design & behavior* (pp. 19–75). New York: Wiley.

Ulrich, E. (1987). Some aspects of user-oriented dialogue design. In P. Docherty (Ed.), *System design for human development: Participation and beyond.* Amsterdam: North-Holland.

Vogel, D.R., & Nunamaker, J.F. (1990). Design and assessment of group decisions support systems. In *Intellectual teamwork: Social and technology foundations of cooperative work* (pp. 511–528). Hillsdale, NJ: Erlbaum.

Vogel, D.R., Nunamaker, J.E., Martz, W.B., Grohowski, R., & McGoff, C. (1989). Electronic Meeting Experience at IBM, *Journal of Management Information System, 6*(3), 25–43.

Volpert, W. (1988). *What working and living conditions are conducive to human development?* (Swedish-German Workshop on the Ammanization of Working Life). Stockholm: Arbetsmiljofonden.

Conceptual Framework and Research Strategy Considerations: The Study of MIS Professional Ideology

K. Gregory Jin
Western Connecticut State University

INTRODUCTION

Past MIS research attention has focused on the power dimension of political process involved in the development of information systems (Franz & Robey, 1984; Keen & Gerson, 1977; Kling, 1980; Markus, 1983a, 1983b, 1984; Robey & Markus, 1984); due emphasis has not been placed on the ideological dimension of the political process. Although some recent studies have dealt with ethical issues in the MIS profession (Couger, 1989; Mason, 1986; Paradice, 1990; Vitell & Davis, 1990), MIS professional ideology has not been treated as a conceptual construct in MIS research.

The study of MIS ideological issues is significant because it contributes to the understanding of how ideological factors affect the role of MIS professionals in the success of MIS development. It would help to enlighten the human and social value implications of the MIS profession beyond its day-to-day operational and technical consciousness in an organizational setting. It would provide MIS professionals and managers with useful ideological guidelines for "managing" ethics problems in MIS.

The importance of organizational ideological considerations has been reflected in recent studies, which have shown that a fundamental ideology (Brunsson, 1982) as a set of basic philosophy, values, beliefs, and "aspirations" plays a key role in the success of corporations (Howard, 1990; Ouchi, 1981; Pascale & Athos, 1981), and that it is also an important determinant of human actions and decision making in the organization (Beyer, 1981; Ravlin & Meglino, 1987). Successful organizations, such as Hewlett-Packard (Ouchi, 1981) and Levi Strauss (Howard, 1990), are known for their fundamental ideologies that would help generate the voluntary, constructive, and dedicated actions of their employees (including MIS professionals). In the case of Levi Strauss, values—a key component of ideology—is a driving force in achieving technological applications and competitive success.

In the same vein, the MIS profession needs its own professional ideology that would generate positive MIS actions and behaviors. Although it would be integrated with an organizational ideology, the MIS ideology should be based on the MIS professional's own vision for, commitment to, and responsibility for seeing that information technology is used dynamically for the benefit of total humanity today and in the coming decade. Such an MIS professional ideology needs to reflect an integrated set of higher human, social, and ethical values (Johnson & Snapper, 1985; Mason, 1986) beyond the operational and technical consciousness of the MIS professional (Jin, 1991). The "higher goals" can be developed along such basic issues as world peace, environmental protection, privacy protection, effective education, and health care (Shneiderman, 1990). A challenging task of university-based researchers and practitioners in the MIS field would be to develop, research, and promote such an MIS Professional Ideology (MPI) jointly with those in other disciplines. This task first would necessitate the recognition of the importance of intensive research on the MPI at various levels—at the MIS project and organizational levels and at the societal and international levels. The MPI researchers then need to formulate a conceptual framework relevant to the real world and an effective and action-based research strategy.

The purpose of this chapter is to discuss a conceptual framework necessary for the study of MIS professional ideology; to review various research concepts, methods, and approaches used in other disciplines in the study of ideology; and to consider relevant research issues, strategies, and perspectives in studying MIS ideological issues.

A CONCEPTUAL FRAMEWORK

A Definition of MIS Professional Ideology

The belief system of MIS professionals based on a set of fundamental human and social values beyond the operational and technical requirements of MIS work may be called an MIS professional ideology (MPI). The MIS professional needs a *satisfying ideology*, an integrated system of basic philosophy, ideas, values, beliefs, drives, and attitudes that posits certain worthwhile goals that realistically satisfy not only one's enlightened self-interest but also the need to uphold higher social values. While recognizing political realities, computer and information system professionals need to develop higher goals along fundamental issues such as "world peace, medical and psychological health care, adequate nutrition and housing, safe transportation, protection of environment, effective education, access to communication and information resources, freedom of expression, support for creative exploration, privacy protection, and socially constructive entertainment and sports" (Shneiderman, 1990).

A positive MIS professional ideology may be considered a cogent source of basic

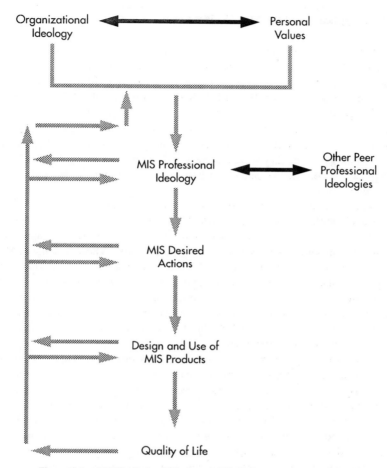

Figure 11.1.   MIS Professional Ideology (MPI) (A Conceptual Framework).

driving forces that would help energize and inspire MIS professionals to take positive constructive actions in the creation and renewal of MIS for higher human and social purposes. Paradoxically, then, in addition to the cognitive, intellectual understanding of MIS technical issues and discrete computer/MIS ethical codes, a positive MIS ideology is needed, in a normative sense, to increase the human drives, capabilities, enthusiasms (Ouchi, 1981) and desired MIS actions of the MIS professional. Such MIS actions would then affect the design and use of MIS products for the MPI higher goals, which would ultimately influence the quality of life. This conceptual framework is depicted in Figure 11.1.

An MPI Application at the MIS Project Level

The author of this chapter in the capacity of an MIS manager observed in the past that certain basic ideological orientations have positive influences on MIS professionals in bringing about their desired behavioral patterns or constructive actions necessary for success in MIS development (Barnard, 1938; Beyer, 1981; Jin, 1991; March & Simons, 1958). The positive ideological orientations (Jin, 1991) of MIS professionals were manifested in their genuine fundamental belief in the higher human and social value of the mission of the MIS projects to which they were assigned. Because they believed in the larger meaning of what they were assigned to do in their projects, they tended to be more proactive, constructive, and enthusiastic in their work than if they did not have a fundamental belief.

To illustrate, in some MIS project situations, driven by an MPI, certain systems professionals working in educational institutions or hospitals seem to take *more* desired positive actions (e.g., cooperative, constructive, and enthusiastic) *more* voluntarily and proactively than some others who do not espouse an MPI. Those lacking an MPI do not seem to conceive a larger goal for which to develop a new system. They think of their professional goal as "designing a system" rather than as contributing to a larger purpose, such as patient care or student education. Those who have an MPI seem to transcend their consciousness of simply "designing systems" (in a technical sense); they would commit to the worthwhile objective of helping the patients or students via their MIS professional contributions.

Some computer programmers, for example, who are engaging in the development of a new student registration system for a large university seem to consider their role as "programming" based on the program specifications given to them by systems analysts in charge of system design. They feel that their daily work assignment is to coding certain program modules during the work hours 8:30 to 5:00. They sometimes do not have a good conception of what the system is for except for their notion that the program modules (e.g., edit or update program) to which they are assigned somehow fit the "new system" required by the organization. They tend not to view their professional role in terms of their contribution to the meaningful human and social goals.

A positive MPI, if the systems analysts and programmers espoused it, would inspire them to genuinely care about the university goal of student education and to contribute to the organizational goals through their professional work. They would want to serve the social and educational goal through their contribution to the timely design of the systems for the benefit of students (or patients) and not just for their employer—the university (or hospital) administration. With the basic belief system, the systems analyst or programmer would be more seriously and enthusiastically disposed to design a system that is really useful for patient care or student education rather than simply for the sake of completing the system within a certain deadline mandated by a project control schedule.

At least two other positive orientations—pragmatism and innovation—seem to coexist with a fundamental ideological commitment and proactive and enthusiastic manifestations (Jin, 1991). In resolving difficult MIS implementation issues, the professionals seem to be pragmatic and flexible; realistically, they are willing to accept human constraints put on the pursuit of idealistically rational goals after a certain critical point. They tend to go through an agonizing appraisal in achieving a balance between political interest reflected in the project control process on the one hand (e.g., holding to the original project deadline set by the MIS department without increasing the original project scope in the face of the user's pressure to add more user requirements) and their genuine concern for serving the user's functional needs on the other (e.g., developing a better system for the benefit of users by accommodating additional user requirements requested by the user, even if that means not meeting the original project deadline). Systems professionals also seem to have an open frame of mind that is conducive to creative exploration of different views and design alternatives in an uncertain and dynamic organizational conditions. This is a partial example of the author's personal observation of positive MIS ideological orientations affecting MIS project implementation.

This concept of MIS professionals' ideology is intended to show its potential impact on their constructive choice behavior patterns or actions in their organizational and social life (Guth & Renato, 1965; Howard, 1990; Ravlin & Meglino, 1987). This is, admittedly, an ideal conception of what an MIS professional ought to be. Ironically, however, it is precisely this idealistic bent that provides raison d'etre of a positive MIS professional ideology. The belief as a basic tenet of the MPI seems to stem from a set of fundamental human and social values to which the MIS professionals commit in an MIS project situation, in an organizational environment, and in a societal or international setting. These values may reflect certain "strong cultural values," which were found to be effective and useful in El Sawy's (1985) study in bringing about desired behavioral patterns in MIS project situations. They may reflect their personal values (Posner & Schmidt, 1992) and/or corporate ideological orientations (Beyer, 1981; Beyer & Trice, 1981). In a global context, they may mirror certain universal good (e.g., human dignity and human right) for mankind as a whole.

MIS Professional Ideology in an Organizational Context

An MIS professional ideology does not exist in vacuum. It is influenced not only by the personal values (England, 1967; Posner & Schmidt, 1992) of the MIS professionals and those of their peer professional group members but also by an organizational ideology professed by the organization's leadership often in the form of a vision or aspiration statement. Recent studies (e.g., Howard, 1990) also emphasized the importance of communicating corporate ideologies to the grass-root employees and empowering the employees based on ideological principles. For example, in its "Aspiration Statement," the Levi Strauss Corporation espoused the empowerment principle that "increases the authority and responsibility of those closest to our products and customers" and that "by actively pushing responsibility, trust, and recognition into the organization, we can harness and release the capabilities of all our people" (Howard, 1990, p. 135). There seems to be increasing evidence for emphasis on empowerment of employees and a self-managed work group concept (Posner & Schmidt, 1992).

Although it is an important indication of the organization's attention to values, the mere existence of a statement of corporate ideologies is not a sufficient condition for organizational effectiveness. Another necessary ingredient for organizational success is demonstration of the fact that people in organizations *genuinely* and *fundamentally believe* in the organizations ideologies. If such a fundamental genuine belief is to exist, the organization's ideological principle must be communicated to its people, understood by its people, and accepted voluntarily by its people. The bottom line is, as the CEO of Levi Strauss stated, "a strategy is no good if people don't fundamentally believe in it" (Howard, 1990, p. 134).

The voluntary acceptance of corporate ideology by its people presupposes that the individual employee's values are congruent with the organization's ideologies. However, in real life discrepancies between the organization's objectives and the individual MIS professional's interests and demands have been reported in recent MIS literature (Kling, 1980; Robey & Markus, 1984; White & Leifer, 1986). MIS professionals have been known to act in pursuit of their professional or political interest rather than in the organization's best interest (Robey & Markus, 1984). White and Leifer (1986) found that IS personnel surveyed considered neither management support nor user involvement as critical to successful system development and suggested that IS personnel lacked cross-functional orientation as IS people viewed the information systems function "as distinct from the rest of the organization" (p. 222). This was illustrated in the case mentioned earlier of systems personnel in a large hospital who indicated during an interview that their mission was to "design systems" without any reference to patient care as the primary mission of the hospital. When doctors and nurses were interviewed, patient care was clearly identified as the primary objective of their being in the hospital.

The conceptual framework discussed earlier suggests the following research question: What are the significant relationships and differences between an MIS professional ideology and the other types of ideologies (e.g., corporate ideology, accountant ideology, and sales professional ideology)? To illustrate, my co-researcher and I have recently undertaken a research project that was intended to investigate such an issue, for example, the influence of an organizational ideology on the ethical attitudes of MIS

Table 11.1.   LEVELS OF MPI DEVELOPMENT AND IMPACT

	MIS Project Level	Organizational Level	Societal Level	Global Level
Organizational Ideology	X	X	X	X
MIS PROFESSIONAL IDEOLOGY	X	X	X	X
Other Professional Ideologies	X	X	X	X

professionals. The project also investigates the differences in the extent of ethicality between MIS professionals and marketing professionals. Another research question would be: What is the impact of MPI on desired MIS actions, design, and use of MIS products, and ultimately the quality of life in different settings? Such significant research issues may be studied at various levels, such as, at the MIS project level, organizational level, societal level, and international level (Table 11.1).

Problems in the Study of MIS Professional Ideology

To study such MPI research issues, we need to be bold enough to admit that it requires special ingenuity to delve into the nebulous and intangible yet real variables—e.g., values and beliefs. Over the years, MIS researchers have focused on investigating more tangible variables such as technical issues, concrete behavioral issues, decision variables, for example, development stages, and political factors involved in MIS implementation. The reason for this seems to be that researching such ambiguous concepts is difficult and time consuming, not conducive to systematic empirical investigations. To borrow Sproull's (1981) explanation of reasons for the difficulty and problems involved in the study of beliefs:

> It is difficult to study beliefs. They cannot be measured directly; only statements about them or artifacts from them are accessible to description and measurement. Furthermore, they may change dramatically over time; thus even an excellent description of beliefs at one time may not accurately predict beliefs at some future time. In addition, the relationships between the beliefs of individual people and shared beliefs present problems; both are important, but shared beliefs do not simply aggregate the beliefs of individuals. (p. 203)

Because the study of MIS ideology entails special kinds of research problems, we need to explore "nonconventional" or innovative research strategy frameworks. We need a research approach for investigating, in depth and over time, the factors affecting the ideological orientations of MIS professionals and the impact of the MPI on their work behavioral processes or MIS actions, project outcome, organizational and social transformation, and international human progress. To this end, in the remainder of this chapter, the author reviews some research concepts, methods, and strategies that have been used and tested in other disciplines in the study of belief, value, and attitudinal dimensions of ideology and that seem to have relevancy and applicability to the study of MPI ideological issues.

RESEARCH CONCEPTS, STRATEGIES, AND PERSPECTIVES

One of the advantages of using ideology as a conceptual construct in MIS research is that it gives "analytical bite" (Pettigrew, 1973), concentrating on certain aspects that "catch something essential in the organizational culture" (Alvesson, 1987, p.12). Sproull (1981) recognizes the theoretical importance of beliefs in organizational analyses as "value premises in decision-making research" (see also Beyer, 1981; Howard, 1990; Kluckhohn, 1951; Ravlin and Meglino, 1987; Simon, 1976).

Sproull (1981) mentions the "four classes of reasons" that justify research interest in beliefs, one of which is that "beliefs cause or influence actions" (p. 218; see also Barnard, 1938; March & Simons, 1958). Sproull (1981) also reports that "by far the most common (research methods) are fixed-response questionnaires and analyses of what can be called revealing statements—for example, transcripts of debates about policy decisions"; and that "a researcher may want to characterize general identity beliefs, by asking respondents to tell *stories* about their organization or its competitors or to describe their ideal organization" (p. 218; see also Mitroff & Kilman, 1976). A recent MIS study used a social action perspective in investigating information systems development by gathering the data based on a series of episodes about recent experiences collected through interviews of the systems project participants (Hirschheim, Klein, & Newman, 1987).

In studying "managerial ideologies and the use of discipline," Beyer and Trice (1981) reported that "all data were obtained in private, face-to-face interviews using an instrument that consisted largely of questionnaire-type items with structured response formats" and "in order to measure managerial ideologies, respondents were asked to what degree they agreed or disagreed with 18 statements reflecting beliefs and values relevant to management" (p. 260). They built scales by averaging responses to those items loading heavily on each factor, as follows: Human Pragmatism scale; Protestant Ethic scale; Laissez-faire philosophy; Social Responsibility scale; and Social Determinism scale. Beyer and Trice (1981) suggest that "additional research is needed to determine whether these results are applicable to managers in other companies, especially companies that espouse different ideologies" (p. 263).

By following the "sociology of knowledge perspective," and for the purpose of his particular research on the managerial control problems related to the employees' alcoholism, Weiss (1986; Weiss & Miller, 1987) studied managerial ideologies as sets of ideas that are predicted by social structural conditions (e.g., increasing organization size and bureaucratization) and that promote the interests of those who promote them, in this case, the interests of management. This idea—ideologies serving the political interests and values of groups who promote them—has been historically a central concern in the field of political science (e.g., Cohen, 1962; Van Dyke, 1957). Weiss (1987) conducted a survey in which he collected data from large corporations with alcoholism programs in operation.

In his research, Eysenck (Eysenck & Wilson, 1978) posited a four-step hierarchical model of attitude organization, which is relevant to the study of ideology (Dator, 1969). At the lowest level he spoke of "specific opinions"; at the next higher level, "habitual opinions"; at the third level, "attitudes"; at the highest aggregate level, "super-attitudes or ideologies," as shown in Figure 11.2.

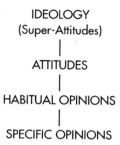

IDEOLOGY
(Super-Attitudes)

|

ATTITUDES

|

HABITUAL OPINIONS

|

SPECIFIC OPINIONS

Figure 11.2.   Eysenck's model of attitude organization (A psychological view).

Eysenck (Eysenck & Wilson, 1978, p. viii) attempted to "integrate the various sociological, historical, political and psychological strands, which contribute to an understanding of ideology". He concentrated on the "much more important issue of the observed inter-relations among attitudes than the simple measurement of attitudes towards a single issue, such as nationalism." (p. viii) Thereby, he sought to "find structures which are close to ideologies," (p. viii) as described by sociologists, political scientists, and others. He, however, did not concern himself with a "belief system" in his discourse (quoted in Dator, 1969, p. 101).

Eysenck (1951) used various psychological instruments and research methods in the study of social attitudes in the context of ideological concepts advanced by sociologists, political scientists, historians, or economist. Eysenck developed a 40-item inventory of Primary Social Attitudes based on his "two-factor theory of attitude structure" or "two orthogonal dimensions": radical-conservative dimension ("R" factor), and tough-minded versus tender-minded dimension ("T" factor). Using the two-factor theory of attitude structure as a basis for measurement, Eysenck and other researchers also investigated progressive and conservative ideologies in their several studies reported elsewhere (Eysenck & Wilson, 1978).

Ravlin and Meglino (1987) studied the effect of values on perception and decision making. They measured work values such as achievement, concern for others, honesty, working hard, positive outlook, helping others, and fairness. They suggested "a need for more research concerning the cognitive processes whereby values influence choice behavior" (p. 672).

The following are research strategies or perspectives that would be relevant to the study of a MIS professional ideology (Mumford, Hirschheim, Fitzgerald, & Wood-Harper, 1985).

Participant Action Research/Action Science Perspectives

Action research involves cycles of action steps taken jointly by a participant researcher and other organizational stakeholders in a real-life organizational setting, for example, diagnosing, action planning, action taking, evaluating, and specifying general findings (as feedback to the first step diagnosing; Susman & Evered, 1978). Keen (1975) hints at a possible application of action research to the study of MIS ideology when he referred to a sociological research that acknowledged the value of action research:

> The data that are obtained through the observer's judicious, but active intervention might not actually be readily available to perception and conception were he *not actively there.* For example, *the careers and ideologies of the hosts are not demonstrably there without his being there; they are created or revealed in and through the interaction of the hosts with the observer.* (quoted in Schatzman & Strauss, 1973, p. 58; emphasis added)

A review of selected perspective observations provides a meaningful rational for the action research approach. Pasmore and Friedlander (1982) successfully used the participative action research method in studying work-related injury problems in order to increase employee involvement in problem solving. This method was chosen after the failure of management to solve the problem using traditional research methods. They concluded that:

> If we, as social scientists, can overcome our preoccupation with artificial rigor imitative of the physical sciences and instead recognize the power we hold to affect human behavior in beneficial ways through our methods of study, our value to organizations and our understanding of organization behavior should increase concomitantly. (p. 361)

One of the implications of their study was that "it has taken problems of a severe nature to force managers to see" (Pasmore & Friedlander, 1982, p. 360) the critical need for changes in organizational structures and behaviors, flexibly through the adoption of useful research methods, such as the participative action research. This was also true in the MIS project situations in which the author conducted a participant action research only after finding that the managers of the user and IS departments were unable to solve the persisting systems project problems with usual means (Jin, 1993; Jin & Franz, 1986). That is, the participant action research served to break away from the "vicious cycles" of entangled dysfunctional behaviors (Masuch, 1985) of the organization that had caused project stagnation. In these cases the participant action research worked well in the solution of real IS project problems and at the same time generated some useful and insightful findings. Such results added to an understanding of the contribution of previous works, for example, the study of situational factors in relation to efficient task accomplishment of the user/IS project teams members (De Brabander & Thiers, 1984).

Another related method that has been used in MIS research in the tradition of Lewin's (1946, 1947a, 1947b, & 1951) action research is Argyris's (1985) action science. His theory-in-use and espoused theory (Argyris, 1983) and the concepts of single-loop and double-loop learning models (Argyris, 1976, 1977) offered an important framework for researching the organization learning involved in the implementation of an MIS (Argyris, 1977; Salaway, 1987). Argyris's espoused theory seems to be significantly related to the concept of MIS ideology in that it refers to the beliefs, values, and attitudes that define effective action in a given context and to the "operating assumption" that define effective action regardless of the context. Recently Salaway (1987]) used Argyris's organizational learning approach to information systems development.

One of the significant ingredients that is mentioned in the statement about the ideologies of successful companies seems to be the beliefs about the "higher value or spiritual values"—"a human value beyond profit to which their [employees'] productive lives are dedicated" (Pascale & Athos, 1981, pp.71–76). For example, in investigating the relationship between the higher values and effective task performance (De Brabander & Thiers, 1984) of MIS employees, participant action research in a field setting would be useful as a supplement to or in conjunction with a quantitative research method. In the past, in their research in different organizational settings, a considerable number of MIS researchers have used participant action research methods (Antill, 1985; Bostrom & Kaiser, 1982; Gibson, 1975; Jin & Franz, 1986; Mumford, 1981; Wood-Harper, 1985).

Although action research may be considered a major research strategy in the study of ideology (along with a quantitative "scientific" research method), there are other innovative research approaches and perspectives that seem to be also relevant. They are briefly considered next.

Open-ended study

In some cases Mintzberg's (1973) "open-ended study" approach may be appropriate, in which "the researcher seeks to develop basic understanding by the process of induction; observational methods and the critical incident method appear to hold the best promises" (p. 197) for the initial exploratory study of MIS ideological issues. Using this approach, Mintzberg (1979) made important observations on MIS.

Ideographic Approach

The role of the researcher as an "insider" is well characterized by the following ideographic approach to organizational behavior research, which:

> is based on the view that one can only understand the social world by obtaining first-hand knowledge of the subject under investigation. It thus places considerable stress upon getting close to one's subject and... emphasizes the analysis of the subjective accounts which one generates by "getting inside" situations and involving oneself in the everyday flow of life—he detailed analysis of the insights generated by such encounters with one's subjects and the insights revealed in impressionistic accounts found in diaries, biographies and journalistic records. (Luthans & Davis, 1982, p. 381)

This approach, also used in policy research, is represented by the research of Mintzberg (1973) in particular. The in-depth study of an MIS ideology may require gathering some data as an insider.

Social Action Perspective

Similar to the approach taken by Mitroff and Kilman (1976), the social action approach to the study of information systems development sees systems development as a series of episodes, each episode is an interaction between the analyst and the user, and can be viewed as an opportunity for improving the likelihood of systems success (Hirschheim et al., 1987). In the tradition of Mannheim (1936), the use of this approach may enlighten the role of MIS ideology in the political processes involved in the systems development.

Protocol Analysis

Recent studies have recognized that there is an increased need for more MIS research in the longitudinal, in-depth, intensive investigation of the interaction, process variables observable in the MIS development process (Boland, 1978; Ginzberg, 1979; Keen, 1975; Ives, Hamilton, & Davis, 1980). Other studies have also put emphasis on the investigation of process variables (De Brabander & Thiers, 1984; Franz & Robey, 1984). For example, Todd and Benbasat (1986) called for increased use of protocol analysis in IS research, which involves detailed, intensive analysis of subprocesses and focuses on a small number of individuals participating in MIS development.

Case Research Strategy

The case research method is defined as examining:

a phenomenon in its natural setting, employing multiple methods of data collection to gather information from one or a few entities (people, groups, or organizations). The boundaries of the phenomenon are not clearly evident at the outset of the research and no experimental control or manipulation is used. (Benbasat, Goldstein, & Mead, 1987, p. 370)

Case research method has also been presented as a way to "answer 'how' and 'why' questions, that is, to understand the nature and complexity of the processes taking place" (p. 370). Numerous studies have been completed in studying the ideological phenomena by using this method.

Phenomenology Approach

Boland (1985) views the phenomenology approach as a preferred approach to research on information systems. Referring to his earlier study (Boland, 1978), he observed that "the later, phenomenological view of the experiment tried to look beneath the surface of outcome to the structures of meaning that gave rise to these particular interpretations by these analysts" (p. 197). Underlying this approach is the philosophical view of information systems that "information systems are constituted by consciousness and are to be found in the intersubjective, intentional actions of human beings, not some mythological rational calculus that stands over us as general law" (p. 198). This premise seems to be quite consonant with the philosophical underpinnings of MIS professional ideology discussed in this chapter.

A Combined Research Strategy

Although recognizing the merits or limitations associated with different research methods, some MIS researchers have began to appreciate a combined strategy of two or more different strategies. Some of the traditional quantitative methods (Beyer & Trice, 1981; Weiss, 1986) may be combined in a creative way with any one or more of the innovative research perspectives considered earlier.

An Illustration of the Use of A Mixed Research Strategy

For the purpose of illustration, to investigate the impact of organizational ideology on the MIS professional ideology that would influence MIS professionals to take constructive and cooperative actions in MIS development process, one may consider the following research question: How or to what extent do different organizational ideologies influence the MIS professional ideology that would generate voluntary and proactive ethical commitment and constructive actions of MIS professionals?

For example, Brunsson's (1982) two basic types of organizational ideologies—fundamental ideology (e.g., emphasis on the intrinsic, higher human, and social values and ethical commitment), and operational ideology (e.g., focus on profit or bottom-line-oriented)—may be related to the MPI orientations.

Consistent with a part of the previous research question, my coauthor and I have recently undertaken a research project to empirically investigate the ethicality of MIS professionals (in comparison to the professional groups in other functional areas) and the influence of organizational ideologies on the ethical attitudes of MIS professionals. We decided to use both the traditional survey method and case study/action research to collect the data. The study conducts a survey of MIS and marketing professionals. The sample is chosen on a systematic sampling basis from the IMS Marketing Association and the IS Association Directories, such as Data Processing Management Associations, Associations for Systems Management, Information Technology Managers Associations, and Society for Information Management. The American Marketing Association directory will be used for marketing professionals.

Qualitative data will be gathered over time from a case study/action research (Argyris, 1985; Benbasat et al., 1987; Bostrom & Kaiser, 1982; Gibson, 1975; Keen, 1975; Lewin, 1946, 1947a, 1947b; Peters & Robinson, 1984; Rapport, 1970; Susman & Evered, 1978), which will be combined with the quantitative data collected from the study instrument. Data gained from interviews and direct observations in the field will be used partially to verify the results of survey and partially to enhance the ability to interpret the results of quantitative research.

Two large corporations were contacted for collaborative research with the managers and professional staff of the organizations. Upon mutual agreement, a joint action research plan was developed to highlight the research objectives and the practical benefits that would accrue to the organizations. On an ongoing basis, the results of action research will be discussed with the management and professional staff of the corporations, and some practical implications of the research findings will be communicated to the organizations in the form of recommendations. The goal of the action research will be to contribute to real problems and organizational learning (Argyris, 1977). After completion of the current research, we plan to conduct a longitudinal study using a case study/action research strategy to gain a deeper understanding of the MIS ideological issues over time.

CONCLUSION

A recent study by Posner and Schmidt (1992) suggests that in the United States a substantial portion of managers of the 1990s, in contrast to those of the 1980s, have increased their awareness of the importance of an ideological orientation (e. g., fundamental value commitment) as a key to the future, that is, the "improvement of the total human community" (p. 90). In an MIS ideological context, one wonders: To what extent is such an increased awareness also true in the MIS profession? The idealistic conception of a positive MIS ideology, as discussed in this chapter, is certainly a challenging notion as we reflect on the following questions. Is this concept of a positive MIS ideology unrealistic at this time? If so, should we abandon it now, or should we strive to achieve this idealistic goal in the future? Do we want to improve our profession by striving to attain higher social and human goals via our professional contributions? The answer should be in the affirmative, as has been emphasized throughout the chapter. These questions also imply the need for more research into MIS ideological issues.

Another significant implication of MPI is related to the question of what the obligations of university-based researchers and MIS practitioners today are in transforming the present MIS profession into something more meaningful to the human society as we are heading toward the 21st century. Those in the MIS profession—MIS practitioners, university-based researchers, and educators—have the responsibility for seeing that higher goals in the context of positive MIS professional ideology are consciously recognized, valued, researched, promoted, and pursued actively in the real world, that is, that information technology is used for the benefit of humanity—not the converse. Shneiderman (1990) made a significant observation in a keynote address in regard to the responsibilities of computer and MIS professionals in the age of information, especially in the coming decade:

> Earlier in this century physicists recognized their responsibility in dealing with atomic energy and vigorously debated the issues. I believe that we in the computing professions must also recognize our responsibilities, set an example of moral leadership by inspiring discussion and influencing colleagues in other fields of science or in engineering, social sciences, medicine, law, etc.

A corollary issue is: Do today's MIS professionals need their own vision (as a basic content of MIS ideology) based on human and social values beyond purely operational or technical objectives (e.g., designing system or programming)? From the author's point of view, such a vision needs to be developed and discussed spiritedly among the MIS professionals and between them and those in other disciplines. An analogy is clearly present in the field of strategic management in that many management scholars support the idea that, to lead an organization to a successful achievement of its mission, its top management or leaders need a vision based on human and social values (Howard, 1990) beyond purely bottom-line-oriented organizational objectives (e.g., profit or market growth). The vision statement defines the meaningful role of organization in relation to a larger system, such as, target customers or, broadly speaking, a human society. This is referred to as an organizational, managerial, or corporate ideology. Likewise, from the author's point of view, MIS professionals need an MIS professional ideology based on their own vision.

An implication of such a positive MIS professional ideology is that we do need MIS professionals who can think with a global perspective and genuinely care about human and social issues and can relate their professional roles to larger human and social goals. Another related issue to be addressed is: Will the 21st century need a renaissance or interdisciplinary "synergistic" man as an MIS professional? Will futuristic MIS professionals be educated in many disciplines other than the narrowly defined MIS field? The affirmative answers to these questions have serious implications for educators and researchers.

To *really* understand and delve into such value-and-belief-based MIS ideological issues, we first need to develop a relevant conceptual framework that incorporates ideology as a significant conceptual construct and defines its relationship to the existing other MIS research models (Beard & Peterson, 1988; Ives et al., 1980; Kling, 1980; Turner, 1982). This chapter represents a small attempt to offer a starting point to satisfy this need. We in the MIS profession can draw from past research work done on ideology and related issues in other disciplines, which tested relevant methodology and measurement instruments and which provided research insight and useful tools. Certain positive MIS ideological orientations (as variables), once identified and operationalized, can be related to other variables studied in previous research, such as corporate ideology, effective task performance, productivity, commitment, cooperative action, and MIS project outcome.

MIS scholars need to collaborate with practitioners in researching the role of MIS professional ideology in different organizations' settings and in a transorganizational context as management scholars have done in their discipline in the past. In doing so, we will need to recognize and use such relevant research strategies as action research creatively and in conjunction with quantitative research methods. Such a combined strategy seems to have been particularly useful when certain research issues have not been resolved successfully with traditional "scientific" research methods (Bostrom & Kaiser, 1982) and especially when the criticalness of problem situations have awakened those with authority and responsibility for actions (Pasmore & Friedlander, 1982).

The deliberation of a relevant conceptual framework and research strategy for the study of MIS professional ideology is timely and necessary. This is so partially because recent MIS research has revealed that the nature of MIS phenomena is political (Franz & Robey, 1984; Hirschheim et al., 1987; Keen & Gerson, 1977; Kling, 1980; Markus, 1983a, 1983b, 1984; Markus & Robey, 1983) as well as technical. To deepen our understanding of the political factors and behavioral issues affecting MIS, we also need to research and understand the ideological dimensions (as well as power dimensions) of political processes involved in MIS.

REFERENCES

Alvesson, M. (1987). Organizations, culture, and ideology. *International Studies of Management and Organization, 17*(3), 4–18.

Antill, L. (1985). Selection of a research method. In Mumford, E., Hirschheim, R., Fitzgerald, G., & Wood-Harper, T.(Eds.), *Research methods in information systems* (pp. 203–215). Amsterdam: Elsevier Science (North-Holland).

Argyris, C. (1976). Single loop and double-loop models in research on decision making. *Administrative Science Quarterly, 21,* 363–377.

Argyris, C. (1977). Organizational learning and management information systems. *Accounting, Organizations and Society, 2*(2), 113–123.

Argyris, C. (1983). Action science and intervention. *The Journal of Applied Behavioral Science, 19*(2), 115–140.

Argyris, C. (1985). *Action science.* San Francisco: Jossey-Bass.

Barnard, C.I. (1938). *The functions of the executive.* Cambridge, MA: Harvard University Press.

Beard, J.W., & Peterson, T.O. (1988). A taxonomy for the study of human factors in management information systems (MIS). In J.M. Carey (Ed.), *Human factors in management information systems* (pp. 7–28). Norwood, NJ: Ablex.

Benbasat, I., Goldstein, D., & Mead, M. (1987). The case research strategy in studies of information systems. *MIS Quarterly, 11*(3), 369–388.

Beyer, J.M. (1981). Ideologies, values, and decision making in organizations. In P. Nystrom & W. Starbuck (Eds.), *Handbook of organizational design* (Vol. II, pp. 166–202). London: Oxford University Press.

Beyer, J.M., & Trice, H.M. (1981). Managerial ideologies and the use of discipline. *Proceedings of the Annual Meeting of the Academy of Management.* Academy of Management.

Boland, R.J., Jr. (1978). The process and product of systems design. *Management Science, 24*(9), 887–898.

Boland, R.J., Jr. (1985). The phenomenology approach: A preferred approach to research on information systems. In E. Mumford, R. Hirschheim, G. Fitzgerald, & T. Wood-Harper (Eds.), *Research methods in information systems* (pp. 193–202). Amsterdam: Elsevier Science (North-Holland).

Bostrom, R.P., & Kaiser, K.M. (1982). Personality characteristics of MIS project teams: An empirical study and action research design. *MIS Quarterly, 6*(4), 43–60.

Brunsson, N. (1982). The irrationality of action and action rationality: Decisions, ideologies and organizational actions. *Journal of Management Studies, 19*(1), 29–44.

Cohen, C. (1962). *Communism, fascism, and democracy: The theoretical foundation.* New York: Random House.

Couger, J.D. (1989). Preparing IS students to deal with ethical issues. *MIS Quarterly, 13*(2), 211–218.

Couger, J.D., Zawacki, R.A., & Opperman, E.B. (1979). Motivation level of MIS managers versus those of their employees. *MIS Quarterly, 3*(3), 47–56.

Dator, J.A. (1969). Measuring attitudes across cultures: A factor analysis of the replies of Japanese judges to Eysenck's Inventory of Conservative–Progressive Ideology.

De Brabander, B., & Thiers, G. (1984). Successful information system development in relation to situational factors which affect effective communication between MIS-users and EDP specialists. *Management Science, 30*(2), 137–155.

El Sawy, O.A. (1985). Implementation by cultural infusion: An approach for managing the introduction of information technologies. *MIS Quarterly, 9*(2), 131–140.

England, G.W. (1967). Personal value systems of American managers. *Academy of Management Journal, 10,* 53–68.

Eysenck, H.J. (1951). Primary social attitudes as related to social class and political party. *The British Journal of Sociology, 11*(3), 198–209.

Eysenck, H.J., & Wilson, G.D. (Eds.). (1978). *The psychological basis of ideology.* Baltimore: University Park Press.

Franz, C.R., & Robey, D. (1984). An investigation of user-led systems design: Rational and political perspectives. *Communications of the ACM, 27*(12), 1202–1209.

Gibson, C.F. (1975). A methodology for implementation research. In R.L. Schultz & D.P. Slevin (Eds.), *Implementing operations research/management science.* New York: American Elsevier.

Ginzberg, M.J. (1979). A study of the implementation process. In R. Doktor, R.L. Schultz, & D. P. Slevin (Eds.), *The implementation of management science* (pp. 85–102). Amsterdam: Elsevier Science (North-Holland).

Guth, W.D., & Renato, T. (1965). Personal values and corporate strategy. *Harvard Business Review, 43*(5), 123–132.

Hirschheim, R. A., Klein, H., & Newman, M. (1987). A social action perspective of information systems development. In *Proceedings of the Eighth International Conference on Information Systems* (pp. 45–56).

Howard, R. (1990, September-October), Values make the company. *Harvard Business Review,* pp. 133–144.

Ives, B., Hamilton, S., & Davis, G. B. (1980). A framework for research in computer based management information systems. *Management Science, 26,* 910–934.

Jin, K.G. (1991). On a positive MIS ideology. In J.M. Carey (Ed.), *Human factors in information systems: An organizational perspective* (pp. 195–216). Norwood, NJ: Ablex.

Jin, K.G. (1993). Overcoming organizational barriers to systems development: An action strategy framework. *Journal of Systems Management, 44*(5), 28–33.

Jin, K.G., & Franz, C.R. (1986). Obstacle coping during systems implementation. *Information and Management, 11*(2), 65–75.

Johnson, D.G., & Snapper, J.W. (1985). *Ethical issues in the use of computers.* Belmont, CA: Wadsworth.

Keen, P.G.W., & Gerson, E.M. (1977, November). The politics of software systems design. *Datamation,* pp. 80–84.

Keen, P.G.W. (1975). *A clinical approach to the implementation of OR/MS/MIS projects.* (Working Paper No. 780-75). Cambridge, MA: Sloan School of Management, MIT.

Kling, R. (1980). Social analyses of computing: Theoretical perspectives in recent empirical research. *Computing Surveys, 12*(1), 61–110.

Kluckhohn, C. (1951). Values and value-orientations in theory of action: an exploration in definition and classification. In T. Parsons and E. A. Shils (Eds.), *Toward a general theory of action* (pp. 388–433). Cambridge, MA: Harvard University Press.

Lewin, K. (1946). Action research and minority problems. *Journal of Social Issues, 2*(4), 34–46.

Lewin, K. (1947a). Frontiers in group dynamics I: Concept, method and reality in social science. *Human Relations, 1,* 5–41.

Lewin, K. (1947b). Frontiers in group dynamics II: Channels of group life-social planning and action research. *Human Relations, 1,* pp. 143–153.

Lewin, K. (1951). Problems of research in social psychology. In D. Cartwright (Ed.), *Field theory in social science: Selected theoretical papers* (pp. 155–169). New York: Harper & Row.

Luthans, F., & Davis, T.R.V. (1982). An ideographic approach to organizational behavior research: The use of single case experimental designs and direct measures. *Academy of Management Review, 7*(3), 380–391.

Mannheim, K. (1936). *Ideology and Utopia.* New York: Harcout Brace & World.

March, J.G., & Simon, H.A. (1958). *Organizations,* New York: Wiley.

Markus, M.L. (1983a). Implementation politics: Top management support and user involvement. *Systems, Objectives, and Solutions,* (6) pp. 293–215.

Markus, M.L. (1983b). Power, politics, and MIS implementation. *Communication of the ACM, 26,* 430–444.

Markus, M.L. (1984). *Systems in organizations.* Marshfield, MA: Pitman.

Markus, M.L., & Robey, D. (1983). The organizational validity of management information systems. *Human Relations, 36*(3), 203–226.

Mason, R.O. (1986). Four ethical issues of the information age. *MIS Quarterly, 10*(1), 5–14.

Masuch, M. (1985). Vicious cycles in organizations. *Administrative Science Quarterly, 30,* 14–33.

Mintzberg, H. (1973). *The nature of managerial work.* New York: Harper and Row.

Mintzberg, H. (1979). *The structuring of organizations.* Englewood Cliffs, NJ: Prentice-Hall.

Mitroff, I.I., & Kilman, R.H. (1976). On organization stories: An approach to the design and analysis of organizations through myths and stories. In R.H. Kelmann, L.R. Pondy, & D.P. Slevin (Eds.), *The management of organization design: Strategies and implementation* (pp. 189–207). Amsterdam: Elsevier Science (North-Holland).

Mumford, E. (1981). Participative systems design: Structure and method. *Systems, Objectives, Solutions, 1*(1), 5–19.

Mumford, E., Hirschheim, R., Fitzgerald, G., & Wood-Harper, T. (1985). *Research methods in information systems.* Amsterdam: Elsevier Science.

Ouchi, W.G. (1981). *Theory Z.* Reading, MA: Addison-Wesley.

Paradice, D.B. (1990). Ethical attitudes of entry-level MIS personnel. *Information and Management, 18,* 143–151.

Pascale, R.T., & Athos, A.G. (1981). *The art of japanese management: Applications for american executives.* New York: Simon and Schuster.

Pasmore, W., & Friedlander, F. (1982). An action research program for increasing employee involvement in problem solving. *Administrative Science Quarterly, 27,* 343–362.

Peters, M., & Robinson, V. (1984). The origins and status of action research. *The Journal of Applied Behavioral Science, 20*(2), 113–124.

Pettigrew, A.M. (1973). *The politics of organizational decision-making.* London: Tavistock.

Posner, B.Z., & Schmidt, (1992). Values and the American manager: An update updated. *California Management Review, 35*(1), 80–94.

Rapport, R. (1970). Three dilemmas in action research. *Human Relations, 23,* 488–513.

Robey, D., & Markus, M.L. (1984). Rituals in information system design. *MIS Quarterly, 8*(1), 5–15.

Ravlin, E.C., & Meglino, B.M. (1987). Effect of values on perception and decision making: A study of alternative work values measures. *Journal of Applied Psychology, 72*(4), 666–673.

Salaway, G. (1987). An organizational learning approach to systems development. *MIS Quarterly, 11*(2), 245–264.

Schatzman, L., & Strauss, A.L. (1973). *Field research: Strategies for a natural sociology.* Englewood Cliffs, NJ: Prentice-Hall.

Shneiderman, B. (1990). *Human values and the future of technology: Declaration of empowerment.* Keynote address for ACM SIGCAS Conference.

Sproull, L.S. (1981). Beliefs in organizations. In P.C. Nystrom & W.H. Starbuck (Eds.), *Handbook of organizational design: Remodeling organizations and their environments* (pp. 203–204). London: Oxford University Press.

Susman, G.L., & Evered, R.D. (1978). An assessment of the scientific merits of action research. *Administrative Science Quarterly, 23*(4), 582–603.

Todd, P., & Benbasat, I. (1986). *Process tracing methods in decision support systems research: Exploring the black box.* (Working Paper No. 1140). Vancouver: Faculty of Commerce and Business Administration, The University of British Columbia.

Turner, J.A. (1982). Observation on the use of behavioral models in information systems research and practice. *Information and Management, 5*(4 & 5), 207–213.

Van Dyke, V. (1957). *International politics.* New York: Appleton Century-Crofts.

Vitell, S.J., & Davis, D.L. (1990). Ethical beliefs of MIS professionals: The frequency and opportunity for unethical behavior. *Journal of Business Ethics, 9,* 63–70.

Weiss, R.M. (1986). *Managerial ideology and the social control of deviance in organizations.* New York: Praeger.

Weiss, R.M., & Miller, L.E. (1987). The concept of ideology organizational analysis: The sociology of knowledge or the social psychology of beliefs. *Academy of Management Review, 12*(1), 104–116.

White, K.B., & Leifer, R. (1986). Information systems development success: Perspectives from project team participants. *MIS Quarterly, 10*(3), 215–224.

Wood-Harper, T. (1985). Research methods in information systems using action research. In Mumford, E., Hirschheim, R., Fitzgerald, G., & Wood-Harper, T. (Eds.), *Research methods in information systems* (pp. 169–192). Amsterdam: Elsevier Science.

Part V
End User Involvement

Importance of Familiarization for System Acceptance: The Case of Voice Mail

Michel Plaisent
University of Québec at Montréal, Canada

Prosper Bernard
INCAE, Costa Rica

INTRODUCTION

E-mail and voicemail, often called store-and-forward systems, refer to a computer-mediated system that facilitates the edition, transmission, storage, and reception of messages. The messages are text-based and/or files in the mail system and the user's voice in the voice-system.

Voice mail is predicted to have a U.S. market of $1 billion in 1993 and $68 million in Canada. In 1988 usage was $280 million in the U.S. for voice mail and $133 million for interactive voice response (Wintrob, 1989). The growth of this market is estimated to be 39% per year. As prices start at reasonable $269 for a PC-based system (Stone, 1989), it is expected that the distribution of this technology will continue to grow.

The interest of voice mail as a study object originates from the scarcity of research in regard to its economic importance and from the fact that its technology may be revealed to be part of the missing link between prophesied widespread use (similar to fax for written information) and real use of an advanced medium for interaction. Understanding about the adjustment of individuals to the introduction of new technologies is limited and needs further investigation (Nelson, 1990).

OBJECTIVES OF THIS STUDY

At the University of Quebec in Montreal, where a voice mail system has been installed for one year in a pilot group—a good approach according to Morin, 1988/1989—many complaints were heard. The high number of persons refusing to record a message and hanging up before leaving any message was troublesome. Complaints to the administration of the university were numerous.

These factors contributed to a decision to conduct a study to determine the level of knowledge about the capacities of the system and the level of satisfaction of its users. The aim of the study was to clarify whether the complaints were coming from the majority or were a manifestation of resistance from a few users. Finally, some rumors were to be verified, namely that the voice system was used as a screen by the pilot group and that the system conveyed a very mechanical image. The telecommunication executive, who initiated the system and was anxious and impatient to expand it, was confident of its positive impact on organizational productivity. He suggested the hypothesis that negative perceptions were due to a lack of user training.

This study attempts to provide a better understanding of the factors leading to voice mail acceptance from users and more specifically examine whether negative perceptions about the voice mail system could be changed through hands-on experience and information.

REVIEW OF THE LITERATURE

Advanced Technology to Support Organizational Communication

The contingency paradigm presents organizations as information-processing entities (Cyert & March, 1963; Galbraith, 1973) that scan and interpret data (Daft & Weick, 1984) in order to reduce uncertainties. These uncertainties originate from a complex and changing environment (Lawrence & Lorsch, 1967) from task complexity and inter-dependencies introduced by differentiations and size (March & Simon, 1969). The contingent approach underlies much behavioral research in MIS (Malone et al., 1987; Panko, 1984; Rockart & Short, 1988; Safayeni et al., 1987; Tapscott, 1980; Trice & Treacy, 1986; Turner, 1984; Yaverbaum, 1988). Viewing the organization as a network of interactive brains demonstrates the importance of communication inside and outside the organization (Katz & Khan, 1966). This is especially true for large businesses (Drucker, 1988).

For years, it appeared that the telephone and the traditional mail service would, for most organizations, be sufficient to handle communications with an acceptable level of efficiency, even though effectiveness of the service was often questioned (Hubert, 1982).

As the pace of doing business accelerates and the environment becomes more uncertain and turbulent, organizations must react faster and with more flexibility (Rallet, 1989). These factors force them to consider technology as a competitive weapon (Lederer et al., 1987; Porter & Millar,1985). Organizations introduce technology in order to improve management practice (Olson & Turner, 1986), personnel productivity, and to gain competitive advantage (Rockart & Delong, 1986; Elias, 1988).

Among the most recent technologies, computer-mediated communication systems appear to be the most promising for organizational, group, and individual productivity, and also for gaining competitive advantage (Rockart & Short, 1988; Treacy, 1986). Among these new technologies, e-mail, fax, and voice mail have been long advocated as solutions to the telephone-tag problem.

Indeed, many studies report problems associated with face-to-face and telephone communications, including costs and telephone-tag (Kerr & Hiltz, 1982) and work disturbance (Mintzberg, 1973; Sullivan & Smart, 1987). A study reported that 67% of calls are less important than the work they interrupt (Kleinschrod, 1989).

These new media can at least complement if not substitute for more traditional media for all users, mainly middle-managers (Millman & Hartwick, 1987) and CEOs (DeLone, 1988). Taken separately, these media are associated with a transition between traditional office communication systems and advanced integrated communication systems (Brantham & Vaske, 1985). As much as 70% of readable information is available in electronic format (Braasch, 1989).

A comparison of the capacity of several alternatives to telephone communications conducted in Canada with 1,490 managers. This study suggests that external communication needs were best filled by fax (90%) as an effective media over the postal service and even over the private carrier. Some organizations even use fax machines for internal electronic mail. Fax technology thus constitutes an efficient system for transmission of images. In 1988, the U.S. fax market was $4 billion.

The main advantages of electronic media include: 1) allowance for spontaneity and asynchronism, 2) the elimination of space and time barriers, 3) increased control over the communication process (e.g., proof of reception), and 4) facilitation of distribution as well as collection of information (Plaisent, 1987; Uhlig, 1977). From a corporate perspective, these technical advantages allow for 1) better coordination (Rockart & Short, 1988; Todd, Nelson, & Adams, 1987), 2) faster decisions (Uhlig, 1982), 3) improved organizational membership, and 4) circulation of more creative ideas (Kaye & Byrne, 1984) and much more.

The voice mail system is more than a sophisticated machine, since it allows for user control, connects groups, and forwards messages. For the receiver, it means freedom from interruption (Uhlig,1982) allowing peak concentration (Parker, 1987). Additionally, the voice mail makes it possible to receive a message from any digital phone at any time, and facilitates forwarding. Voice mail messages tend to be shorter, more efficient, more action oriented, more personal, and less formal (Todd, Nelson & Adams, 1987) than a written memo. However, understanding may be sacrificed by listening to a message rather than reading it.

For the sender, it gives the assurance that the message will be received as soon as possible. The sender can leave a more precise message, with 250% higher useful content (Morin, 1988/1989), less distortion, and no telephone-tag. Studies have shown that only 30% of business first calls succeed (Morin, 1984, 1989; Philip & Young, 1987), that 50% of completed calls were unidirectional and required a long waiting time before being answered. Voice mail also allows sending information to a distribution list (Bruder, Moy, Mueller, & Danielson, 1981), and the automation of answering of standard or frequent calls.

ACCEPTANCE VS RESISTANCE TO COMPUTER-MEDIATED COMMUNICATIONS

The introduction of computerized media to aid communication has been much slower than one would expect (Rallet, 1989). This may be due to lack of proper training (Young, 1984), poor implementation strategy (Weinberg, 1990), lack of concern for changes in social structure (Zuboff, 1982), or design faults. "It's already been implemented! They just aren't using it." (Schultz & Slevin, 1982, p. 88).

Indeed, despite the many advantages associated with electronic messaging, many people feel reluctant to use new media (Grindlay, 1983a; Nickerson, 1981). In the case of the video-phone and in the case of e-mail, the absence of a critical mass of communication partners prolongs the transition period (Morin, 1988/1989; Rushinek & Rushinek, 1986).

In the case of e-mail, messages have to be typewritten by the originator or suffer delay for a chauffeured entry. Keyboarding may be a frustrating and an annoying activity for many; speed and lack of facility on the keyboard can discourage people from using this medium. Reading a message causes verbal cues to be missed and the addressee could accuse the medium of coldness and poverty of expression. Several studies have shown that these input and output limitations (the essence of a communication) were a sufficient reason to discourage someone from using it. Semistructured messages can partially eliminate this constraint by limiting the need for typewriting proficiency and routine information reentry (Malone et al., 1987).

The promoters and retailers of Voice Mail System (VMS) advocate that this medium, while sharing the asynchronism and spontantaneity of e-mail, overcomes e-mail limitations because it relies on a convenient and universally accepted support for communication—the phone—for both input and output (Todd, Nelson, & Adams, 1989). Messages are natural and voices familiar (Sproul & Kiesler, 1986). Speaking has been found to require only 35 to 75% of the time that writing does (Gould, 1982). Voice mail could be perceived as easier to use and more useful (namely for sending, receiving, and manipulating a message) than e-mail (Todd et al., 1987).

None of these computer-mediated systems "possess the immediacy and completeness of feed-back found in a face-to-face context" (Salem & Gratz, 1989, p. 415). Voice mail, although allowing for richer messages than written media, is still not as rich as face-to-face meetings (Lengle & Daft, 1988); on the other hand, the interaction is also different. Voice messages tend to be more formal, shorter, more structured (Morin, 1988/1989) and lack feedback (Brantham & Vaske, 1985). Additionally, there is no recognized etiquette (Kiesler in Brantham & Vaske, 1985). Some critics mentioned the fact that they hated to speak to a machine, or that their interlocutor could use its VMS as a screen (Todd et al., 1987).

Organizations are fortunately or unfortunately made up of individuals with limited rationality (Simon, 1960) and with personal characteristics that are not necessarily congruent with corporate strategies; therefore, systems are often left unused by organizational members (Gould & Lewis, 1985; Manross & Rice, 1986; Pavri, 1987).

In the worst of cases, individuals will react negatively to change and they will resist using the new system. In best cases, they will incorporate the new system into their work habits as long as they perceive that the supplementary effort needed to learn it and to use it is worthwhile given the perceived usefulness of the system (i.e., the reward they can expect from improved productivity due to use of the system (Robey, 1979; Davis, 1989)).

It is generally accepted that it is through use that technology affects performance (Gattiker & Nelligan, 1988; Lucas, 1975; King, Grover & Hufnagel, 1989). The value of a system is a function of the performance it allows (Goodhue, 1986). One premise of technology introduction is that people will use technology to actualize expected gains (Crowston & Treacy, 1986; Ginzberg, 1981), given the task requirements for information (Ugbah, 1986). A divergent view suggests that increased use of computer-mediated communication can lead to organizational ineffectiveness through loss of communication skills following improvement in computer literacy (Salem & Gratz, 1989). Success thus refers to the adequate outcome from implantation in regard to the objectives of the system design based on the user's expected improved performance through system use (Turner, 1982a).

User acceptance can then be seen as the particular conclusion a user draws from his/her attitude toward the use of a system. Some CEOs refuse to use e-mail because they believe it lacks security and is too impersonal (Brantham & Vaske, 1985); others insist on receiving information electronically. The acceptance of the system refers to the intention (degree of willingness) of an individual to use or not to use a system as a consequence of its assessment in regard to his/her needs (Robey, 1979), and the social pressure to use it. This can be measured by the use of the system and by the satisfaction subsequent to use (Kerr & Hiltz, 1982; Nelson & Cheney, 1987). Valid measurement scales of user acceptance are rare (Davis, 1989).

The learning model (Ginzberg, 1981) states that some use will lead to acceptance, which in turn will lead to continued use, then to learning, which will lead to good use, which will improve the decision-making process. Thus, minimal use plays the role of training as an artificial means of giving the subjects a prior experience on which they can build beliefs that will translate into acceptance through attitudes, according to the Fishbein-Ajzen model (1974). This minimal contact with the system would favor ulterior motivation to learn (Mozeico, 1982). Use leads to experimentation and ultimately to adoption (Olfman & Bostrom, 1988. Practice has proven that increased performance (MacGregor & Lee, 1987) and level of computer use proved to be more related to success than the computer training level of users

(DeLone, 1988). Computer literacy is generally acquired through experience (Salem & Gratz, 1989). The extent of PC use and, more precisely, usage diversity has been significantly correlated to prior experience with computers (Lee, 1986). The sequence of the evolutionary model is: a) unfreezing occurs, (i.e., user habits are first questioned and focus is placed on lack of actual behavior), b) new behaviors are introduced (moving), and c) refreezing (acceptance) occurs when a new behavior proves useful.

METHODOLOGY

Our instrument is a questionnaire consisting of three parts. Part A gathers information about the respondents' satisfaction with the system. Part B consists of: 1) two pages of information on the capacities of the systems, how to use main functions (skip the message, help, etc.), and the advantages of using voice mail, and 2) a guided experience through the main functions of the system. Part C consists of a new evaluation of respondent satisfaction with the system.

All items are in the form of 7-point Likert scales on which respondents are asked to code their appreciation of sentences regarding a topic. The questionnaire has been pre-tested with eight persons: five staff members of the telecommunication department, two professors and one professional.

For one week, all employees of the staff department (26.9% of the organization) kept a record of all the messages they received on their voice mail system. When a call was returned, the employee invited the person to participate in the study. Two hundred twelve persons have been invited to participate. This mode of selection induces bias. Indeed, people who called the staff department are not necessarily representative of the organization's population. Despite this bias, this selection method offers great convenience as it guarantees that all these people have used the voice mail system at least once. The questionnaire was mailed simultaneously to all 212 persons. A recall to late-comers was made two weeks after the initial mailing.

EMPIRICAL EVIDENCE

Representativeness of respondents

We received 79 responses out of 212 (i.e., 37.3%) which was judged satisfactory considering the short time limits provided for the experiment. This level of response (37.3%) is sufficient to insure a consistency of 97.5% with a level of confidence of 95%. The respondents have similar occupations (except for the professors for whom the response level was lower than the others, probably because of their more flexible schedule at this time of the year). Age and experience of respondents in regard of the population showed no distortion.

Evaluation of the degree of satisfaction

In order to evaluate satisfaction, two constructs are defined:

SATBEFORE: the mean of 11 questions on satisfaction, asked BEFORE part B of the questionnaire (information/test)

SATAFTER: the mean of 5 questions, asked AFTER part B, where 1 = the most satisfied and 6 = the least satisfied

Global evaluation

The construction of these two latent variables relies on the following hypothesis:

1) different aspects of satisfaction have properties that add up.
2) each measured property has the same importance.
3) the scale's properties indicate adequately the degree of satisfaction.

Results:	Before:	After:
Number	78	78
Average	3.183	2.437
std deviation	0.150	0.133

Thus, according to this scale, (all) respondents would be more or less satisfied and the degree of satisfaction is higher after, meaning that the information (testing) has a positive effect on global satisfaction.

Evaluation according to the degree of familiarity

Satisfaction before:

	N	Mean	test	sig
Connected	20	2.0326	F=26.692	(.000)
Not connected	57	3.5851	T-test= 5.17	(.000)

Satisfaction after:

	N	Mean	test	sig
connected	21	1.6603	F=14.940	(.000)
not connected	57	2.7231	T-test= -3.87	(.000)

The familiarity with the system influences the degree of satisfaction with the voice mail system. The voice mail system is more important than the answering machine to find out the degree of satisfaction. Thus, it seems that satisfaction is a matter of habits in using the system.

Impacts on knowledge

When asked if they knew the system better since they read information and/or could practice, respondents averaged at 2.0232 (n = 71) with 1 = total agreement. They responded differently depending whether that they were connected or not in the following manner:

Connected   mean = 3.1000 (n = 20) slight agreement
Not connected mean = 1.6250 (n = 50) strong agreement
T-test   t= 4.39, prob. = 0.000

These results indicate that the respondents connected to the voice mail system did not learn much. However, the unconnected respondents did learn a lot. Thus information-testing is useful for better knowledge.

CONCLUDING REMARKS

From our results it seems that familiarity with the voice mail system has an effect on the satisfaction of users. Through adequate information and at least some training of users, perception of the system has been changed. There was no need for very long training and costs for training were minimal. The human factor once more proved to be effective and economic.

From our results we recommend the development of training strategies based on practical use rather than on information only. We suggest the study the usage patterns of employees who are actually answering machines in order to prevent resistance.

Our study suffers from many flaws that limit greatly its external validity. First the level of responses was low due to short time limits that inhibited recall of non-respondents. The sampling procedure was not free of bias. The questionnaire was quite complex for closed questions, which always limits severely the information yield. Some questions had a weak response rate. Further studies are needed.

REFERENCES

Braasch, B. (1989). Text management is coming of age. *Canadian Datasystems, 21*(8), 31.

Brantham, C.E., & Vaske, J.J. (1985). Predicting the usage of an advanced communication technology. *Behavior and Information Technology, 4*(4), 327–335.

Bruder, J., Moy, M., Mueller, A., & Danielson, R. (1981). User experience and evolving design in a local electronic mail system. *Computer Message System,* IFIP: 69–77.

Crowston, K., & Treacy, M.E. (1986). Assessing the impact of information technology on enterprise level performance. *Seventh Annual International Conference on Information Systems,* San Diego, California, 14–17.

Cyert & March. (1963). *A behavioral theory of the firm.* Englewood Cliffs, NJ: Prentis-Hall.

Daft, R.L., & Weick, K.E. (1984). Toward a model of organizations as interpretation systems. *Academy of Management Review, 9*(2): 284–295.

Davis, F.D. (1989). Perceived usefulness, perceived ease of use, and user acceptance of information technology. *MIS Quarterly, 13*(3): 319–340.

DeLone, D.W. (1988). Determinants of success for computer usage in small business. *MIS Quarterly, 12*(1): 51–61.

Drucker, P.F. (1988). The coming of the new organization. *Harvard Business Review, 66*(1): 45–53.

Elias, J. (1988). The voice in the machine. *Small Business, 7*(10): 111–114.

Fishbein, M., & Ajzen, I. (1974). Attitudes towards objects as predictors of single and multiple behavioral criteria. *Psychological Review, 81,* 59–74.

Galbraith, J. (1973). *Designing complex organizations.* Redding, MA: Addison-Wesley.

Gattiker, U.E., & Nelligan, T.W. (1988). Computerized offices in Canada and the United States: Investigating dispositional similarities and differences. *Journal of Organizational Behavior, 9*: 77–96.

Ginzberg, M.J. (1981). DSS success: Measurement and facilitation. *Center for Research on Information Systems,* New York University, No. 33.

Goodhue, D. (1986). I/S attitudes: Toward theoretical and definitional clarity. *Center for Information Systems Research,* Massachusetts Institute of Technology, CISR WP No. 141, Sloan WP No. 1833-86.

Gould, J.D. (1982). Writing and speaking letters and messages. *International Journal of Man-Machine Studies, 16:* 147–171.

Gould, J.D., & Lewis, C. (1985). Designing for usability: Key principles and what designers think. *Communications of the ACM, 28*(3): 300–311.

Grindlay, A. (1983a). Managing the trilogy: Office systems, data processing and communications. WP no. 83-07, University of Western Ontario.

Hubert, (1982, February). Organizational information systems: Determinants of their performance and behavior. *Management Science, 28*(2): 138–155.

Katz & Khan (1966). *The social psychology of organizations.* New York: Wiley.

Kaye, A.R., & Byrne, K.E. (1984, june). The impact of a computer-based message system on an organization. *Carleton U. WP.*

Kerr, E.B., & Hiltz, S.R. (1982). *Computer-mediated communication systems: Status and evaluation.* New York: Academic Press.

King, W.R., Grover, V., & Hufnagel, E.H. (1989). Using information and information technology for sustainable competitive advantage: Some empirical evidence. *Information & Management, 17*(2): 87–93.

Kleinschrod, W.A. (1989). With voice messaging you always get the message. The popularity of voice messaging is on the rise—and so is user satisfaction. *Today's Office, 4:* 39–45.

Lawrence, P.R., & Lorsch, J.W. (1967). *Organizationa and environment.* Homewood, IL: Irwin.

Lederer, A.L., Stubler, W.F., Sethi, V., & Ryan, J.C. (1987). The implementation of office automation. *Interfaces, 17*(1): 78–84.

Lee, D.M.S. (1986). Usage pattern and sources of assistance for personal computer users. *MIS Quarterly: 10*(4): 313–325.

Lengel, R.H., & Daft, R.L. (1988, August). The selection of communication media as an executive skill. *The Academy of Management Executive, 2*(3): 225–232.

Lucas, H.C., Jr. (1975). Performance and the use of an information system. *Management Science, 21*(8): 908–919.

MacGregor, J.N., & Lee, E.S. (1987). Performance and preference in videotex menu retrieval: A review of the empirical literature. *Behavior and information Technology, 6*(1): 43–68.

Malone, T., Kenneth, W., Grant, R., Lai, K.-Y., Rao, R., & Rosenblitt, D. (1987). Semistructured messages are surprisingly useful for computer-supported coordination. *ACM Transactions on Office Information Systems, 5*(2): 115–131.

Manross, G.G., & Rice, R.E. (1986). Don't hang up: Organizational diffusion of the intelligent telephone. *Information & Management, 10:* 161–175.

March, J.G., & Simon, A. (1969). Organizations. *DUNOD.*

Millman, Z., & Hartwick, J. (1987). The impact of automated office systems on middle managers and their work. *MIS Quarterly.* 479–491.

Mintzberg, H., (1973). *The nature of managerial work.* New York: Harper & Row.

Morin, M.M. (1988/89). On implementing a voice messaging system. *Optimum, 19*(4): 107–117

Mozeico, H. (1982). A human/computer interface to accommodate user learning stages. *Communications of the ACM, 25*(2): 100–104.

Nelson, D.L. (1990). Individual adjustment to information-driven technologies: A critical review. *MIS Quarterly, 14*(1): 79–98.

Nelson, R.R., & Cheney, P.H. (1987). Training end users: An exploratory study. *MIS Quarterly: 11*(4): 547–559.

Nickerson, R.S. (1981). Why interactive computer systems are sometimes not used by people who might benefit from them. *International Journal of Man-Machine Studies, 15:* 469–483.

Olfman, L., & Bostrom, R.P. (1988). The influence of training on use of end-user software. *Association of Computing Machinery Conference on Office Information Systems,* March 23–25, Palo Alto, CA: 110–117.

Olson, M.H., & Turner, J.A. (1986). Rethinking office automation *DATABASE: 9*(6): 20–28.

Panko, R.R., (1984). Office work. *Office: Technology and People, 2,* 205–238.

Pavri, F. (1987). A model for predicting microcomputer usage. *ASAC 1987 Conference,* Ed. Barki, H., *8*(4): 103–114.

Phillip & Young. (1987). Man-machine interaction by voice: Developments in speech technology. *Information Science Principles and Practice, 13*(1): 3–23.

Plaisent, M. (1987, February). *A test of the usage of a computer-mediated communication system by upper levels of managers in an organization.* Doctoral thesis. University of Quebec.

Porter & Millar. (1985). how information gives you and conpetitive adves... *Harvard Business Review, 63*(4): 149–160.

Rallet, A. (1989). From an organizational network to networked organizations. *Network, 36:* 121–143.

Robey, D. (1979). User attitudes and management information system use. *Academy of Management Journal, 22*(3): 527–538.

Rockart, J.F., & DeLone, D.W. (1986). Executive support systems and the nature of executive work, CISR WP, no 135, *Sloan School of MIT.*

Rockart, J.F., & Short, J.E. (1988). Information technology and the new organization: Towards more effective management of interdependence. *Center for Information Systems Research,* Sloan School of Management, Massachusetts Institute of Technology.

Rushinek, A., & Rushinek, S.F. (1986). What makes users happy? *Communications of the ACM, 29*(7): 594–598.

Safayeni, F., MacGregor, J., Lee, E., & Bavelas, A. (1987). Social and task-related impacts of office automation: An exploratory field study of a conceptual model of the office. *Human Systems Management, 7:* 103–114.

Salem, P.J., & Gratz, R.D. (1989). Computer use and organizational effectiveness: The case of two intervening variables. *Management Communication Quarterly, 2*(3): 409–423.

Schultz, R.L., & Slevin, D.P. (1982). Implementation exchange: Implementing implementation research. *Interfaces, 12*: 87–90.

Simon, H.A. (1960). *The new science of management decision.* New York: Harper.

Sproul, L., & Kiesler, S. (1986, November). Reducing social context cues: Electronic mail in organizational communication. *Management Sciences, 32*(11): 1492–1512.

Stone, M.D. (1989). Replacing the receptionist: PC-Based Voice Mail Systems. *PC Magazine, 8*(1): 186–234.

Sullivan, C.H., & Smart, J.R. (1987). Planning for information networks. *Sloan Management Review.* 39–43.

Tapscott, D. (1980). Towards a methodology for office information communication systems research. *Integrated Office Systems-Burotics.* North-Holland 71–91.

Todd, P., Nelson, R., & Adams, D. (1987). The impact of computer mediated communication systems: A comparison of voice and electronic mail. *Information Systems, 8*(4): 153–160.

Treacy, M.E. (1986, March). Toward a cumulative tradition of research on information technology as a strategic business factor. CISR WP no. 134, *Sloan School of MIT.*

Trice, A.W., & Treacy, M.E. (1986) Utilization as a dependent variable in MIS research, *Sloan* wp 1834-86.

Turner, J.A. (1982a). Observations on the use of behavioral models in information systems research and practice. *Information & Management, 5*: 207–213.

Turner, J.A. (1982b). Observations on the use of behavioral models in information systems research and practice. *Center for Research on Information Systems,* New York: New York University.

Ugbah, S.D. (1986). Computer mediated communication systems: The impact on organizational climate, and information adequacy in organizational settings. *DAI, 47*(10A): 3612.

Uhlig, R.P. (1977). Human factors in computer message systems. *Datamation, 77*(5): 120–126.

Uhlig, R.P. (1982) *The office of the future, vol. 1.* New York: North Holland.

Weinberg, P. (1990). Speaking terms: Although data will be ever more important to telecom managers in the '90s, in the short run voice is still king. *OA Canada's Office Automation Magazine, 6*(1): 32–35.

Wintrob, S. (1989). Voice mail booming but be wary, researcher says. *Computing Canada, 15*(23): 6.

Yaverbaum, G.J. (1988, March). Critical factors in the user environment: An experimental study of users, organizations and tasks. *MIS Quarterly.* 75–88.

Young, T.R. (1984). The lonely micro. *Datamation.* 100–114.

Zuboff, S. (1982, September–October). New worlds of computer-mediated work. *Harvard Business Review.* 142–152.

A Task for Examining Information Chaneling Under Time Pressure

Manouchehr Tabatabai
Fort Hays State University

James Hershauer
Arizona State University

INTRODUCTION

Stabell (1983) states that improving the effectiveness of the decision maker should be a principal objective for decision aid development. He suggests that effectiveness can be improved by appropriate channeling of information processing. Silver (1988, 1990) also discusses the advantages of system restrictiveness. The major reason behind designing restrictive decision aids is to prescribe a preferred information-processing approach.

The two basic information processing patterns in multialternative, multiattribute choice decisions are alternative-based and attribute-based (Svenson, 1979). Information selection strategies using alternative-based processing examine attributes of an alternative before considering the next alternative. By contrast, information selection strategies using attribute-based processing examine alternatives on a single attribute before considering the next attribute. Decision research has found the use of both information processing patterns to be common (see Ford, Schmitt, Schechtman, Hults, & Doherty, 1989, for a summary of 45 studies). Although both patterns have been used, there is evidence to suggest that processing information by attribute is easier (Klayman, 1985; Payne, 1982; Todd & Benbasat, 1991). Paquette and Kida (1988) also found attribute-based processing heuristics to be more efficient and equally effective compared to alternative-based processing heuristics.

Therefore, with increased use of reduced processing strategies (heuristics) in high information loads in order to minimize the cognitive effort (e.g., Biggs, Bedard, Gaber, & Linsmeier, 1985), it may be appropriate to encourage use of attribute-based processing. One way to encourage attribute-based processing is through the restrictive/channeling approach to system design suggested by Silver (1990). Empirical efforts based on appropriate tasks and laboratory software are needed to examine and analyze whether a restrictive/channeling design approach to support a predefined decision process improves effectiveness.

BASIS FOR TASK AND LABORATORY SYSTEM

The main purpose of this chapter is to propose a realistic business decision task and a laboratory setting to enable controlled empirical examination of the effectiveness of alternative-based and attribute-based information channeling when time pressure is present. If access by restrictive information support mechanisms can be shown to affect both the effort and the decision accuracy, then use of particular support mechanisms can be tested and evaluated. Todd and Benbasat (1991) have reported recent empirical testing of flexible decision aids (not restrictive in the sense described by Silver, 1990) using students in an apartment selection task without specific time pressure.

Decision Support Mechanisms

There are two simple decision support mechanisms proposed. One mechanism organizes and displays information by alternative to channel alternative-based processing, whereas the other organizes and displays information by attribute to channel attribute-based processing. In the nonchanneled information-processing pattern (control group), the information is displayed in full and is not organized to channel a specific processing pattern.

Recent research by Todd and Benbasat (1991) indicates that there is a direct relation between information support features available and the information-processing pattern employed. Decision makers tend to use the information in the form in which it is organized in order to reduce cognitive effort and to increase benefit. This means that it is less effortful to take the information as organized and choose strategies to suit such organization than to transform information to fit strategies. Bettman and Kakkar (1977) suggest that organization of information is important because it affects the type of comparisons and consequently the information selection and consideration. They suggest that organization of information into separate lists for each alternative elicits alternative-based processing, whereas organization of information into separate lists for each attribute elicits attribute-based processing.

Other authors have also suggested the consistency of information acquisition and information processing. Newell and Simon (1972) suggest that people search information in a manner consistent with the decision process employed. Svenson (1979) claims that the order in which a decision maker seeks and evaluates the information of a decision problem is related to the cognitive process leading to the final decision.

Cost/Benefit Framework

Payne (1982) proposed a theoretical framework of cost/benefit analysis that accounts for this general finding of contingent behavior. In any one task environment, a decision maker is expected to adopt an information selection strategy that minimizes the effort and maximizes the benefit. The decision-maker cost is primarily the cognitive effort required to use the strategy, such as information selection/acquisition and computational effort. The benefit of a strategy is its ability to produce a correct decision or to minimize errors and reduce the decision time. In a given decision task situation, the decision maker examines costs and benefits of various information selection strategies, and the strategy with the highest expected net benefits is selected.

If a decision maker's only concern is accuracy of choice, then we would expect the additive utility selection strategy to be common. However, evidence does not support that this is the case (Bettman, Johnson, & Payne, 1990; Miller, 1956; Payne, 1976; Svenson, 1979). The cost(effort)/benefit(accuracy) framework of Payne and the suggestion of cost (effort) being weighted more than benefit (accuracy) can explain two important findings of the research. One is the general finding of increased usage of reduced processing (heuristics) strategies and attribute-based processing as task complexity increases (Biggs et al., 1985; Payne, 1976; Payne & Braunstein, 1978; Russo & Dosher, 1983). The other is the acquisition and usage of information in the form in which it is organized and displayed. Todd and Benbasat (1991) suggest that decision makers tend to use the information in the manner in which it is supported.

One implication of the cost/benefit analysis is that reduction of the effort involved in high processing strategies will encourage more usage of such strategies. In a study of supermarket shopping, Russo (1977) supported the influence of information organization form on cognitive cost/benefit tradeoffs. He found a significant change in strategy and performance of shoppers when information was provided by attribute (unit price) in organized lists as opposed to availability of this information next to the products in the usual form on the shelves. Results showed that consumers shopped more effectively (lower average cost of shopping) when information was organized based on unit price (attribute information organization). Tversky (1969) suggests that attribute-based processing is easier because the same unit (attribute) is used when comparing the alternatives. Also, difference calculations are cognitively easier and less error prone within attribute (attribute-based) than between attribute (alternative-based) (Jarvenpaa, 1989). Bettman and Kakkar (1977) argue that the reason for attribute-based processing being easier is that fewer between-attribute comparisons are required.

Russo and Dosher (1983) found overwhelming use of attribute-based processing in a decision task environment in which either alternative-based or attribute-based processing could be used. With the result of this and other experiments, they concluded that attribute-based processing requires less mental effort than alternative-based processing. The greater amount of information may put additional burdens on the processing resources and, hence, elicit the least demanding type of processing.

Jacoby, Kuss, Mazursky, and Trotman (1985) found that the best performers were those who used attribute-based processing, whereas the poorest performers were those who used more alternative-based processing in an environment in which either processing pattern could be used. The reason for better performers being attribute-based processors may be twofold. One is that based on the earlier discussions attribute-based processing is cognitively easier than alternative-based processing, which allows for more processing of available information and hence better performance. The other reason is that in high information load some information is ignored, which means reduced processing (heuristics) strategies are used, and not all the information is examined. However, attribute-based processing provides a general assessment of all the alternatives by examining the most important attributes for them even when some attributes are ignored, whereas alternative-based processing ignores some alternatives totally without any assessment.

Time Constraint in Decision Making

Time pressure (a few minutes in the current context) is another important variable in decision support mechanisms that examine the effectiveness of channeled information processing patterns. Time pressure is important because under severe time constraints the use of a normative decision strategy (expected value maximization) may be infeasible or less attractive (Simon, 1981). Payne, Bettman, and Johnson (1988) suggest that when time pressure exists, the decision maker's choice of strategy is the best available heuristic (reduced processing strategies), rather than deciding between using some heuristics or optimal strategies.

Studies conducted in a laboratory setting always involve at least an implied time pressure when the subject has been asked to participate during a fixed time period. To produce more practically useful findings, laboratory studies should therefore use a task in which time pressure is realistic and explicit. A key contribution of this chapter is the development of a scheduling task with a real time constraint.

Payne et al. (1988) found time constraints to have substantial effects on decision strategies and accuracy of outcome. As a result of their simulation study, they concluded that the most effective strategies are those that process at least some information about all alternatives as quickly as possible. This finding suggests that effective strategies are, in fact, those strategies that use attribute-based processing. They also found a similar result by using decision makers in an experimental setting. The authors concluded that when decision makers faced a severe time pressure, they accelerated their processing, focused on a subset of more important information, and changed their processing toward attribute-based. This implies that a decision maker may believe that a good strategy is to look at the most important information for all alternatives (attribute-based processing) first, then look at other information as time allows.

Therefore, under time pressure, attribute-based processing should process more information and perform better than alternative-based processing. Although attribute-based processing may be more effective under presence of time pressure, this does not identify which particular information selection strategy a decision maker should adopt in a given decision task. It depends on the degree to which a decision maker is willing to trade a decrease in accuracy for savings in effort. This tradeoff might depend on factors such as the decision maker's goal structure, the size of the payoffs, and the need to justify a decision (Payne et al., 1988). This result of attribute-based processing being more effective under presence of time pressure suggests a mixed approach of restriction and flexibility to system design. This might be achieved by restricting decision makers to use attribute-based processing, while allowing any information selection strategy preferred.

LABORATORY ENVIRONMENT

Decision Task

A multiattribute choice decision task has been developed for testing support mechanisms. The following desired characteristics were used in selection of the decision task: (a) a real task that is performed under time pressure, (b) an information load that could be determined and quantified, (c) a task that could be organized and presented in a matrix format with a number of alternatives explained on a set of attributes, and (d) a task suitable for screen display with automatic data capturing by the system.

The task is a scheduling problem that involves a truck dispatching decision (Ahituv & Newmann, 1990; Goetschalckx, 1988; Goetschalckx & Taylor, 1987; Hill, 1982; Lukka & Lukka, 1988). The decision makers are asked to assume the role of a supervisor who schedules truck orders. A hypothetical situation is created in which all trucks are currently scheduled and are ready to leave the depot. At this time a new order is received, and the supervisor is faced with the choice decision of to which currently scheduled truck this new order should be assigned. Assignment to a truck causes several different attributes for a truck's schedule to change. Information values are a reflection of these changes. These values represent the incremental effect on each attribute of adding the new order to each particular truck. The information values on each attribute will be represented on a 7-point scale, ranging from a very negative to a very positive effect.

A 7×7 matrix presents the information values. In this matrix the rows represent the trucks, and columns are attributes upon which truck scheduling is based. The attributes are Pickup Window, Load Distribution, Delivery Quality, Crew Members, Delivery Timeliness, Pickup Service, and Distance Minimization. This set of attributes has been adopted from the truck scheduling literature (Ahituv & Newmann, 1990;

Goetschalckx, 1988; Goetschalckx & Taylor, 1987; Hill, 1982; Lukka & Lukka, 1988). The information values in the matrix are generated using a random number generator. Some adaptations are made, if necessary, to ensure that there are no dominant alternatives. The decision makers are asked to make a series of independent choice decisions, each time with a new matrix of information values. The decision makers are instructed that the information values are the results of models run by the DSS in the background.

Laboratory Tool

A laboratory tool has been developed that involves a multiattribute choice decision task in an experimental setting using a computer-based system (see Appendix A for a brief description of the software and Appendix B for a presentation of the task). The system is designed for Macintosh computer systems and compatibles using a mouse to improve ease of use.

Information organization and presentation is by matrix format for a moderate information load. In low information load mostly compensatory strategies are used, regardless of processing patterns adopted. However, the decision outcome may be different. Thus, research questions can be more appropriately answered by using a higher information load.

The key independent variables supported by the tool are information display and time pressure. The variable on information display has three levels: display of information by alternative, display of information by attribute, and display of information in full (control group).

A symmetrical matrix of the same size is used to present the information in each level. A symmetrical matrix is suggested to make the information load consistent in alternative and attribute information displays. This matrix consists of alternatives (rows), each described on a set of attributes (columns). In the alternative information display, information inquiry is only by rows. For example, an alternative (row) should be identified, and then attributes (columns) of interest can be examined for the identified alternative. In attribute information display, information can only be inquired by columns. For example, an attribute (column) should be identified, and then alternatives (rows) of interest can be examined for the identified attribute. In full information display, all the information is presented on the screen, and thus information can be inquired by any manner.

The other independent variable—time pressure—also has three levels: low (4 minutes), moderate (2 minutes), and high (1 minute). These time pressures are based on the system test findings that are explained later. The low time constraint (4 minutes) allows enough time for most people to complete the task in a compensatory fashion. The moderate time constraint allows just about enough time, and high time constraint allows less time than is generally required to complete the task in a compensatory fashion.

The system is set up so that once the time is expired the users cannot collect any more information. The time left is indicated on the screen using a counting down clock.

The decision makers are told in the instruction sheet that they should not wait for the time to expire in order to make their decision, and they should make their decision at any time they think enough information has been examined to make a choice.

System Test

To confirm that subjects could understand and use the system appropriately, a pilot system test was conducted. Seventeen graduate students enrolled in an information systems course participated in the test. The findings of the test suggested some changes based on the decision makers' performance, postexperiment questionnaire, and group and individual discussions. Subjects found the need for individual cell access after row or column access to be artificial and also desired a workspace. The system has been modified to display information by alternatives or attributes as a whole without the requirement of individual cell selections. Also, a notepad has been added to the system. The data on the usage of the notepad can also contribute in analysis of differences between the information-processing patterns. Improvements and modifications of instruction sheets for both the system as well as the choice decision task have been made.

Determination of appropriate time pressures was also a concern of the system test. The test indicated that 4 minutes and 2 minutes create situations of moderate and high time pressures, respectively, given the choice decision task using the initial system that had 10 alternatives and individual cell access. However, it has been found that 2 minutes and 1 minute are more appropriate for the moderate and high time pressures in the current system. The reduction of the matrix size from 10×7 to 7×7 was necessary to obtain fair comparisons of attribute-based support and alternative-based support. Also, no cell selection is involved in the new system.

Procedures

There are two sets of instruction sheets: one for the system usage, and the other for the choice decision situation. The instructions about the system usage are given to the decision makers a few days in advance. The instructions about the decision situation are provided to the decision makers right before decisions are made. This separation of instruction helps the decision makers fully understand the system and the choice decision task they are facing. Appendix B contains the instructions about the decision situation. A practice task is provided to them before the actual experimental task. They are allowed and recommended to redo the practice task for full understanding.

A description of the decision task with an explanation of the attributes is provided to the decision makers in the decision situation instruction sheets. They are given enough time for rereading and asking questions. The decision makers make three choice decisions in each level of time pressure.

System Features

The decision task is presented by a computer-based system. This system also traces the information selection and collects data on the order of information selection, the amount of time that each selection is examined, and the decision made. This system overcomes problems associated with manual process-tracing methods (information boards, verbal protocol, and eye movement recordings) by elimination of researcher intervention, tighter control over the data collection process, and increased sample size opportunity. This system provides a user-friendly system, subject involvement and motivation, and comprehensive data collection by employing current computer technology. In addition, this system allows simultaneous access to a number of data items and recording of repeated observations of data items. This system, called ISSS=IS^3 (IS^3=Information Selection Strategy System), was developed by the first author using HyperCard on the Macintosh computer system. Appendix A provides a brief description of the system. More detailed documentation and the system itself are available at no charge for related research projects.

REFERENCES

Ahituv, N., & Newmann, S. (1990). *Principal of information systems for management.* Dubuque, IA: Wm. C. Brown.

Bettman, J.R., Johnson, E.J., & Payne, J.W. (1990). A componential analysis of cognitive effort in choice. *Organizational Behavior and Human Decision Processes, 45,* 111–139.

Bettman, J.R., & Kakkar, P. (1977). Effects of information presentation format on consumer information acquisition strategies. *Journal of Consumer Research, 3,* 233–240.

Biggs, S.F., Bedard, J.C., Gaber, B.G., & Linsmeier, T.J. (1985). The effects of task size and similarity on the decision behavior of bank loan officers. *Management Science, 31*(8), 970–987.

Ford, J.K., Schmitt, N., Schechtman, S.L., Hults, B.M., & Doherty, M.L. (1989). Process tracing methods: Contributions, problems, and neglected research questions. *Organizational Behavior and Human Decision Processes, 43,* 75–117.

Goetschalckx, M. (1988). A decision support system for dynamic truck despatching. *International Journal of Physical Distribution and Materials management, 18*(6), 34–42.

Goetschalckx, M., & Taylor, W. (1987). A decision support system for dynamic truck dispatching. *Computers and Industrial Engineering, 13*(1–4), 120–123.

Hill, A. (1982). An experimental comparison of human schedulers and heuristic algorithms for the traveling salesman problem. *Journal of Operations Management, 2*(4), 215–223.

Jacoby, J., Kuss, A., Mazursky, D., & Troutman, T. (1985). Effectiveness of security analyst information accessing strategies: A computer interactive assessment. *Computers in Human Behavior, 1,* 95–113.

Jarvenpaa, S.L. (1989). The effect of task and graphical format congruence on information processing strategies and decision making performance. *Management Science, 35*(3), 285–303.

Klayman, J. (1985). Children's decision strategies and their adaptation to task characteristics. *Organizational Behavior and Human Decision Processes, 35,* 179–201.

Lukka, A., & Lukka, M. (1988). Expert systems: A role in transportation planning. *International Journal of Physical Distribution and Materials Management, 18*(1), 3–8.

Miller, G.A. (1956). The magical number seven, plus or minus two: Some limits on our capacity for processing information. *The Psychological Review, 63*(2), 81–97.

Newell, A., & Simon, H.A. (1972). *Human problem solving.* Englewood Cliffs, NJ: Prentice-Hall.

Paquette, L., & Kida, T. (1988). The effect of decision strategy and task complexity on decision performance. *Organizational Behavior and Human Decision Processes, 41,* 128–142.

Payne, J.W. (1976). Task complexity and contingent processing in decision making: An information search and protocol analysis. *Organizational Behavior and Human Performance, 16,* 366–387.

Payne, J.W. (1982). Contingent decision behavior. *Psychological Bulletin, 92,* 382–402.

Payne, J.W., Bettman, J.R., & Johnson, E.J. (1988). Adaptive strategy selection in decision making, *Journal of Experimental Psychology: Learning, Memory, and Cognition, 14,* 534–552.

Payne, J.W., & Braunstein, M.L. (1978). Risky choice: An examination of information acquisition behavior. *Memory and Cognition, 6*(5), pp. 554–561.

Russo, J.E. (1977). The value of unit price information. *Journal of Marketing Research, 14,* 193–201.

Russo, J.E., & Dosher, B.A. (1983). Strategies for multiattribute binary choice. *Journal of Experimental Psychology: Learning, Memory, and Cognition, 9,* 676–696.

Silver, M.S. (1988). User perceptions of decision support system restrictiveness: An experiment. *Journal of Management Information Systems, 5*(1), 51–65.

Silver, M.S. (1990). Decision support systems: Directed and nondirected change. *Information Systems Research, 1*(1), 47–70.

Simon, H.A. (1981). *The sciences of the artificial* (2nd ed.). Cambridge, MA: MIT Press.

Stabell, C.B. (1983). A decision-oriented approach to building DSS. pp. 221–260. In J. L. Bennett (Ed.), *Building decision support systems.* Reading, MA: Addison-Wesley.

Svenson, O. (1979). Process descriptions of decision making. *Organizational Behavior and Human Performance, 23,* 86–112.

Todd, P., & Benbasat, I. (1991). An experimental investigation of the impact of computer based decision aids on decision making strategies. *Information Systems Research, 2*(2), 87–115.

Tversky, A. (1969). Intransitivity of preferences. *Psychological Review, 76,* 31–48.

APPENDIX A
A BRIEF DESCRIPTION OF IS³

IS³ (Information Selection Strategy System) is an interactive computer-based system that supports decision makers in choice decisions. The system is designed for Macintosh computer systems and compatibles using a mouse to improve ease of use.

There are three IS³ systems of alternative information display, attribute information display, and full information display. Each system includes a series of choice sessions based on the three levels of time pressure (low, moderate, and high). Prior to a choice sessions menu, the system provides users with a practice task consistent with the system form of information display. The menu for a practice task includes a

"Repeat" button for repeating the practice task with different time pressures as many times as needed.

A menu then lists the choice sessions in the order that the users are required to perform them.

Information about the decision task in choice sessions is organized and presented in a matrix format. In order to access information in the matrix, the user must identify the alternative (alternative information display only) or attribute (attribute information display only) desired. The system is configured so that alternative information display users cannot access the information through attributes, and users in the attribute information display cannot access information through alternatives. Once the alternative/attribute of interest has been identified, the cells containing the information for that alternative/attribute are opened and the values revealed. These values stay on until a new alternative/attribute is selected. Users can reaccess an alternative/attribute as often as they wish.

This process of alternative/attribute selection is continued until the user is ready to make a choice. At that time the user must click on the "DECISION" button that appears on the screen. After confirmation, small pointing-hand icons appear on the screen. There is one such icon per alternative. After a valid pointing-hand corresponding to the chosen alternative is clicked, the user is asked to confirm the choice. If the choice is not confirmed, the user is given the opportunity to make another choice. Clicking a "Yes" to confirm the choice causes the system to return to the main menu and terminates the current choice session for a given information display and time pressure.

The system also provides the users with a notepad. The notepad can be accessed by clicking on the "NOTEPAD" button appearing on the screen. This is a write-only notepad in which users can jot down their notes without being allowed to erase anything. The notepad is a blank screen with a "Go Back" button that returns to the main screen.

The remaining time is indicated on the screen by a clock that counts down. The users are disallowed from further alternative/attribute selection once the required time is expired and the small pointing-hand icons appear for the choice to be made.

APPENDIX B
THE MOVERS COMPANY

It is another summer morning in Tempe, AZ. The supervisor who schedules the trucks in The Movers Company (TMC) has again received enough orders to schedule all seven trucks available. The trucks are all set and ready to leave the depot. The supervisor is browsing through the schedule while watching drivers prepare to leave. The office is very quiet until the sound of a phone ring breaks the silence. It is a call from a customer to place an order whose moving job has been previously given a quote assessment by an evaluator of TMC. However the customer needed more time to accept the offer. Because the order is a worthy one, and from a loyal customer, the supervisor cannot reject it.

Because there is no idle truck, the only option left is to allocate this order to one of the currently scheduled trucks.

While closing in on the departure time, the problem facing the supervisor is to decide which truck should get the new order. The supervisor quickly enters basic information about the new order with respect to the currently scheduled trucks into the computer. Further evaluation is provided in the background by the decision support system (DSS). He is thankful that this computer system with a matrix arrangement of resulting information is available to him. He can now examine the arranged data and make his decision about which truck to assign for the new order. While looking at the data, he is aware that time is clicking away, and the decision of which truck schedule can best fit the new order must be made quickly.

Situational Assumptions

Assume you are the supervisor of TMC. In each of the following decision situations there are seven trucks that a new order can be assigned to. Your task will be to choose one truck in each situation to assign the new order.

Decision Situations

There are several independent decision situations. In each decision situation you are to choose one truck from among seven to handle the new order. Assignment to a truck causes several different criteria for a truck's schedule to change. Information values from the DSS a are reflection of these changes. These values represent the incremental effect on each criterion of adding the new order to each particular truck. The information values for each item of information (values within each cell of the matrix) will be represented on a 7-point scale, ranging from very negative effect to very positive effect. Models are run in the background by the DSS to obtain these values. Some of these models are quite complex and related to a special "Traveling Salesman" model. Because no single choice of a truck receives perfect scores (7) on all information criteria, your subjective judgment as a supervisor is required to make the final decision. It is now your task to explore the information resulting from running the DSS in order to choose one truck to assign this new order to.

You have a series of independent decisions to make. Each of these decisions represents a similar situation for different days. You may take a short break between decisions to clear your mind. Please note that there is no relationship between decisions and information values from one decision to the next. There are always seven truck schedules to consider because this is the number of trucks available in TMC.

Performance/Evaluation Criteria

The following are the seven criteria used in truck scheduling at TMC with their brief description.

1. Pickup Window: Customer specified time window for pickup including priority orders and special services. It is important to pick up customer orders within their specified time windows to keep them satisfied.
2. Delivery Timeliness: On-time delivery request by the customers. Delivery should be made when customers want it. The customers specify the time zone of delivery. Delivery at any other time may inconvenience the customers, which creates dissatisfaction.
3. Load Distribution: Load distribution proportional to the truck size. To balance the truck schedules, and work hours among the drivers including overtime. It is important to keep the drivers and their union satisfied by an equal assignment of work hours.
4. Pickup Service: The preset amount of time specified by management of TMC to be spent on each pickup order for quality service. This avoids any possibility of damage due to rush work. For years, TMC has had a good reputation of safe service, and it is important to keep it that way.
5. Delivery Quality: The management of TMC has a set of rules and policies to maintain quality of transportation and delivery. These rules include a preset amount of time to be spent on each delivery order. This avoids unsafe delivery due to rush transportation and delivery.
6. Distance Minimization: Minimization of the overall travel distance reduces the transportation cost to the corporation. This means increased profit. Thus, it is important to keep the drivers within the specified zone in order to minimize travel distance, time, and cost.
7. Crew Members: To help pickup and delivery for faster and better service, crew members are needed. Assignment of extra crew members to a shipment should be avoided. Consideration should be given to utilization of crew members to balance work hours.

The Effects of Individual
Differences on User Satisfaction

Allison Harrison
Mississippi State University

Kelly Rainer
Auburn University

INTRODUCTION

End-user computing (EUC) is widely regarded as one of the most significant phenomena in the information systems (IS) field over the past decade (Ball & Harris, 1982; Benson, 1983; Brancheau & Wetherbe, 1987; Dickson, Leitheiser, Nechis, & Wetherbe, 1984; Hartog & Herbert, 1986). EUC is defined in this chapter as the direct, hands-on use of computers by persons with problems for which computer-based solutions are appropriate (Carr, 1987; Doll & Torkzadeh, 1989; Hackathorn & Keen, 1981; Sprague & McNurlin, 1986).

Many authors have noted the explosive growth in the number of organizational personnel who make direct use of computers in their work (Alavi & Weiss, 1985–1986; Benjamin, 1982; Rockart & Flannery, 1983). The increasing number of employees practicing EUC suggests that they have diverse individual characteristics. Not only are more people involved in EUC, but their roles have changed significantly (Davis & Olson, 1985). These people have assumed a wider range of computing responsibilities, such as interacting with applications, obtaining data, specifying and producing output, as well as others (Cotterman & Kumar, 1989; Igbaria & Nachman, 1990).

The diversity and number of people involved in EUC, coupled with their increasing computing sophistication, means that EUC is of critical importance to organizations but is difficult to effectively manage. With these points in mind, practicing managers clearly should be able to assess the success of EUC. However, little research exists that provides these managers with guidelines toward evaluating EUC success. For example, Cheney, Mann, and Amoroso (1986) noted the need for more empirical research on the factors which influence EUC success.

End-user satisfaction is considered a viable proxy for EUC success (e.g., Baroudi & Orlikowksi, 1988). End-user satisfaction is defined as the affective attitude expressed toward a specific computer application by the end user (Doll & Torkzadeh, 1988). If end-user satisfaction is to be the surrogate measure for EUC success, the factors associated with end-user satisfaction should be examined.

CORRELATES OF END USER SATISFACTION

The correlates of user satisfaction can be grouped into two categories: factors associated with the end-user environment and factors associated with the end user. Factors associated with the end-user environment include characteristics of the IS environment and characteristics of the organization. Factors associated with the end user, also known as individual differences, are characteristics of the individual, including demographic traits, personality characteristics, and cognitive traits.

The majority of the research examining the antecedents of user satisfaction explores environmental factors. Table 14.1 shows the environmental factors, grouped into six categories, that were noted in 13 empirical studies of user satisfaction. Interestingly, with the exception of computer literacy and understanding of and confidence in computer systems, none of these factors pertains to individual characteristics.

Table 14.1.   Correlates of End User Satisfaction

Characteristics of information provided by the computer systems

* accuracy—1,2,6,8,9,11,12	* informative—4,5
* timeliness—1,2,6,8,9,11	* helpful—4,5,11
* precision—1,2,8,9,12	* useful—4,11
* reliability—1,2,8,12	* desirable—4
* currency—1,2,3,8,9	* meaningful—4,5,11
* completeness—1,2,12	* good—4
* format—1,8,9,11	* important—4,5
* volume—1,2	* valuable—4
* relevancy—1,2,4,5,6,8,9,12	* effective—4
* clarity—5,6,8,9	* necessary—4
* ease of understanding—8	* significant—5,11
* sufficient—8,9	* readable—5,6,11
* meets user needs—4,8,9	* concise—6

Relationship between user and IS department

* priorities determination—1,2	* feeling of participation—1,2,12,13
* chargeback method of payment for services—1,2	* feeling of control—1,2
* relationship with IS staff—1,2,12,13	* microcomputer policies—10
* means of input/output with IS department—1,2	* communication with IS staff—1,2,12,13

Characteristics of IS department
 * technical competence of IS staff—1,2
 * attitude of IS staff—1,2,12
 * schedule of products, services—1,2,7
 * time required for new development—1,2,7,12
 * presence of information center—10

 * vendor support—1,2
 * response/turnaround time—1,2
 * presence of hotline—10
 * processing of change requests— 1,2,7,12

Relationship between IS department and general management
 * organizational competition with the
   IS department—1,2
 * organizational position of the IS department—1,2

 * top management involvement—1,2

 * decentralized organization—13

User interaction with the computer systems
 * degree of training—1,2,12
 * convenience of access—1,2,3
 * understanding of computer systems—1,2,12
 * confidence in the computer systems—1,2
 * user computer literacy—13
 * depth of information requirement analysis—13

 * languages used—1,7
 * expectations—1,2,7
 * perceived utility—1,2
 * job effects—1,2
 * interactive applications—13

Characteristics of the computer systems
 * error recovery—1,2
 * security of data—1
 * documentation—1,2
 * flexibility of computer systems—1,2
 * integration of computer systems—1,2
 * promptness of equipment delivery—7
 * cost effectiveness of productivity aids—7
 * percentage of mainframes—7
 * compatibility of peripherals—7
 * percentage of microcomputers—7
 * compatibility of programs—7

 * easy to use—8,9
 * fast response time—3,7
 * efficient—7,8
 * dependable—8
 * user friendly—8,9
 * system cost—7
 * number of users—7
 * number of systems—7
 * average system life—7
 * system expandability—7
 * percentage minicomputers—7

Legend:
 1 = Bailey and Pearson (1983)
 2 = Ives, Olson, and Baroudi (1983)
 3 = Raymond (1987)
 4 = Gallagher (1974)
 5 = Larcker and Lessig (1980)
 6 = Swanson (1974)

 7 = Rushinek and Rushinek (1986)
 8 = Doll and Torkzadeh (1988)
 9 = Doll and Torkzadeh (1989)
 10 = Bergeron and Berube (1988)
 11 = Zmud (1979)
 12 = Baroudi and Orlikowski (1988)
 13 = Montazemi (1988)

With the growth in the number and sophistication level of end users, the impact of these individual differences, if any, should be examined. This is not to say that the environmental characteristics are not important or are less important. The literature clearly indicates the importance of the environmental characteristics; however, if additional factors affecting user satisfaction can be identified, then user satisfaction and, therefore, EUC success could possibly be more readily attained. The purpose of this research is to examine the relationship between characteristics of the individual end user and end-user satisfaction.

LITERATURE REVIEW AND PROPOSITION GENERATION

Zmud (1979) addressed the influence of individual differences on Management Information Systems (MIS) success by placing individual difference variables into three categories: demographics, personality, and cognitive style. Demographic variables are personal characteristics such as age, gender, education, and experience with computers. Personality variables relate to the individual's cognitive and affective structures used to understand events and people. Cognitive style represents the individual's modes of perceptual and thinking behavior.

Zmud's categorization of individual difference variables is used to outline the review of the literature. Propositions regarding the relationship of each individual difference variable and user satisfaction follow the discussion of each variable.

Demographics and Personal Characteristics

Gender.

Prior research has examined the relationship of gender and computer-related outcomes. Computer use has been perceived to be a male-oriented activity, and males have also demonstrated a greater liking for the computer (Wilder, Mackie, & Cooper, 1985). Heinssen, Glass, and Knight (1987) suggested that women are more likely than men to be more anxious about and dissatisfied with computers. These findings suggest the following:

Proposition 1:   Females will demonstrate less satisfaction than males.

Age.

Raub (1981) and Nickell and Pinto (1986) found older employees to demonstrate negative attitudes toward computers. Age was significantly related to system success in a recent study by Igbaria and Parasuraman (1989). They found age to be negatively related to user satisfaction. Thus, based on previous research:

Proposition 2:   Older end users will exhibit lower levels of end user satisfaction than younger end users.

Computer Experience.

Levin and Gordon (1989) found subjects owning computers more motivated to familiarize themselves with computers and to possess more affective attitudes toward computers than did subjects not owning computers. Kasper and Cerveny (1985) concluded that end-user experience and EUC success were positively related. Igbaria and Nachman (1990) also found experience of the end user to be significantly related to EUC success. These findings suggest:

Proposition 3:   End users with more computer experience will demonstrate higher levels of satisfaction than end users with less experience.

Education.

Davis and Davis (1990) found end users with higher levels of education to perform significantly better in a computer training environment. Several studies have reported a negative relationship between education and computer anxiety (Gutek & Bikson, 1985; Igbaria & Parasuraman, 1989; Raub, 1981). Lucas (1978) found that less educated individuals possess more negative attitudes toward information systems than individuals with more education. Such findings suggest:

Proposition 4:   End users with more education will demonstrate higher levels of satisfaction than less educated end users.

Computer skill level.

The relationship between end-user computer skill level and user satisfaction remains largely unexplored. Pratkanis and Greenwald (1989) suggest that an attitude such as satisfaction may be a function of the roles and tasks a person must perform in a given situation. Melone (1990) recommends further research on the influence of the required use of technology on user attitudes. In relation to user computer skill, Baroudi, Olson, and Ives (1986) and Igbaria and Nachman (1990) found strong relationships between user satisfaction and system utilization. These findings suggest:

Proposition 5:   End users with more computer skill will indicate a greater level of satisfaction.

Personality.

The personality variables represent the affective component of individual differences. These variables should reflect the individual's feelings or emotions regarding computers and computer use (Igbaria & Parasuraman, 1989). Personality variables include various types of anxiety and attitudes. Computer attitudes demonstrate the individual's degree of like or dislike for computer use, whereas computer anxiety indicates the tendency for an individual to be apprehensive about computer use.

Computer attitudes.

In a survey of end users, Mandell (1989) found that many subjects viewed computers as dehumanizing in nature. Furthermore, these subjects thought that computers gave organizations power and control over workers. Based on the belief that individuals' attitudes toward an object influence their behavior toward the object, Arndt, Clevenger, and Meiskey (1985) reported that subjects regarding the computer with positive attitudes had significantly more computer use than subjects with pessimistic views. These finding lead to the following proposition:

Proposition 6:   End users with more positive attitudes toward computers will demonstrate higher levels of satisfaction than those with negative attitudes.

Computer anxiety.

Heinssen et al. (1987) found that individuals with higher computer anxiety possessed lower self-confidence in their abilities and demonstrated poorer performance outcomes than subjects with lower computer anxiety. Igbaria and Parasuraman (1989) suggested that computer anxiety is a key variable related to system success and concluded that computer anxiety is related to greater dissatisfaction with the system. These findings suggest:

Proposition 7:   End users indicating higher computer anxiety will exhibit lower levels of satisfaction.

Cognitive Style.

Cognitive style refers to the way an individual collects, analyzes, evaluates, and interprets data. Igbaria and Parasuraman (1989) suggested that the attention to detail required for computer work lends itself to a more analytical or systematic cognitive style. However, Vernon-Gerstenfeld (1989) found that subjects with a preference for abstract thinking were more likely to adopt a computer for use on their job. Similarly, Davis and Davis (1990) found intuitive thinkers to outperform all other cognitive styles in a training environment. The conflicting findings in the cognitive style literature lead to the following general proposition:

Proposition 8:   Cognitive style will vary among end users demonstrating high or low levels of satisfaction.

METHODOLOGY

The research study was conducted during the fall of 1990 to investigate the effects of individual differences on user satisfaction. The authors mailed a multipart questionnaire to salaried personnel at a large university in the southern United States. The questionnaire was not sent to hourly personnel because the authors wanted to restrict the population to knowledge workers. The 9-page, 250-item questionnaire required approximately 30 minutes to complete. The respondents were assured anonymity.

The first part of the questionnaire gathered demographic data on the respondents. The second part sought data on individual characteristics of each respondent. The final section addressed the user satisfaction of each respondent. Suggested changes made after two pretests were incorporated into the final instrument.

The survey population consisted of the 3,488 knowledge workers of the university. Seven hundred and seventy-six usable responses were received for a response rate of 22.3%. The sample included respondents from four job categories: faculty (43%), technical (7%), administrative (20%), and clerical (30%). These percentages approximate the proportions of each category in the population. Fifty-one percent of the respondents were male, and 72% possessed at least a bachelor's degree. The mean age of the respondents was 38 years, and they averaged 7.5 years of experience with computers.

The sample is notable for several reasons. First, it includes respondents from every administrative and academic department in the university. Second, respondents represent all ranks in each job category: clerical (Secretary I to Administrative Assistant IV), technical (Research Technician I to Research Technician VIII), faculty (Instructor to Professor), and administrative (Department Head to Vice President). Third, the response rate is noteworthy, considering the length of the survey instrument.

Nonresponse bias was checked with random telephone calls to 40 people who had not completed the questionnaire. (A follow-up mailing was prohibited by university regulations.) All stated that the length of the questionnaire was the reason they had not responded. The 40 respondents agreed to complete the questionnaire. T-tests comparing the demographic variables revealed no significant differences between the first and second groups of respondents. The conclusion was reached that nonresponse bias was not present, and that the results could be generalized to the university population of salaried employees.

Measures

To assess individual differences and user satisfaction, the study used a series of existing scales. The following section describes each scale and the variable it measures.

Computer anxiety.

Computer anxiety was measured by the 19-item Computer Anxiety Rating Scale (CARS; Heinssen et al., 1987). Because the CARS had not been factor analyzed, the authors performed an exploratory factor analysis of the scale. The principle component factor solution with an orthogonal rotation resulted in two factors with eigenvalues greater than 1. The first factor, containing statements such as "I hesitate to use a computer for fear of making mistakes I cannot correct" consisted of 10 statements. This factor, labeled fear, yielded an internal consistency reliability coefficient of .85. The second factor consisted of eight questions, including statements such as "I am confident that I can learn computer skills." This factor was labeled anticipation and resulted in an internal consistency reliability coefficient of .84.

Computer Attitudes.

Computer attitudes were measured by the 20-item Computer Attitude Scale (CAS; Nickell & Pinto, 1986). This scale was originally designed to measure attitude as a single construct, but exploratory factor analysis revealed three independent factors. An orthogonal rotation resulted in a three-factor solution with eigenvalues in excess of one.

Factor one, labeled pessimism, contained eight items. An example statement is "Soon our lives will be controlled by computers." The internal consistency reliability for the pessimism factor was .82.

The second factor embedded in the CAS, labeled optimism, consisted of seven items relating to the positive aspects of computers. An example statement is "The use of computers is enhancing our standard of living." This factor had an internal consistency reliability coefficient of .79.

The third attitudinal factor relates to the belief that computers are intimidating. Labeled intimidation, this factor consisted of four statements, for example, "Computers make me uncomfortable because I don't understand them." The internal consistency reliability coefficient for this factor was .86.

Cognitive Style.

Cognitive style was assessed with the Kirton Adaption-Innovation Inventory (KAI; Kirton, 1976). The 32-item survey included three subscales measuring trait components of the adaptor-innovator dimension. The Originality subscale describes the creative individual. The Methodical Weberianism subscale describes the person who is precise, reliable, and disciplined. The Mertonian conformist subscale identifies the bureaucratic individual who respects authority and rules. The internal consistency reliability coefficients for the three factors were .66, .68, and .82, respectively.

Skill Level.

The Computer Self-Efficacy Scale (CSE; Murphy, Coover, & Owen, 1989) was used to measure the respondents' perceptions of their capability regarding specific computer-related knowledge and skills. Respondents expressed their perceptions on 32 statements using 5-point Likert scales, ranging from (1) strongly disagree to (5) strongly agree.

The 32 statements addressed specific computer skills ranging from elemental abilities to more advanced, complex skills. The CSE had an internal consistency reliability coefficient of .95.

This study employs the CSE because each of the 32 statements represents a discrete, task-specific, work-related outcome. The authors felt that the specific nature of each statement reduced the possibility of varying interpretations by the respondents.

End-user satisfaction.

End-user satisfaction was measured by the 12-item scale developed by Doll and Torkzadeh (1988). Respondents replied to each statement on 5-point Likert scales, ranging from (1) strongly disagree to (5) strongly agree. The scale had an internal consistency reliability coefficient of .93.

RESULTS

The study utilized multiple regression analysis to examine the impact of individual differences, including demographics and personal characteristics, personality, and cognitive variables, on the satisfaction level of the respondents. Table 14.2 summarizes the variables used in the model. Table 14.3 presents the variable means, standard deviations, correlations, and reliability coefficients. Table 14.4 reports the results of the ordinary least-squares regression analysis.

Table 14.2. Descriptions of Variables

Dependent Variable: User Satisfaction

Independent Variables

Personal Characteristics

Age: age of respondent
Gender: 0=male; 1=female
Education Level:
    1= some high school
    2= high school diploma
    3= technical school
    4= some college
    5= college diploma
    6= some graduate school
    7= graduate degree
Experience: years of hands-on computer use
Skill Level: computer-related knowledge and skills

Personality

Computer Anxiety

Fear: apprehension and fear associated with computer use
Anticipation:
    confidence and comfort with the idea of learning and using computer skills

Computer Attitudes

Pessimism: belief that computers are dominating and controlling humans
Optimism: belief that computers are helpful and useful
Intimidation: belief that computers are intimidating

Cognitive Style

Weberian: cognitive style of precise, reliable, disciplined individual
Mertonian: cognitive style of bureaucratic individual
Originality: cognitive style of creative individual

Demographic Variables

One of the five propositions regarding the influence of demographic variables on user satisfaction was supported. The computer skill level of the end user was positively related to user satisfaction. There was no significant finding for gender or age as related to user satisfaction. Level of education and years of computer experience proved significant, however, in negative direction. As education level increases and as years of computer experience increases, the results of this study indicate that user satisfaction will be lower.

Table 14.3. Descriptive Statistics[a]
Means, Standard Deviations, Correlations, and Reliabilities[b]

Variables	Means	S.D.	1	2	3	4	5	6	7	8	9	10	11	12	13	14
1. Gender (0=male, 1=female)	.49	.50														
2. Age (years)	37.52	10.46	-.28													
3. Education Level	5.69	1.54	-.47	.31												
4. Experience	7.74	6.12	-.30	.37	.27											
5. Fear	4.06	.59	-.13	.02	.17	.31	**.85**[b]									
6. Anticipation	4.30	.52	.09	-.05	-.05	.14	.54	**.84**								
7. Pessimism	3.74	.71	-.15	.02	.22	.19	.51	.34	**.82**							
8. Optimism	4.18	.56	.02	.04	-.01	.10	.32	.53	.35	**.79**						
9. Intimidation	4.08	.80	-.07	-.09	.06	.25	.76	.48	.48	.28	**.86**					
10. Math Anxiety	3.57	.97	-.20	.03	.18	.20	.40	.17	.24	.12	.34	**.96**				
11. Weberian	3.51	.55	.17	-.02	-.14	-.03	.05	.17	.03	.19	.06	.07	**.68**			
12. Mertonian	3.01	.53	.17	-.07	-.26	-.13	-.25	-.02	-.23	-.04	-.20	-.01	.30	**.82**		
13. Originality	3.51	.40	-.12	.06	.08	.13	.27	.19	.16	.26	.21	.12	.11	-.29	**.66**	
14. Skill	116.81	14.83	-.08	-.13	-.03	.32	-.60	.47	-.30	.26	-.59	.35	.09	-.12	.27	**.95**

[a] N=620   [b] Reliabilities shown in **bold** on diagonal.

Table 14.4. Results of Regression Analysis
Dependent Variable: User Satisfaction

Variables	Beta	t
Personal Characteristics		
Gender	.052	.962
Age	−.001	−.044
Education	−.056	−3.19***
Experience	−.009	−1.95*
Skill Level	.009	5.63***
Personality		
Computer Anxiety		
Fear	−.098	−1.44
Anticipation	.166	2.69**
Computer Attitudes		
Pessimism	−.087	−2.19**
Optimism	.103	2.05*
Intimidation	.061	1.33
Cognitive Style		
Weberian	.038	.84
Mertonian	.183	3.60***
Originality	.051	.73
R^2 .28		
Adjusted R^2 .26		
N 620		

* $p < .05$
** $p < .01$
*** $p < .001$

Personality Variables

Three of the personality variables yielded results to support the proposed relationships of computer anxiety and computer attitudes to user satisfaction. Anticipation, a latent variable of computer anxiety, was positively related to end-user satisfaction. Anticipation represents the absence of anxiety, thereby supporting the proposition that end users with lower levels of anxiety would report higher levels of satisfaction.

Pessimism and optimism, latent variables of the computer attitudes construct, were also significant predictors of end-user satisfaction. As predicted, end users with more pessimistic attitudes toward computers reported lower levels of satisfaction, and users with positive attitudes toward computers indicated higher levels of satisfaction.

Cognitive Style

A relationship between cognitive style and user satisfaction was also identified. The Mertonian cognitive style was a significant predictor of higher levels of user satisfaction. The remaining two latent variables of cognitive style were not significant.

DISCUSSION

The findings of this study strongly suggest that the antecedents of user satisfaction include variables in addition to than those associated with the organization and its information systems. The human factors, or individual differences, of the end users account for 26% of the variation in satisfaction. Because previous research has employed user satisfaction as a surrogate measure for EUC success, the findings of this study have several implications for the management of EUC.

The positive relationship between computer skill level and user satisfaction means that the more highly skilled users exhibit greater satisfaction. A possible explanation is that skilled users may view themselves as more independent, more self-reliant, and with greater ability to use the computer at their own discretion without needing assistance. Therefore, they accomplish their work more readily.

The negative relationship between education and satisfaction is unexpected for two reasons. First, the finding could possibly be an artifact of this sample. The respondents' average education level of 5.69 (see Table 14.2 for education levels) stems from the use of a university as a research site. Respondent education levels possibly are higher than other types of organizations; therefore, the negative relationship between education and satisfaction may not universally apply. Second, the more educated the respondent, the more he or she might expect from computer systems, with the likely result of disappointment.

The finding that years of experience with computers is negatively related to user satisfaction was also unexpected. On closer examination, however, we note that years of experience does not mean that respondents have more knowledge or skill regarding computer use. For example, clerical or IS personnel could have many years of experience using computers doing the same tasks such as word processing or COBOL programming, respectively. These persons may reach a plateau of skill, experience diminishing marginal utility, and therefore report lower satisfaction.

A positive attitude and a lack of anxiety toward computer use both contribute to increased satisfaction. Likewise, a pessimistic attitude diminishes satisfaction. In spite of these findings, little evidence exists to indicate that researchers or practicing managers are addressing these relationships. Organizations should develop training and education efforts aimed at reducing anxiety and eliminating negative attitudes. These efforts should go beyond simply eliminating negative attitudes to encouraging positive attitudes.

Respondents who are rule-oriented and disciplined exhibit the cognitive style related to increased satisfaction. This finding follows from the fact that computer use tends to be structured and rule-oriented (e.g., programming in procedural languages such as COBOL and use of application software packages). Clearly, the cognitive style mentioned earlier is the closest fit to today's computer interaction. In the future, however, graphical user interfaces, object-oriented programming, fuzzy logic, and so on, may change the manner in which end users interact with computer systems. This situation may alter the fit between the user's cognitive style and his or her mode of interaction with the computer.

CONCLUSIONS

Practicing managers can exercise control over three of the human factors variables affecting user satisfaction, namely, computer skill level, computer anxiety, and computer attitudes. The greatest opportunity to alter these individual differences lies with training and education efforts. Skill, attitudes, and anxiety can be audited prior to instituting training or education programs. These programs can then be customized for end users, based on their individual differences.

Knowledge of user satisfaction levels is critical, considering that this variable is often used as a surrogate for EUC success. Previous research has largely examined the relationship between environmental factors and user satisfaction. The purpose of this research was not to diminish the importance of these factors but to investigate an additional set of factors that affect user satisfaction. This study accomplishes this purpose. The findings suggest that researchers and practicing managers should consider individual differences as well as environmental characteristics when attempting to measure user satisfaction.

REFERENCES

Alavi, M., & Weiss, I.R. (1985-1986). Managing the risks associated with end-user computing. *Journal of Management Information Systems, 2*(3), 5–20.

Arndt, S., Clevenger, J., & Meiskey, L. (1985). Students' attitudes toward computers. *Computers and the Social Sciences, 1*(3–4), 181–190.

Bailey, J.E., & Pearson, S.W. (1983). Development of a tool for measuring and analyzing computer user satisfaction. *Management Science, 24*(5), 530–545.

Ball, L., & Harris, R. (1982). SMIS members: A membership analysis. *MIS Quarterly, 6*(1), 19–38.

Baroudi, J.J., Olson, M., & Ives, B. (1986). An empirical study of the impact of user involvement on system usage and information satisfaction. *Communications of the ACM, 29*(3), 232–238.

Baroudi, J.J., & Orlikowski, W.J. (1988). A short form measure of user satisfaction and notes on use. *Journal of Management Information Systems, 4*, 44–59.

Benjamin, R.I. (1982). Information technology in the 1990's: A long range planning scenario.

MIS Quarterly, 6(2), 11–31.

Benson, D.H. (1983). A field study of end-user computing: Findings and issues. *MIS Quarterly, 7*(4), 35–45.

Bergeron, F., & Berube, C. (1988). The management of the end-user environment: An empirical investigation. *Information and Management, 18*, 107–118.

Brancheau, J., & Wetherbe, J.C. (1987). Key issues in information systems—1986. *MIS Quarterly, 11*(1), 23–46.

Carr, H.H. (1987). Information centers: The IBM model vs. practice. *MIS Quarterly, 11*(3), 325–340.

Cheney, P.H., Mann, R.I., & Amoroso, D.L. (1986). Organizational factors affecting the success of end-user computing. *Journal of Management Information Systems, 3*(1), 65–80.

Cotterman, W., & Kumar, K. (1989). User cube: A taxonomy of end users. *Communications of the ACM, 32*(11), 1313–1320.

Davis, L.D., & D.F. Davis. (1990). The effect of training techniques and personal characteristics on training end users of information systems. *Journal of Management Information Systems, 7*(2), 93–110.

Davis, G.B., & Olson, M. (1985). *Management information systems: Conceptual foundations, structure, and development,* (2nd ed.). New York: McGraw-Hill.

Dickson, G.W., Leitheiser, R.L., Nechis, M., & Wetherbe, J.C. (1984). Key information system issues for the 1980's. *MIS Quarterly, 8*(3), 135–148.

Doll, W.J., & Torkzadeh, G. (1988). The measurement of end user computing satisfaction. *MIS Quarterly, 12*(2), 259–274.

Doll, W.J., & Torkzadeh, G. (1989). A discrepancy model of end-user computing involvement. *Management Science, 35*(10), 1151–1171.

Gallagher, C.A. (1974). Perceptions of the value of a management information system. *Academy of Management Journal, 17*(1), 46–55.

Gutek, B.A., & Bikson, T.K. (1985). Differential experiences of men and women in computerized offices. *Sex Roles, 13* (3-4), 123–136.

Hackathorn, R., & Keen, P.G.W. (1981). Organizational strategies for personal computers in decision support systems. *MIS Quarterly, 5*(3), 21–27.

Hartog, C., & Herbert, M. (1986). 1985 opinion survey of MIS managers: Key issues. *MIS Quarterly, 10*(4), 351–361.

Heinssen, R.K., Glass, C.R., & Knight, L.A. (1987). Assessing computer anxiety: Development and validation of the computer anxiety rating scale. *Computers in Human Behavior, 3*, 49–59.

Igbaria, M., & Nachman, S.A. (1990). Correlates of user satisfaction with end-user computing. *Information and Management, 19*(2), 73–82.

Igbaria, M., & Parasuraman, S. (1989). A path analytic study of individual characteristics, computer anxiety, and attitudes toward microcomputers. *Journal of Management, 15*(3), 373–388.

Ives, B., Olson, M., & Baroudi, J.J. (1983). The measurement of user information satisfaction. *Communications of the ACM, 26*(10), 785–794.

Kasper, G.M., & Cerveny, R.P. (1985). A laboratory study of user characteristics and decision-making performance in end-user computing. *Information and Management, 9*(2), 87–96.

Kirton, M. (1976). Adaptors and innovators: A description and measure. *Journal of Applied Psychology, 61*(5), 622–629.

Larcker, D.F., & Lessig, V.P. (1980). Perceived usefulness of information: A psychometric examination. *Decision Sciences, 11*(1), 121–134.

Levin, T., & Gordon, C. (1989). Effect of gender and computer experience on attitudes toward computers. *Journal of Educational Computing Research, 5*(1), 69–88.

Lucas, H.C. (1978). Empirical evidence for a descriptive model of implementation. *MIS Quarterly, 2*(2), 27–52.

Mandell, S.F. (1989). Resistance and power: The perceived effect that computerization has on a social agency's power relationships. *Computers in Human Services, 4*(1–2), 29–40.

Melone, N.P. (1990). A theoretical assessment of the user-satisfaction construct in information systems research. *Management Science, 36*(1), 76–91.

Montazemi, A.R. (1988). Factors affecting information satisfaction in the context of the small business environment. *MIS Quarterly, 12*(2), 239–256.

Murphy, C.A., Coover, D., & Owen, S.V. (1989). Development and validation of the computer self-efficacy scale. *Educational and Psychological Measurement, 49*, 893–899.

Nickell, G.S., & Pinto, J.N. (1986). The computer attitude scale. *Computers in Human Behavior, 2*, 301–306.

Pratkanis, A.R., & Greenwald, A.G. (1989). A socio-cognitive model of attitude structure and function. In L. Berkowitz (Ed.), *Advances in experimental social psychology,* (Vol. 22, pp. 137–144). New York: Academic Press.

Raub, A.C. (1981). *Correlates of computer anxiety in college students.* Unpublished doctoral dissertation, University of Pennsylvania.

Raymond, L. (1987). Validating and applying user satisfaction as a measure of MIS success in small organizations. *Information and Management, 12*(4), 173–180.

Rockart, J.F., & Flannery, L.S. (1983). The management of end-user computing. *Communications of the ACM, 26*(10), 776–784.

Rushinek, A., & Rushinek, S.F. (1986). What makes users happy? *Communications of the ACM, 29*(7), 594–598.

Sprague, R.H., Jr., & McNurlin, B.C. (Eds.) (1986). *Information systems management in practice.* Englewood Cliffs, NJ: Prentice-Hall.

Swanson, E.B. (1974). Management information systems: Appreciation and involvement. *Management Science, 21*(2), 178–188.

Vernon-Gerstenfeld, S. (1989). Serendipity? Are there gender differences in the adoption of computers? A case study. *Sex Roles, 21*(3–4), 161–173.

Wilder, G., Mackie, D., & Cooper, J. (1985). Gender and computers: Two surveys of computer-related attitudes. *Sex Roles, 13*(3–4), 215–288.

Zmud, R.W. (1979). Individual differences and MIS success: A review of the empirical literature. *Management Science, 25*(10), 966–979.

The Role of User Cognitive Skills in Information Display: A Follow-up Study

Hulya Yazici
Portland State University

INTRODUCTION

Graphical representations and pictures are generally preferred to other type of information formats. However, when it comes to understanding the role of graphics in decision making, we have little in the way of conclusive research (DeSanctis, 1984; Jarvenpaa & Dickson, 1988). This is especially true for understanding a decision maker's cognitive abilities. For instance, cognitive style, which was examined in various studies, is a broad cognitive measure to apply the cognition classification in practice (Keen & Scott Morton, 1978). Another factor of the discrepancy is the type of task employed. As recently explained in an article by Vessey (1991), a cognitive fit between the task type and the problem representation exists. The premise of this chapter is that both task and cognitive abilities contribute to the research of information formats. This chapter reviews the relevant empirical research and discusses the theoretical basis for the task and cognitive skill relationship.

PRIOR RESEARCH

Several studies on task type and the use of information formats have been reported in the literature. The interest herein focuses on research examining the effects of user cognitive differences and display formats at low-and high-task complexity. A summary of these studies is shown in Table 15.1.

Table 15.1 indicates that according to the level of complexity of the decision task,

Table 15.1. Summary of Previous Research in Decision Support Systems Involving Display Modes

Reference	Task Complexity	Decision Maker Chars	Display Chars	Findings
Benbasat & Dexter, 1985 & 1986	High	Field Dependence/ Independence	Tabular/Graphical/ Color	* Multicolor reports show better profit performance * Field-dependents perform better w/multicolor; no difference for field dependents * Under time constraint, combined displays result in higher performance
Davis, Davis, & Schrode, 1987	High	Decision-Making Style	Tabular/Graphical/ Raw/Summarized Graphical/Tabular	* Sensitive-feeling, intuitive-feeling, intuitive-thinking people perform better w/tabular displays * Intuitive-feeling people perform well when the combination of graphics and summarized data is used; sensitive-feeling people perform well with tabular-raw or tabular-summarized types
Garceau, Oral, & Rahn, 1988	High	Cognitive Style	Tabular/Graphical	* In intelligence phase, logical/tabular and intuitive graphical produced high-quality, longer response time and low-decision confidence with graphical * In design phase, equal outcomes for both display types
Lucas, 1981	High	Heuristic/Analytic (Barkin)	CRT/Hardcopy/ T & G/ T on CRT	* Heuristics using graphics showed best simulation results. Also, graphics provided better problem understanding * Hard-copy group had superior performance on problem understanding * Use of both graphical and tabular displays gave higher simulation outputs.
Pracht & Courtney, 1986	High	Field Dependence/ Independence	Graphics/ Nongraphics	* Field-independents performed better with graphics-system, field-dependents with nongraphics system in problem structuring

Study	Level	Quantitative Skill	Format	Findings
Blocker, Moffie, & Zmud, 1986	High		Tabular/Graphic	* An interaction effect between report format and quantitative skill is found. People who scored high on quantitative skill performed better using tabular displays * High-experienced people showed higher decision confidence using color graphical displays
Hoadley, 1990	Low	None	Pie, Bar, Line Charts, Color	* Faster decisions made with pie, bar charts, and tables with color. Pie and line charts with color and mono tables produced more accurate results. Same accuracy is obtained by using colored and mono bar charts.
Jarvenpaa, 1989	Low	None	Attribute, Alternative, and Grouped Bar Charts	* In information acquisition, attribute bar charts and, in evaluation task, alternative charts are more effective * Task and format interaction is found significant
Lalomia, Coovert, & Salas, 1988	Low	None	Tabular/ Graphical	* In locating a number, faster performance is obtained with tabular displays. In trend analysis, graphical displays provided faster and more accurate decision making.
Nibbelin, 1988	Low	Field Dependents/ Independence Domain Expertise	Tabular/Graphical Combined/Single	* Field-independents performed better with data-only displays and field-dependents with data/graph and data/faces displays * Domain expertise had an influence on decision accuracy
Powers, Corda, Sanchez, & Shneiderman, 1984	Low	None	Combined/Single Format	* In non-recall task, tabular increased comprehension. Combination of graphical and tabular displays gave most accurate performance
Sparrow, 1989	Low	None	Graph type (Pie, bar, stacked bar charts), Single/Multiple line graphs, spreadsheet	* Spreadsheets are good for conveying specifics, trends, and accumulation; conveying the limits of a data set, stacked bar charts are more appropriate * For proportions, pie charts and single-line graphs and for conveying conjunction, trends, and limits, multiple-line graphs are appropriate

the consistency of the results varies. For instance, the findings are inconsistent when the performance is observed using high-complexity tasks involving problem structuring, problem solving, and strategic decision making. However, dealing with low-complexity tasks such as data reading, information acquisition and evaluation, and trend analysis, we can conclude that tables are accurate in extracting specific values, and graphics are better in trend analysis and finding relationships among the problem elements.

The inconsistency in results is also observed when user cognition is included in the study along with the task complexity. For instance, Nibbelin (1988) found out that when using a low-complexity task such as predicting bond ratings based on financial information, high analytics perform better with a data-only format and less analytics with combined data and graph formats. In examining high-complexity tasks such as strategy formulation, a study by Garceau, Oral, and Rahn (1988) agrees with this conclusion for the intelligence phase of the decision making that includes data search and evaluation. However, during the design phase, which requires not only data evaluation but also a formulation of the problem, none of the formats is superior for any cognition group. Likewise, Pracht and Courtney's (1986) research gives contradictory results. In their study, graphics actually aids field independents or high analytics dealing with a problem structuring task. The study by Davis, Davis, and Shrode (1987) suggests that different types of displays should be considered for different cognitive style groups.

These studies show that the impact of user cognition is easily determined when dealing with low-complexity and high-complexity tasks that require a series of mental processes and create a difficulty obtaining consistent results. From these studies, we can conclude the following:

1. Task complexity is an important factor determining which display format gives higher decision performance.
2. Decision-maker cognitive characteristics interact with task complexity.

The next section explains creativity and reasoning ability, considered as the user cognitive characteristics of the research. The section is followed by the research results and comments.

COGNITIVE ABILITIES

The interaction of task complexity and user cognitive characteristics leads to a careful examination of the mental processes involved during the decision-making tasks. This study is concerned with user cognitive abilities that have been found significant in determining the use of graphics and imagery in problem-solving activities (Loy, 1991; Richardson, 1983). The cognitive abilities of the problem solver determine the type and quality of the mental representations developed during the problem-solving process (Greeno, 1973; Loy, 1991).

One cognitive ability likely to interact with representational mode is the creative potential of the user. Creativity is the ability to visualize and imagine problems, see connections between disparate areas, and form a variety of ideas (Torrance, 1974). It is the ability to combine prior learning experiences with the components of a current problem (Armistead & Burton, 1987-88). Creative persons have the ability to imagine and visualize the situations as well as the ability to have a simultaneous view of all arguments that have been presented, which in turn facilitates problem understanding and solving (Forisha, 1975; Kaufmann, 1980). Thus, creative individuals might be more able to use previous experiences as a basis for encoding and interpreting information presented in different modes, such as graphical, tabular, text, and so on.

The ability to imagine is also significant for the use of graphics combined with other formats. Richardson (1980) refers to this process as "visual imagery," in which the formation of visual images results in improved memory performance: Imagery activates an input's representation in visuospatial code, enhancing discriminability and short-term recall. Here, imagery is seen as having an effect on long-term recall by creating a consistent organization of the cues activated; that is, the information is more readily retrievable from memory for use in later decision making. Thus, graphics is an aid to better visualizing and generating images that enhance short-and long-term recall and provide a better interpretation of the information. Thus, an interaction of creativity with graphical formats is theoretically expected.

Another cognitive ability to interact with representation mode is reasoning. Reasoning is the ability to observe and use all relevant facts of a problem and to approach the problem in a systematic, step-by-step manner. Individuals with high reasoning abilities can differentiate between relevant and irrelevant facts and can isolate and control the variables associated with the problem (Nummedal, 1987). Individuals having high reasoning abilities are likely to approach problems logically and generate correct solutions to the problems. However, individuals with high reasoning abilities tend to think analytically in structuring the elements of the problem, in other words, their thinking process is rather discrete or serial. Each element is processed individually rather than continuously or through parallel processing of all problem elements. It seems that they may not benefit from an aid in the form of graphics to visualize the problem in a holistic sense. It is expected that a tabular format would be a proper aid for high analytics or individuals with high reasoning abilities.

RESULTS AND DISCUSSION

The purpose of the study was to explore the interaction effect between the decision maker's cognitive abilities and the system's display formats. An experiment was conducted to show the effectiveness of the display mode, particularly graphical and tabular modes, represented simultaneously, and user cognitive abilities on the quality of problem formulation and problem solutions. Table 15.2 summarizes the results of these experiments, where graphics refers to the simultaneous display of graphs and tables.

Table 15.2. Results of the Experiments

System's Display Format Interacts with Individual's Cognitive Skills

Graphics and Creativity
- Highly creative individuals benefit from graphics
- Graphics does not improve the performance of less creative individuals

Graphics and Reasoning Ability
- Less analytical individuals benefit from graphics
- Graphics impair the performance of highly analytical individuals

Simple Effects
- Graphics alone do not improve decision quality
- Creativity alone does influence decision quality
- Reasoning ability alone does not influence decision quality

The decision task employed in these studies is a high-complexity task that involves problem understanding/formulation and solving tasks for a semistructured management case study. As indicated in Table 15.2, significant interaction effects of display formats and cognitive abilities were found. However, the effects of display format alone were not determined. This agrees with the cognitive fit theory defined by Vessey (1991), as well as with the conceptual framework described earlier. Because of the complexity of the task to be tested, the influence of graphics varies according to the cognitive processes involved in different phases of the decision making.

Furthermore, the interaction effects of creativity and reasoning ability with the display formats show that a fit exists between these formats and user cognitive abilities. The simultaneous representation of graphical and tabular modes fits with the creativity of the individuals. Creativity is the ability to combine prior experiences with the elements of a problem by being able to visualize all the arguments of the problem. Representing graphics and tabular modes improves the decision quality of highly creative people by complementing their visualization abilities because this system "fits" their approach to problem solving of broadly comprehending the problem elements.

On the contrary, the wholistic understanding the display mode provides is not an aid for individuals with high reasoning ability because these individuals tend to be analytic and discrete thinkers who are not likely to use holistic representations of the problem. But the graphics system aids individuals with low reasoning ability by structuring the information for them and helps them to develop a more complete understanding of the problem. Consequently, the research results offer practitioners a message by providing flexible system features to help less creative and highly analytical individuals.

The question that remains to be answered is what would be a further direction in extracting the types of display modes to be used that deal with high-complexity tasks. In other words, how can the simple (main) effects of display formats on decision quality be empirically demonstrated when dealing with high-complexity tasks?

CONCLUSIONS

As Vessey (1991) indicates, there is a match between representation format and task: Tables are symbolic data representations, and graphs are spatial data representations. Vessey tests the cognitive fit theory by analyzing simple problem-solving tasks—the ones that involve information acquisition and evaluation. As she notes, testing of the cognitive fit theory was useful for examining fairly simple, decision-making tasks. Furthermore, when dealing with more complex tasks, where strategy formulation/selection is the key, more research is needed to analyze the effects of display formats on decision-making performance.

The study shows that when dealing with high-complexity tasks, cognitive characteristics of the individuals come into perspective. In a problem-solving situation, cognitive abilities play a significant role. Creativity is an important variable in decision making. It has always been considered a significant characteristic of managers. Complex decision-making tasks involve judgment and heuristic thinking. Experience can also be considered a contributing factor. Although the study does not indicate any effect on the level of experience, field research using manager subjects could possibly demonstrate that effect.

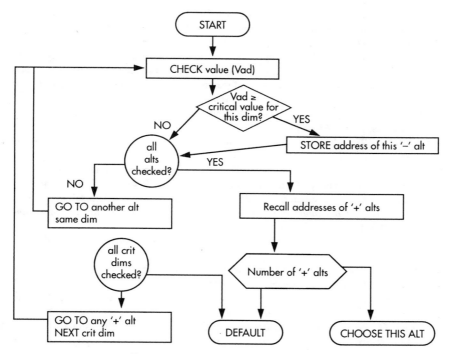

Figure 15.1. Elimination by Aspects Strategy.

Based on these remarks, a model for further research in system displays as problem-solving aids would be valuable. Figure 15.1 shows a model developed for this purpose. As previous research showed, examining cognitive processes provides more insight to determine problem-solving aids. The effects of cognitive abilities provide a specific understanding of how an individual will develop solution strategies for the decision task at hand. Creativity might explain how individuals develop perceptual/imaginal processes when formulating a decision task. Reasoning ability, which is also a measure of analytical thinking, might explain how individuals select from different solution strategies to come up with the best problem solution.

The primary purpose of this chapter was to provide a follow-up for the user interface research. The proper use of information display modes may enhance the decision process. Testing of the model proposed herein will help to clarify the significance of task and cognitive process variables for successful use of these displays. Future research should focus on cognitive processing and determine a solid theory for interface design.

REFERENCES

Armistead, L.P., & Burton, J.K. (1987–88). Creative computer problem solving. *Computer Scheduling, 4*(3–4), 47–53.

Benbasat, I., & Dexter, A.S. (1986). An experimental evaluation of graphical and color-enhanced information presentation. *Management Science, 31*(11), 1348–1364.

Blocher, E., Moffie, R.P., & Zmud, R.W. (1986). Repost formats and task complexity: Interaction in risk judgments. *Accounting, Organizations, and Society, 11*(6), 457–470.

Davis, D., Davis, R.D., & Schrode, W. (1987). Decision support systems (DSS) design for operations managers: An empirical study of the impact of report design and decision style on effective choice. *Journal of Operations Management, 7*(1–2), 47–62.

DeSanctis, G. (1984). Computer graphics as decision aids: Directions for research. *Decision Sciences, 15*(4), 463–487.

Forisha, B.D., (1975) Mental imagery verbal processes: A developmental study. *Developmental Psychology, 11*(3), 259–267.

Garceau, S., Oral, M., & Rahn, R.J. (1988). The Influence of data-presentation mode on strategic decision-making performance. *Computer Operations Research, 15*(5), 479–488.

Greeno, J.G. (1973). The structure of memory and the process of problem solving. In R.L. Solso (Ed.), *Contemporary issues of cognitive psychology: The loyola symposium*, (pp. 105–133). New York: Wiley.

Hoadley, E.D. (1990). Investigating the effects of color. *Communications of the ACM, 33*(2), 120–125.

Jarvenpaa, S.L. (1989). The effects of task demands and graphical format on information processing strategies. *Management Science, 35*(3), 285–303.

Jarvenpaa, S.L., & Dickson, G.W. (1988). Graphics and managerial decision making: Research based guidelines. *Communications of the ACM, 31*(6), 764–774.

Kaufmann, G. (1980). *Imagery, language and cognition.* Norway: Universitetsforlaget.

Keen, P.G., & Scott-Morton, M.S. (1978). *Decision support systems: An organizational perspective.* reading, MA: Addison-Wesley.

Lalomia, M.J., Coovert, M.D., & Salas, E. (1988). Problem solving performance and display preference for information displays depicting numerical functions. *SIGCHI Bulletin, 20*(2), 47–51.

Loy, S.L. (1991). The interaction effects between general thinking skills and interactive graphics-based DSS to support problem structuring. *Decison Sciences, 22*(4), 846–868.

Lucas, H.C. (1981). An experimental investigation of the use of computer-based graphics in decision making. *Management Science, 27*(7), 757–768.

Nibbelin, M.C. (1988). *Effects of mode of information presentation and perceptual skill on bond rating change decisions: A laboratory study.* Unpublished doctoral thesis, Florida State University.

Nunmedal, S.G. (1987). Developing reasoning skills in college students. In *Applications of cognitive psychology: Problem solving, education, and computing* (pp. 87–97). Hillsdale, NJ: Erlbaum.

Powers, M., Conda, L., Sanchez, P., & Shneiderman, B. (1984). An experimental comparison of tabular and graphic data presentation. *International Journal of Man-Machine Studies, 20*, 545–566.

Pracht, W., & Courtney, J.F. (1986). A visual user interface for capturing mental models in model management systems. In *Proceedings of the Nineteenth Annual Hawaii International Conference on System Sciences,* (pp. 535–541).

Pracht, W., & Courtney, J.F. (1986). An experimental comparison of tabular and graphic data presentation. In *Proceedings of the Nineteenth Annual Hawaii International Conference on System Sciences,* (pp. 535–541).

Richardson, J.T.E. (1983). Mental imagery in thinking and problem solving. In *Thinking and reasoning: Psychological approaches.* Boston: Routeledge & Keegan Paul.

Sparrow, J.A. (1989). Graphical displays in information systems: Some data properties influencing the effectiveness of alternative forms. *Behaviour and Information Technology, 8*(1), 43–56.

Torrance, E.P. (1974). Torrance tests of creative thinking, norms-technical manual. Bensenville, Ill: Scholastic Testing Service.

Vessey, I. (1991). Cognitive fit: A theory-based analysis of the graphs versus tables literature, *Decision Sciences, 22*(2), 219–240.

Part VI
Methodological Issues

Measurement Issues in the Study of Human Factors in Management Information Systems*

Peter R. Newsted*
W. David Salisbury
The University of Calgary

Peter Todd*
Queens University

Robert W. Zmud
Florida State University

INTRODUCTION

Theories, Constructs, and Measurements

Theories require constructs and constructs depend on measurement; therefore, there can be no theories without measurement. Measures per se can be very reproducible (i.e., reliable), but in the simplest sense measurement yields nothing more than a

* Chapter developed from a Panel Discussion at the 4th Symposium on Human Factors in Information Systems, Phoenix, Arizona, February 27–28, 1992.

Peter R. Newsted's work in this chapter was partially funded by the Social Sciences and Humanities Research Council of Canada whose support is gratefully acknowledged. Peter Todd's part was assisted by the Natural Sciences and Engineering Research Council of Canada, whose support is also gratefully acknowledged.

response to a question or experimental manipulation. Unfortunately most measurements in management information systems (MIS) are not governed by natural or derived laws but by fiat where "there exists a common-sense concept that on a priori grounds seems to be important but for which there are no direct measures" (Sethi & King, 1991, p. 457). Constructs are more than just measurements. The concept of a construct gives measurement meaning, suggesting a higher level of abstraction than simple measurement. At the highest level of abstraction, constructs are aggregated to form a theory.

Numerous things can be measured and considered part of a construct, but the domain of a construct should be prescribed. Many measures—and their associated constructs—are specific to a given context, and care must be taken if they are to be used in a generic fashion in broader theories. Care must also be taken when generic survey instruments are used in a specific situation.

Unfortunately, even though most researchers will admit to the truth of these conclusions, much published work is flawed in its disregard for measurement issues and correct designs. It is the goal of this chapter to review these issues in hopes of promoting higher quality in all forms of MIS research that require measurement.

Process versus Content

Both the content of theories and the process of creating them are important. The first section of this chapter (authored by Robert Zmud) gives an overview of some of the process issues—especially considering the context of measurements. Next, Peter Newsted and David Salisbury discuss results and methodologies in the specific area of surveys, whereas Peter Todd concludes with a review of issues in laboratory experiments. Although these are not the only methodologies in human factors in management information systems (HF/MIS) research (cf. Kraemer, 1991, for a list of other methodologies, such as case-based research, mathematical models, and software systems demonstrations), the bulk of work has been done in these two areas.

CONSTRUCT MEASUREMENT ISSUES IN MANAGEMENT INFORMATION SYSTEMS RESEARCH

The creative development and effective utilization of constructs is a primary determinant of the quality of scholarship undertaken in any field of study, including those associated with the broad field of MIS research. Essentially, constructs reflect the labels assigned to abstract representations of phenomena of interest to a body of researchers. Because they are abstract entities, constructs are easily fabricated, easily manipulated, and broadly interpretable. However, such characteristics can produce both advantages and disadvantages. Constructs serve two main roles in support of the scholarly development of a field of study.

First, constructs serve as the language through which theoretical ideas and research findings are communicated among researchers. Ideally, constructs should be relevant to a variety of domains with a field of study but very tightly defined. If a construct's relevance is limited, it will not attract the attention of many of the researchers in the field. Without such attention, the construct will neither attract critical attention to itself nor will it inform the future direction of research. If a construct is loosely defined, its creators' intentions may very well be misinterpreted and, hence, be too broadly or too narrowly or simply incorrectly applied.

Second, constructs serve as the medium through which conceptual notions and research models are articulated, intellectually explored, and formally specified by a researcher (or team of researchers) in the process of research. Ideally, constructs should be quite malleable but in an quasi-elastic sense, such that the conceptual notion can be easily reshaped but will tend to return to its original configuration unless extremely strong forces, such as logical or analytical arguments, exert themselves. When constructs are embedded within research models to be explored through empirical methods, concern shifts from that associated with intellectual exercises to that associated with operationalization. Constructs are empirically operationalized through the use of measurement scales. Simple constructs such as those that represent unidimensional phenomena are operationalized with a single scale; more complex constructs that represent multidimensional phenomena are operationalized with multiple scales. As much has been written on scale construction and assessment, these topics are not be covered here other than to emphasize the requirement that scales be both valid (capturing data that reflect the specific construct being measured) and reliable (comprised of items that singularly and collectively portray consistent nuances of the construct being measured). Instead, two concerns associated with construct measurement are addressed:

- Definitional concerns associated with conceptual ambiguity and conceptual overlap
- Concerns associated with construct-context interaction.

Definitional Concerns

When a construct is ambiguously defined, it becomes virtually impossible to reach consensus on the nature of the items used to comprise measurement scales. This not only causes obvious problems for scale developers and scale adopters but also for journal referees. If a referee is either confused about the nature of a construct or interprets the construct differently than did the researcher, it is highly likely that the referee will view the researcher's attempt to operationalize the construct to be faulty. Thus, researchers must attend to the careful definition of their research constructs, especially when prior efforts toward construct definition have been equivocal.

Conceptual overlap can occur in at least three ways:

- The constructs involved represent phenomena that have common elements

- The phenomena represented by one construct are actually subelements of the second construct
- Different constructs from different disciplines may refer to the same phenomena.

In any of these situations, it is quite probable that very similar items are likely to be included within the scales used to measure both constructs. With common items, one would expect scales to be correlated even if there was no compelling reason to believe that the focal constructs were associated. As a consequence, a portion of the association observed between scales must be attributed to the instrumentation rather than to any actual association between the phenomena being examined. Another problem that arises when excessive conceptual overlap exists among two constructs in a research model is that research propositions or hypotheses directed at these constructs become tautological in nature.

Generic versus Context-Specific Scales

Most scales tend to be constructed in a generic fashion in order to increase the extent to which the results of a study can both be generalized to contexts other than that exam-

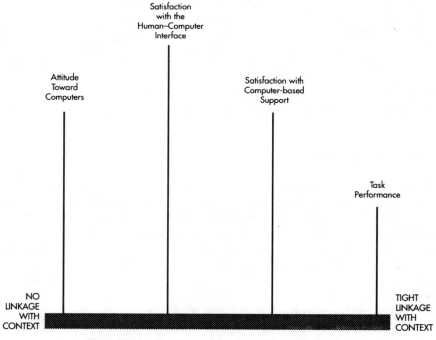

Figure 16.1.   A Continuum of Construct Linkage with Context.

ined in the study and be readily interpreted as informing the body of theory to which the study is directed. All constructs, however, can be viewed as being located on a continuum reflecting the extent to which a construct is intellectually linked with experientially based phenomena. Figure 16.1, for example, places four conceptually similar constructs on such a continuum.

In measuring an individual's attitude toward computers, it is desirable that there be separation between this general belief and specific, recent behavioral episodes that an individual may have experienced. However, some linkage is still desirable as the manner in which computers are generally applied (and, hence, are viewed by individuals) does vary depending on the context involved. On the contrary, measures of task performance must be inextricably tied to the specific nature of the task for which computer-based support is being provided. Other constructs, such as satisfaction with the human–computer interface and satisfaction with computer-based support are perhaps best conceptualized as possessing an intermediary linkage with the context. That is, although some of the elements of the constructs might be generic in nature, others must be directly related to the context in order to provoke appropriate subject responses. Most often, such intermediately located constructs are complex, multidimensional constructs. When faced with such a construct, it might be advisable for the researcher to consider replacing the construct with a set of related constructs, each of which is located toward either end of the previous continuum.

An Empirical Study

These concerns apply to a number of the constructs commonly examined in human–computer interaction research. Of particular importance when working with such constructs are:

- the use of generic instruments to operationalize constructs that have strong linkages to the task context,
- a likely increased incidence of confounded measurement when generic measures are used to operationalize constructs that overlap conceptually.

In order to illustrate these concerns, an experiment was designed to gather data on subject responses regarding the following three of the four constructs displayed in Figure 16.1: attitude toward computers, satisfaction with the computer interface, and satisfaction with computer-based support. Perceptual measures were used to gather subject responses regarding each construct. Generic instruments were used for the all three instruments, as well as a context-specific instrument for satisfaction with computer-based support.

Procedures.

The student career counseling center at Florida State University has acquired a high-quality interactive software package (SIGIPLUS) that students can utilize in order to better understand career values and options. Researchers working at this center have developed a context-specific instrument that assesses a student's satisfaction with the information gained from interacting with the software. Using volunteer student subjects who were utilizing the center as a normal part of their university life, responses were collected to four instruments:

- A context-specific instrument assessing a student's satisfaction with the SIGIPLUS software package developed by researchers at Florida State University (Peterson, Ryan-Jones, Sampson, and Reardon, 1994)
- The Doll and Torkzadeh (1988) generic instrument assessing a user's satisfaction with an information system
- A generic attitude toward computer instruments developed by a doctoral student at Florida State University (Saga, 1991)
- A satisfaction with the computer interface instrument developed by researchers at the University of Maryland (Chin, Diehl, & Norman, 1988)

The attitude instrument was completed prior to a subject's use of the SIGIPLUS package, and the other three instruments were completed after this usage. The order of the two satisfaction with computer-based support instruments was switched for half of the subjects.

Results.

Factor and reliability analyses were performed on subject responses for each of the instruments. The subscales shown in Table 16.1 were produced by these

Table 16.1.   Subscales Associated with Each Study Instrument

Attitude Toward Computers	
• Enjoy	I find computers to be an enjoyable aspect of my life
• Nonthreatening	I do not view computers as a threatening aspect of my life
• Simple	I do not view computers or computer use as particularly difficult
Satisfaction with the Computer Interface	
• Screen	Quality of screen displays
• Message	Quality of screen messages
• Learning	Extent to which the interface facilitates learning about the software
Satisfaction with Computer-Based Support (Generic)	
• Content	Quality of content of computer outputs
• Accuracy	Quality of accuracy of computer outputs
• Format	Quality of the formats used with computer outputs
• Ease of Use	Extent to which computer is easy to use
• Timely	Quality of the timeliness of computer outputs
Satisfaction with Computer-Based Support (Context-Specific)	
• Recommendations	Quality of career recommendations
• Self-Understanding	Quality of information provided on personal values/interests
• Career Understanding	Quality of the information provided on careers

Table 16.2. Significant Correlations ($p<.05$) Among Study Variables

	Enj.	Non.	Sim.	Scr.	Mes.	Lea.	Con.	Acc.	For.	Eas.	Tim.	Rec.	Sel.	Car.
Enjoy														
Nonthreatening	0.34													
Simple	0.35	0.44												
Screen			0.51											
Message			0.42	0.70										
Learning		0.25		0.49	0.45									
Content				0.25										
Accuracy			0.33	0.46	0.47	0.26	0.45							
Format			0.31	0.59	0.59	0.31	0.51	0.50						
Ease of Use				0.45	0.41	0.36	0.31	0.41	0.55					
Timely				0.55	0.54	0.34	0.35	0.59	0.48	0.59				
Recommendations							0.63							
Self					0.25		0.36	0.32	0.33			0.63		
Career				0.28	0.30		0.52	0.37	0.39	0.27	0.40	0.58	0.31	

analyses. Correlations among the study variables are provided in Table 16.2. Three main observations arise from these correlations. First, certain subscales from the three generic instruments do show some association, even though the computer attitude instrument is fairly distant from the other two instruments. Notice that the absolute value of these correlations is quite similar, and that no association was found between the generic attitude and the context-specific satisfaction instrument. Second, most of the subscales of the generic satisfaction instrument address interface issues, with only the content subscale focusing on contextual issues associated with satisfaction with computer-based support. This suggests that serious concerns may exist regarding the nature of the (generic) measures frequently being used as dependent variables in human–computer interaction research. In particular, is the primary research objective focused on determining interface quality or on task performance? Third, these instruments do not appear to fully capture the complex natures of the constructs being examined. Clearly, much further work directed at instrument development and assessment is needed for human–computer interaction research.

Implications.

Hopefully both this presentation and the findings just discussed provide a compelling argument that researchers examining human–computer interaction must be more aware of the theoretical and methodological dangers of (a) utilizing conceptually ambiguous and overlapping constructs in research models, and (b) the relative appropriateness of applying generic and context-specific instrumentation. Strong efforts must be taken both to articulate and differentiate the research constructs that populate a research model and to finely discriminate among the multidimensional nature of complex constructs. Too often, model propositions begin to take the appearance of tautologies; and, again too often, although the focus of a particular research study is on a particular facet of a construct, the instrumentation used does not directly assess the aspect.

Researchers must also begin to recognize the distinction between generic and context-specific instruments and to appropriately apply both forms of instruments. All too often generic instruments are applied when the nature of the research question being examined demands a context-specific instrument. Perhaps one explanation for the inconsistency of much MIS literature may be the overutilization of generic measurement instruments. Finally, it is important to recognize that generic measures can serve two roles in MIS research. First, they often are the most appropriate approach for gathering data on a construct given a particular research model and question. Second, their existence can productively guide the development of context-specific instruments when the nature of a research model and question indicates that generic measures are inappropriate.

A REVIEW OF SURVEY INSTRUMENTS IN
MANAGEMENT INFORMATION SYSTEMS

The Calgary Surveys Query System

To further the study and development of both generic and context-specific surveys, the Calgary Surveys Query System (CSQS) has been developed as a repository of information, constructs, and characteristics of data acquisition instruments seen in the MIS literature. Each identified article with an instrument has been described on more than 20 dimensions. This approach follows Swanson's (1991) suggestion that the context, method, and references are important to a researcher in evaluating a potential survey. CSQS draws from more than 30 journals that have been scanned since 1970. The list of journals has been revised in succeeding versions to reflect the "hit rate" of finding articles that use survey instruments. CSQS has a software front-end to allow searching in a variety of ways. It is fully relational so that interested researchers can join or otherwise manipulate any of its underlying tables. It is compiled and runs without the software used to develop it. The original CSQS paper in *The Information System Research Challenge: Survey Research Methods* (Newsted, Munro, & Huff, 1991) is based on CSQS 2.0. This version of CSQS contained 672 articles through early 1988.

A key feature of the database is that instruments that are seen to be roughly reliable and valid have their studied constructs coded using the Barki, Rivard, and Talbot (1988) scheme. This system contains over 1,100 key words with nine top-level categories that each branch into numerous subcategories—up to four levels deep. This approach is significant in that it has been validated by a survey of MIS researchers who indicated it was a "complete" approach as less than 3% of proposed key words were not in the hierarchy.

It is important to note that constructs in CSQS are those suggested in each article by the article's authors. In very few cases has sufficient work been devoted to their creation to consider them "true" constructs that have been rigorously developed. Interested researchers may find it useful to refer to the recent paper by Sethi and King (1991), which lists eight appropriate steps in the development of a "true" construct.

Efforts have been taken to make CSQS itself as reliable as possible. These are described in detail in Newsted et al. (1991). Significantly the identification and coding of constructs has been done by multiple reviewers whose consistency has been periodically measured and found to be acceptable following typical guidelines suggested in the area of library science (Preschel, 1972).

Versions of CSQS.

CSQS 2.3 was publicly released and substantially the same as CSQS 2.0 with the addition and correction of a number of entries. CSQS is currently in Version 3.0, which has 1,031 complete entries and 469 partial entries. These partial entries are just citation information for articles that are referenced as containing development information on an instrument being used in the complete or "primary" entry. CSQS 3.0 has entries through mid-1991 for most journals. It also has an improved front-end to further facilitate searching for instruments. Articles continue to be coded using the Barki et al. (1988) scheme. However, although all articles with surveys are still entered into the CSQS, the Barki coding is now done only for those that meet the "relaxed" guidelines suggested by Zmud and Boynton (1991). Although these could be more rigorous, it is felt that they are a very useful filter that provides articles that are likely of the greatest value to the majority of researchers. This follows the overall philosophy used in the development of CSQS, where the goal has been to be inclusive rather than exclusive.

The Zmud and Boynton criteria.

These criteria require:

* A scale composed of multiple items
* Information so that a reader can find and use the instrument
* A description in a refereed source
* Evidence of at least a minimal effort to assess a scale's psychometric properties.

Within CSQS, it has not been difficult to determine if an instrument in an article meets the first three of these criteria. The last one, however, is much more difficult. If a study mentioned that it used Cronbach's alpha for reliability or factor analysis to determine the consistency or validity of constructs, it was included. However, if a study was coded as "none reported" for one of these measures, this implied that reliability or validity had possibly been determined in a previous, referenced study and further investigation was required. To do this, the authors of CSQS working in various teams of two carefully examined each such article that had already been coded by a research assistant. In all cases they came to an agreement as to whether an instrument was acceptable. Frequently this involved determination that the instrument had its reliability and validity previously assessed (e.g., the Myers-Briggs Type Indicator—Myers, 1962; the Job Diagnostic Indicator—Hackman & Oldman, 1975, etc.).

In other cases in which an instrument was "adapted from" another author, a judgment was made based on a subjective appraisal of the rigor that was seen and the overall quality of the journals involved. In general, this was a fairly lenient process that included all articles with instruments that had some psychometric effort expended on them. It is unfortunate that this leniency was required, but as Straub (1989) pointed out, "the primary and prior value of instrument validation has yet to be widely recognized" (p. 147). In the future it is hoped that a much more rigorous screening can be used.

The state of surveys in MIS.

As can be seen in Figure 16.2, there has been a steady increase in the use of surveys since 1970. Although it appears that things have dropped off in recent years, this is unlikely to be the case. In particular, it is expected that more surveys will be discovered for 1991, when all journals produce their final 1991 issues.

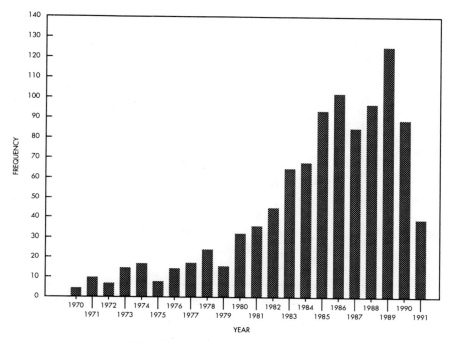

Figure 16.2. MIS Survey Frequency by Year.

As can be seen in Figure 16.3, when the reliability and validity are plotted over years, there has been a definite improvement in the quality of surveys from less than 20% of surveys having these characteristics in the early 1970s to nearly half of them in more recent times. This characterization of reliability and validity has been done very generously, in which articles that indicated no reliability or validity but implied that it had been determined in the previous study were coded as having these properties. A more realistic view of the psychometric properties of instruments is seen in the lower line, which shows the portion of articles meeting the Zmud and Boynton (1991) criteria. Unfortunately, little more than one third of the recent articles are meeting even this minimal level of psychometric respectability.

Surveys in human factors in MIS.

Turning now to the subarea of human factors within MIS, Figures 16.4 and 16.5 show comparable patterns for survey instruments in HF/MIS. The data for these figures are based on a subset of articles from CSQS that deal with human factors. Articles were selected if they fit within the Beard and Peterson (1988) taxonomy. This taxonomy covers the five following major areas:

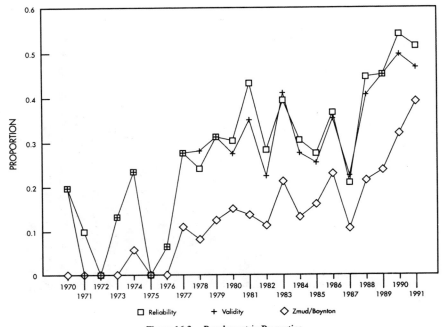

Figure 16.3.   Psychometric Properties

- Human-Computer Interaction: Ways in which the computer and user communicate
- Interface Specification Tools: Detailed design techniques for the computer-user interface
- Information Presentation: How the data are displayed to the user (graphics, text, windowing, etc.)
- System-User Documentation: Documentation and communication procedures to assist the user in accomplishing tasks
- End-User Involvement: Methods used to get users involved in system design, implementation, use, etc.

This taxonomy was used for a number of reasons. First, it has survived for a number of years. It has also been incorporated relatively unchanged into other taxonomies (e.g., Killingsworth, Kletke, Mackay, Trumbly, & Carey, 1992; Martin, 1992). From a content point of view, no new areas have been suggested that are not included in it. Finally, purely ergonomic work that deals with mainly physical aspects of human factors is not included in this taxonomy.

Human factors-based articles were systematically selected from CSQS. Initially the two present authors and the full-time research assistant (who maintains the CSQS) examined the CSQS information on 20 randomly selected articles and independently tried coding them as to whether they fit into this taxonomy. Ready agreement was achieved on 14 of the 20. After minimal discussion and examination of the original articles, agreement was reached regarding the remaining six. This process served primarily to train the second author in this classification procedure. During this process, a number of heuristics were developed to guide the inclusion of articles. These guidelines included:

- The study itself was evaluated as fitting into the taxonomy not just the instrument
- An article was included if in doubt—following the CSQS philosophy of being inclusive ather than exclusive
- Consideration of just an "attitude" about MIS was not considered sufficiently relevant to human factors for inclusion
- The characteristics of a tool had to be discussed; a report of just a tool's usage was not sufficient for its inclusion
- If end-user computing was discussed, fairly major end-user involvement was required for inclusion
- Articles that just reported on frequency of various kinds of computer use were not included.

To further determine the reliability of this procedure, the two authors independently coded an additional random sample of 5% of all articles (51 of 1,031). In this

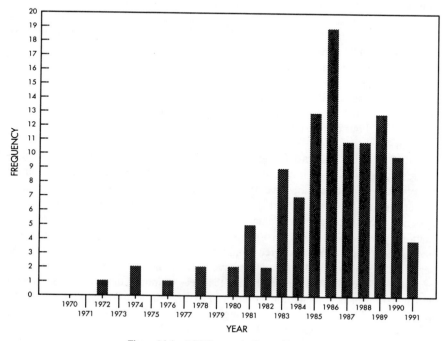

Figure 16.4.   MIS Surveys in Human Factors.

Table 16.3.   Number of Articles that Fall in Each Category of the Beard and Peterson Taxonomy.*

	Frequency	Percent Meeting Zmud and Boynton Criteria
Human-Machine Interaction	26	19
Interface Specification Tools	10	0
Information Presentation	19	21
System-User Documentation	10	40
End-User Involvement	58	22

*Totals to more than the 112 articles identified because some articles fall into multiple categories; 25 articles in total were identified that met the Zmud and Boynton criteria.

process they also identified which of the five areas of the taxonomy the article most appropriately fit. After a second such sample, Cohen's (1960) Kappa of .70 was obtained. This is within an acceptable range (cf. Briggs, Bedard, Gaber, & Linsmeier, 1985) and suggested that the second author could proceed independently to classify the remaining articles in the CSQS. This was done.

The results of this procedure identified 112 articles that are distributed over time as seen in Figure 16.4. Significantly, there does seem to be a drop-off in such studies in recent times that is more dramatic than in the general area of MIS. This is likely due to a decreased interest in end-user involvement and end-user computing by MIS researchers in the last several years. Table 16.3 shows that this has been the primary area of study in the five human factors areas in the 112 identified articles.

With respect to the psychometric properties of surveys in HF/MIS, Figure 16.5 indicates slight improvement over time but not as systematic a relationship as was seen for MIS nor as high a percentage of articles meeting the Zmud and Boynton criteria. Also the high points in reliability in 1981 and 1990 are based on relatively few articles. Four of five total articles were indicated as reliable in 1981 and 8 out of 10 in 1990.

It should be stressed that these 112 articles are only from management information systems—which is a dominant but not the only area that makes up human factors. Although it is a subjective diagram, Carey's (1991) breakdown of areas making up human factors in information systems—not just management information systems—does show a preponderance of coverage in the area of management information systems. Table 16.3 also shows that a concentration of work in end-user involvement and to a lesser degree human-machine interaction and information presentation are the main MIS areas that have been studied in human factors. Clearly, one would not expect MIS to emphasize the areas of information specification tools and system user documentation as much in MIS. Although the numbers are small, Table 16.3 also shows that a relatively high percentage of articles in system user documentation did meet the Zmud and Boynton criteria. Unfortunately, the average over all areas is only 20%.

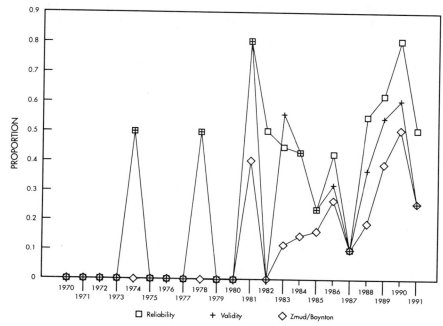

Figure 16.5. Psychometric Properties.

Theories based on surveys.

As a goal of theory construction—be it based on surveys or other data—is the identification of constructs, it is useful to examine the constructs that have been identified within the areas of Beard and Peterson taxonomy. Table 16.4 lists the constructs studied by survey instruments from the 25 (out of 112) articles that met the Zmud and Boynton criteria. They are grouped based on how their "parent" article was classified in the taxonomy. As can be seen from this list, there are a number of constructs that clearly seem part of human factors as well as some that are on the periphery—but which were part of an article judged to have a human factors emphasis. As a next step in theory construction, relationships must be determined between these constructs (in order to aggregate them into a theory). Those within a given study have already had their relationships examined, but links between other constructs from different studies must also be determined for broader theories to be produced. Meta-analysis is required to do this (cf. Glass, McGraw, & Smith, 1981).

Meta-analysis requires knowledge of sample size, variance, and a correlation value in each study. This data are only available in a fraction of studies so comparison is very difficult. A further problem here is the determination of the appropriate context for relations that have been identified. Generic and specific measures should not be indiscriminately related. If major meta-analysis is done, it may ultimately be possible

Table 16.4. Constructs in Human Factors (from Survey Studies that meet the Zmud and Boynton Criteria, ordered following the Beard and Peterson Taxonomy).[*]

AREA OF TAXONOMY

System-User Documentation
- ease of use of software
- helpfulness of documentation
- importance of documentation
- potential effect of improvement in documentation
- satisfaction with documentation
- the meaning of documentation to users
- user documentation quality (3)
- user satisfaction
- user satisfaction with system

End-User Involvement
- accuracy function of EUC satisfaction
- accuracy of system
- anxiety about using computers
- attitude of users toward end-user computing
- availability and accessability of hardware
- availability and accessability of software
- collaboration of users and IS in systems development
- content function of EUC satisfaction
- decision environment characteristics
- decision maker characteristics
- desired involvement in computing activity
- development methodologies
- DSS characteristics
- ease-of-use function of EUC satisfaction
- end-user satisfaction
- end-user satisfaction with computing activity
- format function of EUC satisfaction
- impact of system on organization
- implementation process characteristics
- information dissatisfaction
- information satisfaction
- information satisfaction of end users
- IS function quality
- leadership style of managers
- level of experience using computing systems
- nature of decision making
- perceived involvement in computing activity
- perceived quality of the information systems department
- perceived system usefulness
- problem solving competence in systems development
- process satisfaction
- process satisfaction of end users
- quality of development practice in systems development
- quality of relationship between users and IS in systems development
- resource constraints
- self-determination of end users
- self-determination
- software system characteristics

- stress
- stress level of end users
- success of system
- system complexity
- system usage
- system usefulness
- task satisfaction
- task satisfaction of end users
- timeliness function of EUC satisfaction
- use of system
- user attitudes to system being implemented
- user information satisfaction
- user involvement (4)
- user involvement in system development
- user involvement, design stage
- user involvement, implementation stage
- user satisfaction
- user satisfaction, from control strategies
- user satisfaction–system success
- utilization of end-user computing
- worth of system

Human–Machine Interaction
- gender/power aspects affecting human–computer communication
- job satisfaction
- level of anxiety toward computer
- operator productivity
- perceived ease of use of IT
- perceived usefulness of IT
- perceptions of the power of computers

Human–Machine Interaction and End-User Involvement
- effects of work environment on employees
- job satisfaction
- stressors

Information Presentation
- affects of presentation medium
- evaluation of DSS
- influence of color and information presentation
- opinions of graphical and color-enhanced information presentation
- satisfaction
- subject ratings of the information presentation used
- subjective factors in documentation use

---

* Numbers in parentheses indicate frequency greater than one.

---

to develop a higher level of theory that shows how more than just a handful of constructs are related. Borrowing a metaphor from the physical sciences, one might envision such relations as constituting a "periodic table" of constructs in MIS/HF.

The Periodic Table of Elements is a grouping of basic chemical elements based on their molecular weights. A periodic table of MIS/HF constructs would show what areas have already been researched and how they are related, as well as provide a framework for future additions to the table. For example, the inert gases (helium, argon, krypton, etc.) were as yet undiscovered when the original Periodic Table was built, and the table itself suggested that these "holes" should be filled—as they ultimately were—by the new elements. Although one hopes this idea is feasible, researchers have hardly begun to develop the basic constructs, let alone do the required meta-analysis of how they are interrelated. It is also unlikely that a single dimension such as molecular weight will emerge to guide this grouping.

Thus this section can only begin the task suggested by Benbasat (1991): "Each construct should be cross-referenced to the empirical studies in which it was used in order to understand the empirical linkages between constructs, and as a test of the theoretical linkages between them" (p. 184).

The idea of a periodic table of MIS/HF constructs is already *loosely* developed by Beard and Peterson (1988) as they try to put existing research into identifiable categories. However, the list of variables that have been studied in survey instruments and that are listed earlier should allow further development of this structure. Meta-analysis is required, but this comprehensive list (at least in the recent survey literature) should give some direction for this task *and* caution researchers as to the importance of correct measurement and well-founded instruments.

In the general area of MIS, an overview of survey findings has already been started by Kraemer and Dutton (1991) with a revised version of the Ives, Hamilton, and Davis (1980) MIS taxonomy. They provide a list of survey results in a propositional inventory. This "outline" is probably the closest anyone has come thus far to a periodic table based on survey data. Unfortunately only 98 articles are included. Kraemer and Dutton admit this is not exhaustive, and ultimately nonsurvey work should be included as well. As helpful as this inventory is, no filter as to the quality of article is incorporated. Even Zmud and Boynton's basic guidelines would be very helpful.

MEASUREMENT ISSUES IN EXPERIMENTAL HF/MIS RESEARCH

Issues in Experimentation

The problems that have been identified in dealing with survey instruments also carries over to the area of laboratory experiments. In a review of the methodological approaches taken to research in the administrative sciences, Podsakoff and Dalton (1987) described the typical laboratory experiment as one focusing on the individual, using students as subjects with a sample size of approximately 115 and measuring attitudes and perceptions. They report that in general the typical study does *not* share information about the construct validity of the various metrics. Although their focus was on studies in organizational behavior, there is little reason to suspect that other areas in the administrative sciences, including MIS, are substantially different (Jacoby, 1978;

Straub, 1989). Although weak or poorly validated measures are not peculiar to experimental research (Schwab, 1980), the existence of such measurement weaknesses may be most critical in experimental work given the objectives of experiments to: test predictions derived from theory under controlled, unconfounded conditions; and build theoretical systems (Kerlinger, 1986). If MIS experimentation is compared to these standards, it would fare reasonably well in the first role but the latter seems neglected.[1] Weick (1984) emphasised the need to conduct more MIS research that is geared toward theory building.

Furthermore, it would seem that much MIS experimentation has a different goal altogether, namely, evaluation or validation of systems or features. That is, the purpose of the research is to compare alternative systems or system features, such as tabular versus graphical representation, in order to determine which features lead to superior performance on some variable of interest. These variables typically center on issues of efficiency and effectiveness with which a system can be learned and used to complete a task. Thus, this research emphasizes an "engineering" objective rather than a "knowledge building" one. In examining the issue of measurement in MIS human factors research it is useful to keep the engineering versus theory testing/building objectives in mind. One might argue that the latter approach is simply one that is not well thought out and represents "weaker" research. However, it may be the case that this type of testing and validation is most often conducted by system designers who are interested in the merits (or demerits) of their design approach and not necessarily the underlying cognitive, affective, or social causes (or consequences) of the effects that they observe. This has implications for how they manipulate treatment conditions and also for the fineness of the measures that they employ.

In these cases less formal studies, perhaps with "quick and dirty" measures, may provide adequate information to advance design. Such an approach can be quite valuable in light of the fact that many will argue that the development of constructs and measures cannot occur at the outset of research into an area, but rather that it will occur as knowledge about a phenomena is accumulated. If this is indeed the case, then small informal experiments may provide a good environment in which to develop and refine measurement tools.

Ultimately the application of the experimental method requires reliable and valid operational measures of constructs. Neither the generation nor testing of substantive theory can be undertaken in the absence of valid and reliable measures (Schwab, 1980). In spite of the increasing attention being paid to methodological issues in particular and measurement issue in specific in MIS research (see Barki & Hartwick, 1989; Baroudi & Orlikowski, 1989; Davis, 1989; Melone, 1990; Straub, 1989) it seems that MIS researchers still pay inadequate attention to measurement issues in the execution of studies. This problem appears to be even more acute in experimental research. The remainder of this chapter explores some of the

---

[1] An alternative explanation might be the existence of a publication bias against such work.

issues surrounding measurement with a particular emphasis on measurement in laboratory experimentation.

Linking Measurement with Theory

Theory, dependent and independent variables.

As just discussed, theory and measurement are closely interrelated, and nowhere is this more evident than in the design of experimental studies. The selection of treatment variables and their manipulation, and the selection and measurement of specific dependent variables, are predicated on the relationship between theoretical constructs of interest.[2] Thus, in theory-driven experimental research the selection of what to measure should not be an issue. The difficulty, rather, lies in initially selecting the "right" theory on which to base a study and in deciding how to measure and manipulate the theoretical constructs of interest. In other words, being unclear as to what should be measured in an experiment should be taken as a clear signal that the ideas being tested are not well formulated.

This state of affairs seems to be a rather common occurrence, even in so-called theory-testing work. The attention paid to selection or development of theory often seems inadequate. Precise reasons for the presence of certain dependent measures and the relationship of those measures to the independent variables is not always articulated. More often than not such relationships remain implicit. They may be clear in the minds of the researcher but often less so in the minds of the reader or reviewers. The more time spent precisely defining constructs and the relationships between those constructs, the more likely a good job will be done in operationalizing the required measure.

Unfortunately such precision can seldom be achieved through any single study. The process of measurement development and refinement will, by necessity, be a time-consuming one. Clear and meaningful definitions are often the last things to come from a stream of research, and to expect them at the outset may be asking too much. At the same time, to encourage the development of useful and robust measures it is essential that such work is recognized and rewarded in the academic system. Recent MIS research gives more reason for hope in this regard with the publication of a number of papers that have an exclusive measurement focus (e.g., Baroudi & Orlikowski, 1989; Moore & Benbasat, 1991; Straub, 1989; among others).

It will be virtually impossible to derive good measures without working through an iterative process of definition, operationalization, and testing. The recent paper by Moore and Benbasat (1991) provides an excellent example of how such a measurement process proceeds and indicates the degree of effort and diligence that is required

---

[2] The relationship may be explicitly defined by some extant theory, or may be part of an implicit model held by the researcher. In either case the model should directly indicate the selection of dependent and independent variables.

for "good" measurement. This approach is consistent with the argument of Cooke and Campbell (1979) that measurement should not and cannot be developed in isolation and prior to empirical work; rather, good measures are the result of both significant theoretical development and empirical testing. Thus, to properly evaluate measures and measurement techniques in an area, it is important to look at a body of research and not simply single studies.

Theory and the Constraint of Measurement.

The previous section takes the somewhat traditional view that theory is essential to measurement. Another useful perspective is to recognize the degree to which reliance on theory can constrain measurement and inhibit discovery. This is basically Weick's (1984) argument that "believing is seeing." To the extent that theory defines the relevant dependent variables, it also excludes *seemingly* irrelevant variables. Thus, variables are excluded from measurement that may be of interest but that cannot be accommodated by existing theory. In addition to the extent that one relies on existing theory to determine what should be measured empirically, it is difficult for empiricism to inform and aid theoretical progress in an area except by negative results. Thus, pure theory-driven measurement may lead to support for a theory, or disconfirmation of a theory but it is less likely to lead to discovery. Indeed, the opposite argument is that overdevotion to a particular theory will limit the scope of investigation and inhibit progress in a field.

Weick has argued that MIS suffers from "devotion" to a theoretical perspective that tends to see rationality in all things. In a recent review of the philosophical assumptions underlying much MIS research, Orlikowski and Baroudi (1991) showed evidence of a similarly narrow perspective to research in North America. This devotion to theory and method serves to restrict the types of theories that are admissible and the types of measurements that will be taken. All in all, this emphasis on a single theoretical approach reduces the likelihood of uncovering or generating appropriate theory that could account for anomalous or inconsistent results.

The decision support system (DSS) literature provides a good example of this. Empirical work in this area tends to be rooted in the notion that a well-designed DSS should lead to more effective decision making. This belief is grounded in the seldom articulated model of bounded rationality. In the face of equivocal experimental results, researchers often assume poor experimental design, poor measurement, inadequate operationalization of the decision aid, inappropriate tasks, and the like. They seldom, however, question the theory underlying the research, and thus measures of other potentially relevant variables may not be taken. By questioning the theoretical underpinnings of a body of research, it is possible to generate a new view of the problem. For example, if one questions the premise that a decision maker is a capacity-constrained information processor who would like to "do better" but cannot and instead assumes the decision maker is an "effort minimizer" (who does not necessarily want to "do better"), one can generate quite a different set of predictions about the potential impact of a DSS. Furthermore, this alternative view suggests that variables such as decision strategy and decision-making effort might be as important, if not more important, than decision quality. By exploring the range of theoretical explanations for a phenomena, richer measures and greater insight can be developed.

Measurement for "What," "How," and "Why."

This section reviews the purpose of different measures in terms of identifying that a relationship exists (what), determining the means by which a relationship is formed (how), and determining the underlying cause of the relationship (why). Different forms of measurement will be appropriate, depending on the objectives of the experimenter.

Does design variable x influence measurement y? Measurement with the objective of determining if some relationship exists between specific design variables and measurements of interest such as performance or ease of use are traditionally used in exploratory research. This can be the researcher's version of a "what-if" problem, in which measurement is guided more by intuition than theory. Such a measurement approach would be found in validation and testing studies with engineering objectives. Designers who believe that their approach represents a way to improve learning rates or ease of use, or reduce errors, might set up an experiment that compares their design feature to some benchmark. They may only be interested in the impact of the new design and may have little interest in formally determining how or why the new design does or does not work.

How does design variable x affect the value of y? Measurement with this objective seeks to understand the causal relationships that exist between dependent and independent variables of interest. This often leads to a search for moderating variables (or antecedent conditions) that will help to uncover more precisely the relationships between dependent and independent variables. Such an approach tends to be more strongly theory-driven, seeking to understand the precise route and degree by which the measures are influenced. To this end the researcher is typically engaged in directed research that is based on insight into the behavior of the system user and the user's capacities and limitations. Research of this type may be carried out in the context of a broader theoretical model and employ a multivariate approach to determine the interrelationships among variables. Questions of "how" may often focus on changes in process and examine what happens during an experiment between the onset of stimulus and the completion of some task.

Why does design variable x affect the value of y? Investigations of this sort will most often be looking for lower-level cognitive, perceptual, or affective explanations of system impacts. That is to say, the focus of such work will typically be on uncovering the way in which a system design feature influences or enhances some underlying ability or predisposition, thus causing differences in performance. Such studies often look at very narrow ranges of behavior and employ small, more atomic-level tasks to try to capture underlying mechanisms that cause certain outcomes. Thus, these studies may simply explain how a result occurs by positing lower-level explanations than have been considered previously.

Classifying Measures

Outcome versus process measures.

A key focus in much human factors research in MIS has been on the outcomes of system use. This is consistent with the engineering objective of such research to determine the performance impacts of a design intervention. By contrast, process measures focus on how the system itself is used and how any design alternatives influence system usage patterns or user behavior. Thus, process measures emphasize the direct measurement of behavior while a user is interacting with the system.

Process tracing measures have become more common in human factors research in MIS to obtain greater insight into how and why information systems influence user behavior and performance. By examining what occurs between the introduction of a stimulus, via some experimental treatment, and the production of a response, as measured by an outcome variable, significant insights can be gained into how and why relationships exist between different constructs.

Process measures are also a useful way to combine theory-testing and theory-building research. In a traditional input/output experiment one plans to measure certain variables, but invariably, after the experiment is conducted, results are discovered that lead to questions about other measures. If process data have been collected, it is often possible to assess (at least in a preliminary fashion) these alternate measures and to pursue unexpected or conflicting findings. Thus, process data, because of its richness, provide measures for phenomena of interest that are defined a priori but also support the emergence or discovery of new hypotheses.

Perceptual versus behavioral measures.

An experimental research setting is somewhat unique in that it typically allows the researcher free reign to measure a variety of factors both perceptual and behavioral. By contrast, researchers in field settings are more likely to rely on perceptual measures. Access to actual behaviors is simply more limited in field settings and may consume a greater amount of resources or be practically unobtainable.

For example, in examining interface issues we may be equally interested in what the user does with the system (in terms of behavior) and what the user thinks of the system (in terms of perceptions). Both sets of factors play a role in the acceptance and usage of the system. Although it would be desirable to measure both aspects within a given study, there is a tendency for researchers to employ or emphasize one approach to measurement over the other. Those who focus on behavior implicitly or explicitly believe that actions and performance measures are the most important factors in determining the impact and suitability of a system measure. Their strength lies in the fact that they represent actual behavior with the system, and their interpretation is less prone to respondent biases.

Advocates of perceptual measures, on the contrary, often argue that "perception is reality," and that the actual behavior of users with systems will be moderated by their perceptions of and attitude toward both the system and the context in which they are using it. This true understanding of user behavior may only arise through measurement of user perceptions. Ideally, of course, both sets of measures provide useful information, and it is in experimental settings that the researcher is in the unique position of being able to capture both sets of measures.

Obtrusive versus unobtrusive measures.

In most experimental settings it will be difficult to completely disguise the fact that measurement is taking place, thus purely unobtrusive measure are unlikely. At the same time it is seldom the case that all measurements of interest are fully understood by the participants in the study. Typically, this would be viewed as undesirable as it can lead to hypothesis guessing and other expectancy effects. Thus, experimental measures typically will fall along a measurement continuum from relatively unobtrusive to obtrusive. Often researchers will have options as to how obtrusive data collection will be, even when they have decided on the need for specific items to be measured. For example process traces may be gathered via verbal protocols that are, by definition, highly intrusive. At the same time, similar measures of process might be gathered through system interactions that are logged automatically and unobtrusively as the user performs a task. In general, all other things equal, unobtrusive measures should be favored to the extent that the experimenter is interested in natural behavior.

As the example here illustrates, researchers in MIS are in the unique position to be able to capture many measures of interest unobtrusively using computer-based techniques. In studies in which measures of time, performance, or system use are taken, these measures can be captured while the subject interacts within the experiment. The precise nature and timing of the measures need not be apparent to the subjects. This affords several benefits. Observations can be taken more frequently and often at a finer level of detail than is possible when human intervention is required. Automated measures make disguising certain measures simpler. Furthermore, subjects and lab assistants are not burdened with data collection, and thus more can be accomplished within the fixed duration of the laboratory task.

Quantitative versus qualitative measures.

North American MIS research has over time stressed (and some would argue overstressed) the primacy of quantitative measures that permit the application of statistical techniques. This tendency is even more clearly seen in experimental research. Although it is common, it need not be an essential characteristic of experimental studies. Observational techniques that incorporate the qualitative analysis of text, speech, and nonverbal communication that occurs during an experiment may provide useful insights into the behavior of system users, as well as into such things as user–designer interactions. The interplay between the control afforded by experimental conditions and the richness available from qualitative measures and analysis techniques should be more fully explored.

Special Issues in Measurement Development and Validation for Experiments

This section deals with three issues that are common in much experimental research in the information systems field. Although these issues also present themselves in other research methods (such as surveys), they are particularly important to experimental research and to some extent can be identified as factors constraining the advancement of knowledge in various areas.

The construct validation process.

As a practical point it seems that measurement of dependent variables often occurs as an afterthought in much experimental MIS research. Indeed, this may be the case in much experimental research in the organizational sciences. A review of methods by Podsakoff and Dalton (1987) indicated that the typical laboratory experiment in organizational behavior provided little indication that the measures used had been tested for construct validity. Similar results have been found in marketing, and this result is probably true of MIS research as well. Although there has been a healthy increase in articles that focus on measurement issues in MIS (e.g., Davis, 1989; Moore & Benbasat, 1991; Straub, 1989; among others), this work generally emphasizes measurement in field settings, and experimental research moves forward with seemingly little appreciation of the construct validation issues. Although considerable effort typically goes into the design of experimental treatments, the process seems to stop short of developing and validating useful, reliable, and valid measures of dependent variables of interest. For example, although one is often interested in user "performance" or effectiveness with a system, that construct may be defined in a wide variety of ways. There are few standard definitions of performance. Indeed, such measures may be so highly task-dependent that it will not be possible to define such measures.

Thus, at the very least, researchers must begin to pay increasing attention to the measures used in experimental settings and encourage the use of common validated scales. Facilitating this is one of the major goals of CSQS, which has been described earlier in this chapter. Furthermore, it is essential that new measures that are introduced for experiments receive more than a cursory attempt at validation, and that more than simple measures of reliability be reported in research findings. Unfortunately, this move toward generic multipurpose measures may result in more difficulties given the arguments of Zmud (see discussion earlier in this chapter).

Manipulation and measurement—the role of the manipulation check.

Manipulation checks are measures that are employed, usually as part of the development of treatment conditions and after treatments have been applied in an experiment, to determine if the treatment, as intended by the researcher, was the one actually experienced by the subjects. Thus, if one manipulates mood in an experimental setting there should be some evidence that subjects in different conditions were in fact in different moods. Similarly, if task complexity is manipulated, subjects should perceive one task as more complex than another.

Experimental MIS research does not often employ manipulation checks to determine the effect of the experimental treatments. Such measures are important and particularly critical when experimental treatments involve perceptual manipulations. The absence of manipulation checks may be rooted in the tradition of using tangible manipulations, in which participants in a study work on different systems or are presented with different forms of information. In such cases the manipulations may be so certain and obvious as to make manipulation checks irrelevant. However, as the study of interaction between system features and various task variables increases, it becomes more important to determine if manipulation of, for example, increasing information load really has any effect on a user's perception of the task. Moreover, if one views the information load manipulation as being somehow related to task complexity, then it is essential to measure whether participants in different experimental conditions differ in perceptions of task complexity. Even in cases in which manipulations appear obvious, they may not be so. For example, some early research in information presentation used treatments that confounded the information form (e.g., table or graph) with other factors, such as color, making interpretations difficult. Manipulation checks can help to uncover such problems and should be as much a part of the development of a measurement strategy in an experiment as the dependent variables.

Measurement of covariates.

The measurement of covariates is another particularly difficult area. It is difficult to decide what appropriate covariates are and then to obtain good measures of those variables or constructs. Many variables that we collect as covariates (age, sex, computer experience) seem to be obtained because of tradition rather than because there is a good reason to collect them. Although the collection of extraneous covariates may be unlikely to cause significant problems in an experiment, it is fruitless to try to cast a wide net without some guidance as to *appropriate* covariates. This points back to the importance of theory in determining relevant measures, both of specific constructs of interest and of covariate measures. By collecting the "right" covariates, where right is defined as those that are important to a theoretical argument, richer explanations of "how and why" a phenomena occurs can be provided. Judicious use of covariate measures can also help to rule out alternative explanations or indicate the limitations within which results need to be interpreted. On the contrary, the overuse of covariates may take the place of properly formulating the problem and thus could be detrimental.

The Pragmatics of Measurement in Experimentation

There are a variety of issues associated with actually taking measurements in experimental studies. Some of these issues are enumerated next. The list does not purport to be exhaustive; rather, it represents a subset of issues that are commonly considered by researchers when establishing experimental procedures. Although these issues may each appear minor, taken together they can influence the overall quality and success of an experiment.

Timing of measures.

When should measures be collected during a study, and how often should measurement be made? Certain measures can only be taken at defined points in time; however, the majority of issues surrounding the timing and frequency of measurement are at the discretion of the researcher. Although such things as performance on a task should typically be measured after the fact, a researcher may also choose to take repeated measures of task performance over time to get at issues such as learning rates and take follow-up measures days or weeks later to look at retention. Both the timing and frequency of measures can affect the behavior of subjects. For example, frequent measures of performance over the course of a study may lead to conservative behavior so as not to get "caught" making a mistake. By contrast, measuring performance at the end of a sequence of a task may cause more erratic behavior over the course of the task. It may also result in the researcher missing much of the behavior of interest in a study.

Common concerns such as fatigue and testing effects need to be considered as part of the decision of when to measure. Researchers must decide if measures other than the primary dependent variables, such as demographics, covariates, or manipulation checks, should be taken. Recording such measures after the primary experimental task is preferable in that such measures cannot interfere or interact with the task. However, taking such measures at the end of an experimental session also leads to the risk of hurried or incomplete responses due to a desire for completion. The measures themselves may also be influenced by the outcome or experience of the subject during the study.

Experimenter effects.

The influence of the experimenter on the data collection process is one that is well understood and can most easily be avoided by having experiments administered and data collected by assistants who are "blind" to the nature of the hypotheses under study. At the same time, it may be important for an assistant to know the nature of certain measures to aid in interpretation if need be during data collection. This will be especially true for perceptual and attitudinal measures collected via questionnaires. Of course, the risk associated with this is the possible introduction of bias into the study.

Online data capture.

As indicated earlier, online data capture affords many advantages in terms of timing, frequency, precision, and degree of obtrusiveness. Thus, where possible in experiments, it would be preferable to capture data online. Similarly, automated data collection using online questionnaires is desirable because it can be blended in with the experimental task and cause less disruption. It may also be more engaging for subjects, and thus they may attend more carefully to their responses. Finally, such online data capture brings data to the researcher in a more efficient way, which facilitates analysis and reduces the likelihood of errors.

The only real disadvantage of such data collection is the cost associated with software development. Online measures of performance, timing, and system use may preclude the use of much commercially available software that cannot be modified to accommodate these needs. Thus, costs become higher as special-purpose experimental systems must be developed. There may also be a danger with online data capture in that it will bias the researcher toward the use of quantitative measures at the expense of observational and perceptual data.

Postexperimental debriefing.

Data collected from postexperimental debriefings can be very useful in assisting with the interpretation of results from an experiment and in providing a more qualitative interpretation of the impact of the treatment conditions. The opportunity to use such sessions seems to be overlooked (at least to the extent that it is reported in published literature). This may simply be due to the fact that such results are often collected by research assistants, and that their richness and insight is lost to the experimenter. It may also be the case that such observations are taken in a less than systematic fashion and thus are difficult to interpret. Finally, there may be an inherent bias of experimenters, who tend to rely on structured and quantifiable measures against such data. Whatever the reasons it would seem that data collected after an experiment through interviews or unstructured questionnaires could be a valuable resource in helping to answer how and why questions and in helping to interpret unexpected results.

Measurement and deception.

Often some degree of deception is employed—in an experiment at least to the extent that the participants are not aware of the precise nature of hypotheses under study. It may also be the case that they are not always aware of the nature or purpose of different measures being taken. Researchers need to decide in establishing measures what subjects can and cannot know in terms of the purpose of the experiment. The need to establish informed consent to participate should lead the researcher to disclose any information that would not jeopardize the outcome of the study. When deception is necessary it is important that measures still be taken in a context that is plausible to the participant. To the extent that the measures being taken appear unnatural given the experiences of the participant, behavior may be influenced, and results may become an artifact of the particular setting.

Measurement effects and confounding.

The possible effects of deception on measurement is one example of possible confounding between experimental setting and measures. It is also possible that the type and timing of measures can interact with treatment conditions in various undesirable ways. As was mentioned previously under timing of measures, both timing and frequency of measures may cause changes in user behavior. Similarly, measures that force subjects to choose between conflicting objectives may lead to problems. For example, if an experiment measures both time and accuracy (and the subject is aware of this), each subject may respond differently to the treatment in trying to optimize those measures. Some may try to strike a balance between the two, whereas others may emphasize one or the other. Thus, experimenters must take care to establish procedures where the measurements themselves do not influence and confound the effect of the treatments.

CONCLUSION

Why Isn't the Right Thing Done?

Little that has been discussed about measurement in this chapter is either novel or new. Although the training of researchers may have emphasized measurement issues to differing degrees, most understand and appreciate the need for valid and reliable measures. At the same time, few take the time to ensure that the measures are either valid or reliable. Often there is no compelling reason for taking the measures that are made. This begs the question: Why isn't the right thing done?

There are likely several answers to this question, and most are based on one's own interests and motivations as a researcher. First, developing measures is often characterized as a boring and time-consuming task that requires largely technical skills and generates minimal prestige. Thus, there is little extrinsic motivation to develop and test measures. It requires an inordinate amount of time and may not result in any longer term payoff in terms of such things as career recognition. A second key reason may be impatience on the part of a researcher. Typically in conducting a study there are ideas to test, and one is impatient to discover results that are motivating and potentially rewarding. Measurement and instrument development are simply roadblocks on the way to attaining those results and are to be surmounted in the most efficient way possible. Even in experimental settings, in which attention to detail is often a watchword, the time and effort consumed by issues relating to manipulations and to maintaining internal control may consume available resources leaving measurement issues as simply an afterthought.

Finally, many of the topics researchers emphasize are transient. They are hot topics today and of little interest tomorrow. Attention is only paid to measurement in established areas where the measures may have some permanence and may help to resolve complex issues. For areas that may be of no interest some months down the road, there is little point in spending large amounts of time on measurement issues. Thus, researchers are often conditioned to view measurement as an afterthought. As mentioned, there is some indication that this is changing in the MIS literature with increasing publication of papers relating to measurement issues and a greater use (however rudimentary) of reliability and validity measures in surveys. As the reward system begins to emphasize the importance of measurement and also begins to expect that measurement issues be addressed in reported research, measurement techniques are likely to improve. The reviewing and refereeing process for all future articles should have a psychometric property checklist that all authors are required to meet. This should include pretesting, reliability, and validity as a minimum requirements. With an increase in quality, all researchers will be able to put more faith into the work that is published.

REFERENCES

Barki, H., & Hartwick, J. (1989). Rethinking the concept of user involvement. *Management Information Systems Quarterly, 13*, 53–63.

Barki, H., Rivard, S., & Talbot, J. (1988). An information systems keyword classification scheme. *Management Information Systems Quarterly, 12*, 298–309.

Baroudi, J., Orlikowski, W. (1989). The problem of statistical power in MIS research. *Management Information Systems Quarterly, 13*, 87–109.

Beard, J.W., & Peterson, T.O. (1988). A taxonomy for the study of human factors in management information systems (MIS). In J. Carey (Ed.), *Human Factors in Management Information Systems,* (pp. 7–25). Norwood, NJ: Ablex.

Benbasat, I. (1991). Commentary on survey measures and instruments in MIS: Inventory and appraisal. In K.L. Kraemer (Ed.), *The Information Systems Research Challenge: Survey Research Methods,* (pp. 181–184). Boston: Harvard Business School Press.

Briggs, S.F., Bedard, J.C., Gaber, B.G., & Linsmeier, T.J. (1985). The effects of task size and similarity on the decision behavior of bank loan officers. *Management Science, 31*, 970–987.

Carey, J.M. (Ed.). (1991). *Human factors in management information systems: An organizational perspective,* Norwood, NJ: Ablex.

Chin, J.P., Diehl, V.A., & Norman, K.L. (1988). Development of an instrument measuring user satisfaction of the human-computer interface. *Proceedings of the CHI '88 Conference: Human Factors in Computing Systems,* (pp. 213–218).

Cohen, J. (1960). A coefficient of agreement for nominal scales. *Educational and Psychological Measurement, 20*, 37–46.

Cooke, T.D., & Campbell, D.T. (1979). *Quasi-experimentation: Design and analysis for field settings.* Boston: Houghton Mifflin.

Davis, F.D. (1989). Perceived usefulness, perceived ease of use and user acceptance of information technology. *Management Information Systems Quarterly, 13*, 319–340.

Doll, W.J., & Torkzadeh, G. (1988). The measurement of end-user computing satisfaction. *Management Information Systems Quarterly, 12*, 259–274.

Glass, G. V., McGraw, B., & Smith, M.L. (1981). *Meta-analysis in social research.* Beverly Hills: Sage.

Hackman, J.R., & Oldman, G.R. (1975). Development of the job diagnostic survey. *Journal of Applied Psychology, 60*, 159–170.

Ives, B., Hamilton, S., & Davis, G.B. (1980). A framework for research in computer-based management information systems. *Management Science, 26*, 910–934.

Jacoby, J. (1978). Consumer research: A state of the art review. *Journal of Marketing, 42*, 87–96.

Kerlinger, F.N. (1986). *Foundations of behavioral research.* New York: holt, Rhinehart and Winston.

Kraemer, K.L. (Ed.). (1991). *The information systems research challenge: Survey research methods,* Boston: Harvard Business School Press.

Kraemer, K.L., & Dutton, W.H. (1991). Survey research in the study of management information systems. In K.L. Kraemer (Ed.), *The information systems research challenge: Survey research methods*, (pp. 3–57). Boston: Harvard Business School Press.

Killingsworth, B., Kletke, M.G., Mackay, J., Trumbly, J.E., & Carey, J.M. (1992). Human factors in information systems: A position treatise. In J.M. Carey (Ed.), *Human factors in management information systems*, (pp. 1–24). Norwood, NJ: Ablex.

Martin, M.P. (1995). Human factors in management information systems: A taxonomy. In J.M. Carey (Ed.), *Human factors in management information systems*, (pp. 25–39). Norwood, NJ: Ablex.

Melone, N. (1990). Theoretical assessment of user satisfaction construct in information systems research. *Management Science, 36,* 76–91.

Myers, I.B. (1962). *The Myers-Briggs Type Indicator.* Palo Alto, CA: Consulting Psychologist Press.

Moore, G. C., & Benbasat, I. (1991). The development of an instrument to measure the perceived characteristics of adopting an information technology innovation. *Information Systems Research, 2,* 192–222.

Newsted, P.R., Munro, M.C., & Huff, S.L. (1991). Data acquisition instruments in mnagement information systems. In K.L. Kraemer (Ed.), *The information systems research challenge: Survey research methods*, (pp. 187–209). Boston: Harvard Business School Press.

Peterson, G.W., Ryan-Jones, R.E., Sampson J.P., Jr., & Reardon, R.C. (1994). A comparison of the effectiveness of three computer-assisted guidance systems: DISCOVER, SIGI, and SIGIPLUS. *Computers in Human Behavior, 10,* 189–198.

Podsakoff, P.M., & Dalton, D.R. (1987). Research methodology in organizational studies. *Journal of Management, 13,* 419–441.

Preschel, B.M. (1979). *Indexer consistency in perception of concepts and in choice of terminology.* Unpublished doctoral dissertation, Columbia University, ERIC Document #063942.

Saga, V. (1991). *Development of an attitude toward computers instrument.* (Working Paper). Gainesville: Florida State University.

Schwab, D.P. (1980). Construct validity in organizational behavior. In B.M. Staw & L.L. Cummings (Eds.) *Research in Organizational Behavior,* (pp. 3–44). Greenwich: JAI Press.

Sethi, V., & King, W.R. (1991). Construct measurement in information systems research: An illustration in strategic systems. *Decision Sciences, 22,* 455–472.

Straub, D.W., Jr. (1989). Validating instruments in MIS research. *Management Information Systems Quarterly, 13,* 147–170.

Swanson, E.G. (1991). Commentary on survey measures and instruments in MIS: Inventory and appraisal. In K.L. Kraemer (Ed.), *The information systems research challenge: Survey research methods*, (pp. 185–186). Boston: Harvard Business School Press.

Weick, K.E. (1984). Theoretical assumptions and research methodology selection. In F.W. McFarlan (Ed.), *The information systems research challenge*, (pp. 47–85). Boston: Harvard Business School Press.

Zmud, R.W., & Boynton, A.C. (1991). Survey measures and instruments in MIS: Inventory and appraisal. In K.L. Kraemer (Ed.), *The information systems research challenge: Survey research methods*, (pp. 149–184). Boston: Harvard Business School Press.

Author Index

A

Ackerman, F., 85, 94, *96*
Adams, D., 161, 162, 163, *169*
Addo, T. B. A., 4, 7, *10*
Ahituv, N., 67, 70, *80, 175, 178*
Ajzen, I., 163, *167*
Alavi, M., 183, *195*
Alvesson, M., 144, *152*
Amoroso, D. L., 184, *196*
Anderson, J. R., 55, *65*
Anderson, R., 131, *134*
Antill, L., 147, *152*
Applegate, L. M., 122, 132, *133*
Argyris, C., 146, 150, *152*
Armistead, L. P., 203, *206*
Arndt, S., 187, *195*
Athos, A. G., 137, 147, *155*
Axelrod, R., 85, 92, *95*

B

Bailey, J. E., 185, *195*
Bair, I., 122, *133*
Ball, L., 183, *195*
Barki, H., 219, 220, 229, *240*
Barnard, C. I., 140, 144, *152*
Baroudi, J., 184, 185, 187, *195, 196,* 229, 230, 231, *240*
Bastianutti, L., 132, *134*
Bartimo, J., 35, *49*
Bates, M. J., 55, *65*
Bavelas, A., 160, *168*
Beach, L. R., 68, *80*
Beard, J. W., 151, *152,* 221, 228, *240*
Beck, B., 32, *33*
Bedard, J. C., 172, 173, *178,* 224, *240*
Benbasat, I., 112, *119,* 148, 150, *152, 155,* 171, 172, 173, *179,* 200, *206,* 228, 230, 235, *240, 241*
Benjamin, R. I., 183, *195*
Benson, D. H., 183, *196*
Benson, S., 122, *134*
Bergeron, F., 185, *196*

Berggren, C., 127, *133*
Bertin, J., 4, *10*
Berube, C., 185, *196*
Bettman, J. R., 172, 173, 174, 175, *178, 179*
Beyer, J. M., 137, 140, 141, 144, 149, *152*
Biggs, S. F., 172, 173, *178*
Bikson, T. K., 187, *196*
Billings, R. S., 69, *80*
Bjorkman, T., 127, *133*
Blocher, E., 201, *206*
Boland, R. J., 84, *96,* 148, *153*
Boose, J. H., 92, *96*
Bostrom, R. P., 121, *133,* 147, 150, 152, *153,* 163, *168*
Boynton, A. C., 220, 221, *241*
Braasch, B., 161, *166*
Bradshaw, J. M., 92, *96*
Brancheau, J., 183, *196*
Brantham, C. E., 161, 162, 163, *166*
Braunstein, M. L., 173, 174, 175, *179*
Briggs, R., 32, *33*
Briggs, S. F., 220, 224, *240*
Brooks, F. P., 112, *119*
Brown, A. L., 55, *65*
Brown, L. A., 101n, 104, *106, 107*
Bruder, J., 162, *166*
Brunsson, N., 137, 149, *153*
Burton, J. K., 203, *206*
Byrne, K. E., 161, *167*

C

Call, H. J., 87, *96*
Campbell, D. T., 231, *240*
Campbell, K. S., 94, *96*
Card, S. K., 14, 19, *25*
Carey, J. M., 222, 224, *240, 241*
Carmel, E., 32, *33*
Carr, H. H., 183, *196*
Carroll, J. M., 16, 24, *25,* 53, 65, *65,* 102, 103, *106*
Cerveny, R. P., 186, *196*
Chamran, R., 129, *133*
Chan, L., 86, *96*

Cheney, P. H., 163, *168*, 184, *196*
Cherns, A. B., 124, 130, *133*
Chin, J. P., 216, *240*
Clevenger, J., 187, *195*
Cohen, C., 144, *153*
Cohen, J., 224, *240*
Conda, L., 201, *207*
Conrath, D. W., 86, *96*
Cooke, T. D., 231, *240*
Cooper, J., 186, *197*
Cooper, W. A., 132, *134*
Coover, D., 190, *197*
Coovert, M. D., 201, *207*
Cotterman, W., 183, *196*
Couger, J. D., 137, *153*
Courtney, J. F., 200, 202, *207*
Critenden, R., 33, *33*
Cropper, S., 85, 91, 94, *96*
Crowston, K., 163, *166*
Cummings, T. G., 130, 132, *133*
Cyert, 160, *167*

D

Daft, R. L., 83, *96*, 160, 162, *167*
Dalton, D. R., 228, 235, *241*
Danielson, R., 162, *166*
Dator, J. A., 144, 145, *153*
Davis, D., 200, 202, *206*
Davis, D. F., 187, 188, *196*
Davis, D. L., 137, *155*
Davis, F. D., 163, *167*, 229, 235, *240*
Davis, G. B. 148, 151, *154*, 183, *196*, 228, *240*
Davis, L. D., 187, 188, *196*
Davis, L. E., 124, 130, *134*
Davis, R. D., 200, 202, *206*
Davis, T. R. V., 147, *154*
DeBrabander, B., 146, 147, 148, *153*
DeLone, D. W., 161, 164, *167, 168*
DeMarco, T., 94, *96*, 111, 112, *119*
Dennis, A. R., 27, 32, *33*, 132, *134*
DeSanctis, G., 3, *10*, 199, *206*
Dewar, R. E., 35, 36, *49, 50*
Dexter, A. S., 200, *206*
Dickson, G. W., 3, *10*, 183, *196*, 199, *206*
Diehl, V. A., 216, *240*
Dilla, W. M., 84, *96*
Docherty, P., 122, 130, *134*
Doherty, M. L., 171, *178*
Doll, W. J., 183, 184, 185, 190, *196*, 216, *240*
Dosher, B. A., 173, *179*
Drucker, P. F., 160, *167*
Dudley, T., 36, *49*

Dutton, W. H., 228, *241*

E

Eddy, D. M., 86, *97*
Eden, C., 84, 85, 94, *96*
Egido, C., 36, *49*
Eijnatten, M. F., 124, *134*
Elias, J., 161, *167*
Elliott, O., 124, 130, *135*
Ells, J. G., 36, *49*
Elsawy, O. A., 141, *153*
Emery, F. E., 130, *134*
England, G. W., 141, *153*
Evered, R. D., 146, 150, *155*
Eysenck, H. J., 144, 145, *153*

F

Fischer, G., 83, *96*
Fishbein, M., 163, *167*
Fitzgerald, G., 145, *155*
Flannery, L. S., 183, *197*
Ford, J. K., 171, *178*
Ford, J. R., 102, 103, *106*
Forisha, B. D., 203, *206*
Franz,, C. R., 137, 146, 147, 148, 152, *153*
Friendlander, F., 146, 152, *155*
Fussell, S. R., 84, *96*

G

Gaber, B. G., 172, 173, *178*, 224, *240*
Galbraith, J., 160, *167*
Gallagher, C. A., 185, *196*
Gallupe, R. B., 132, *134*
Gane, C., 94, *96*
Garceau, S., 200, 202, *206*
Gattiker, U. E., 163, *167*
George, J. F., 27, *33*
Gerson, E. M., 137, 152, *154*
Gerwin, D., 124, *134*
Gibson, C. F., 147, 150, *153*
Ginzberg, M. J., 148, *153*, 163, *167*
Gittins, D., 36, *49*
Givon, T., 83, *96*
Glass, C. R., 186, 188, 189, *196*
Glass, G. V., 225, *240*
Goetschalckx, M., 175, 176, *178*
Goetz, J. P., 56, *65*
Goldstein, D., 148, 150, *152*
Goodhue, D., 163, *167*
Gordon, C., 186, *197*
Gould, J. D., 162, 163, *167*
Gowda, R. G., 112, 117, *120*

Grant, R., 160, 162, *168*
Gratz, R. D., 162, 163, 164, *169*
Greeno, J. G., 202, *206*
Greenwald, A. G., 187, *197*
Grindlay, A., 162, *167*
Grohowski, R., 122, *135*
Grover, V., 163, *167*
Gruding, J., 83, *96*
Guillemette, R. A., 101, 102, 103, 104n, 105, *106, 107*
Gurley, K., 124, *134*
Gutek, B. A., 187, *196*
Guth, W. D., 141, *153*

H

Hackathorn, R., 183, *196*
Hackman, J. R., 220, *240*
Hakiel, S. R., 36, *49*
Halstead, M. H., 114, *120*
Hamilton, S., 148, 151, *154,* 228, *240*
Hanna, D., 124, *134*
Harper, R. R., 130, 131, *134*
Harris, R., 183, *195*
Hartog, C., 183, *196*
Hartwick, J., 161, *168,* 220, 229, *240*
Haskell, N., 103, *107*
Hasselblad, V., 86, *97*
Heath, C., 132, *134*
Heinssen, R. K., 186, 188, 189, *196*
Herbert, M., 183, *196*
Herbst, P., 124, *134*
Hill, A., 175, 176, *178*
Hiltz, S. R., 161, 163, *167*
Hirschheim, R. A., 144, 145, 148, 152, *153, 155*
Hoadley, E. D., 4, 5, 8, *10,* 201, *206*
Hollander, E., 127, *133*
Howard, R., 137, 141, 142, 144, 151, *153*
Huber, G. P., 28, *33*
Hubert, 160, *167*
Huchingson, R. D., 35, *49*
Huff, A., 84, *96*
Huff, S. L., 219, *241*
Hufnagel, E. H., 163, *167*
Hughes, J. A., 130, 131, *134*
Hults, B. M., 171, *178*

I

Igbaria, M., 183, 186, 187, 188, *196*
Irby, C., 37, *50*
Ives, B., 148, 151, *154,* 185, 187, *195, 196,* 228, *240*

J

Jacoby, J., 174, *178,* 228, *240*
Janis, I. L., 85, *96*
Jarvenpaa, S. L., 3, *10,* 173, *178,* 199, 201, *206*
Jenkins, A. M., 3, 4, 5, *10*
Jin, K. G., 140, 141, 146, 147
Johansen, R., 122, *134*
Johnson, D. G., 138, *154*
Johnson, E. J., 68, 69, 71, 72, 73, *80,* 173, 174, 175, *178, 179*
Jones, C., 94, *96*
Joyner, E. R., 4, 7, *10*

K

Kacmar, C., 36, *49*
Kaiser, K. M., 147, 150, 152, *153*
Kakkar, P., 172, 173, *178*
Kasper, G. M., 186, *196*
Katz, 160, *167*
Kaufmann, G., 203, *206*
Kaye, A. R., 161, *167*
Keen, P. G. W., 137, 146, 148, 150, 152, *154,* 183, *196,* 199, *206*
Keeny, R. L., 86, *96*
Kenneth, W., 160, 162, *168*
Kerlinger, F. N., 229, *240*
Kern, H., 127, *134*
Kerr, E. B., 161, 163, *167*
Khan, 160, *167*
Kida, T., 171, *179*
Kiesler, S., 162, 163, *169*
Killingsworth, B., 222, *241*
Kilman, R. H., 144, 148, *154*
Kimbal, R., 37, *50*
King, W. R., 163, *167,* 212, 219, *241*
Kingdom, U., 132, *134*
Kirton, M., 190, *196*
Klayman, J., 69, 70, 71, *80,* 81n, 171, *178*
Klein, H., 144, 148, 152, *153*
Kleinmuntz, D. N., 69, 70, *80*
Kleinschrod, W. A., 161, *167*
Kletke, M. G., 222, *240, 241*
Kling, R., 137, 142, 151, 152, *154*
Kluckhohn, C., 144, *154*
Knight, L. A., 186, 188, 189, *196*
Koicke, K., 127, *134*
Kolodny, H., 124, *134*
Kraemer, K. L., 212, 228, *241*
Krauss, R. M., 84, *96*
Kuhlthau, C. C., 55, *65*
Kumar, K., 183, *196*
Kuss, A., 174, *178*

L

LaDuc, L., 94, *96*
Lai, K-Y., 160, 162, *168*
Lalomia, M. J., 201, *207*
Lam, N., 15, *26*
Landow,, G. P., 93, *96*
Landsdale, M., 36, *50*
Larcker, D. F., 185, *196*
Latremouille, S., 14, 15, *26*
Lauer, T. W., 4, 7, *10*
Lawrence, P. R., 160, *167*
Leatherwood, M. L., 84, *96*
LeCompte, M. D., 56, *65*
Lederer, A. L., 161, *167*
Lee, D. M. S., 164, *167*
Lee, E., 14, 15, *25, 26,* 160, 163, *168*
Leifer, R., 142, *155*
Leitheiser, R. L., 183, *196*
Lemke, A., 83, *96*
Lengel, R. H., 83, *96,* 162, *167*
Lessing, V. P., 185, *196*
Levin, T., 186, *197*
Levinson, S. C., 83, *96*
Lewin, K., 146, 150, *154*
Lewis, C., 163, *167*
Linsmeier, T. J., 172, 173, *178, 178,* 224, *240*
LIster, T., 111, 112, *119*
Lorsch, J. W., 160, *167*
Loy, S. L., 202, *207*
Lucas, H. C., 163, *167,* 187, *197,* 200, *207*
Luff, P., 132, *134*
Lukka, A., 175, 176, *179*
Lukka, M., 175, 176, *179*
Luthans, F., 147, *154*
Lyytinen, K. J., 132, *134*

M

MacGregor, J., 15, *25, 26,* 160, 163, *168*
Mackay, J., 222,, *241*
Mackett-Stout, J., 35, 36, *50*
Mackie, D., 186, *197*
Malone, T., 160, 162, *168*
Mandell, S. F., 187, *197*
Mann, L., 85, *96*
Mann, R. I., 184, *196*
Mannheim, K., 148, *154*
Manross, G. G., 163, *168*
Mantei, M. M., 103, *107*
March, J. G., 140, 144, *154,* 160, *167, 168*
Marcus, S. A., 69, *80*
Markus, M L., 137, 142, 152, *154, 155*
Martin, A., 122, *134*

Martin, J., 15, *26*
Martin, M. P., 222, *241*
Martz, W. B., 122, *135*
Mason, R. O., 137, 138, *154*
Masuch, M., 146, *154*
Mazur, S. A., 102, 103, *106*
Mazursky, D., 174, *178*
McCall, J., 83, *96*
McEwen, S., 14, 15, *26*
McGoff, C., 122, *135*
McGraw, B., 225, *240*
McKendree, J., 16, *25*
McNurlin, B. C., 183, *197*
McTear, M., 55, *65*
Mead, M., 148, 150, *152*
Meglino, B. M., 137, 141, 144, 145, *155*
Meiskey, L., 187, *195*
Meister, D., 103, *107*
Melone, N. P., 187, *197,* 229, *241*
Meyerowitz, N., 93, *96*
Millar, 161, *168*
Miller, G. A., 173, *179*
Miller, L. E., 144, *155*
Miller, W. A., 87, *96*
Millman, Z., 161, *168*
Mintzberg, H., 147, *154,* 161, *168*
Mitchell, T. R., 68, *80*
Mitman, R., 122, *134*
Mitroff, I. I., 144, 148, *154*
Moffie, R. P., 201, *206*
Montazemi, A. R., 86, *96,* 185, *197*
Moore, G. C., 230, 235, *241*
Moran, T. P., 14, *25*
Morin, M. M., 160, 161, 162, *168*
Morrel-Samuels, P., 32, *33*
Mosier, J. N., 14, *26*
Moy, M., 162, *166*
Mozeico, H., 163, *168*
Mueller, A., 162, *166*
Mumford, E., 145, 147, *155*
Munro, M. C., 219, *241*
Murphy, C. A., 190, *197*
Myers, I. B., 220, *241*

N

Nachman, S. A., 183, 186, 187, *196*
Nechis, M., 183, *196*
Nelligan, T. W., 163, *167*
Nelson, D. L., 159, *168*
Nelson, R. R., 161, 162, 163, *168, 169*
Neumann, S., 67, 70, *80*
Newell, A., 19, *25,* 172, *179*

Newman, M., 144, 148, 152, *153*
Newmann, S., 175, *178*
Newsted, P. R., 219, *241*
Ngwenyama, O. K., 132, *134*
Nibbelin, M. C., 201, 202, *207*
Nickell, G. S., 186, 189, *197*
Nickerson, R. S., 162, *168*
Norman, D. A., 14, *26*, 102, *107*
Norman, K. L., 15, *26*, 216, *240*
Nunamaker, J. F., 27, 32, *33*, 132, *134, 135*
Nunmedal, S. G., 203, *207*
Nyhan, B., 132, *134*

O

Oldman, G. R., 220, *240*
Olfman, L., 163, *168*
Olson, M., 161, *168*, 183, 185, 187, *195, 196*
Oral, M., 200, 202, *206*
Orlikowski, W., 184, 185, *195*, 229, 230, 231, *240*
Ostwald, J., 83, *96*
Ouchi, W. G., 137, 139, *155*
Owen, D. L., 86, *96*
Owen, S. V., 190, *197*

P

Paap, K. R., 15, *26*
Panko, R. R., 160, *168*
Paquette, L., 171, *179*
Paradice, D. B., 137, *155*
Parasuraman, S., 186, 187, 188, *196*
Pascale, R. T., 137, 147, *155*
Pasmore, W. A., 124, 130, 132, *134*, 146, 152, *155*
Patterson, J., 36, *49*
Pava, C. H., 124, *134*
Pavri, F., 163, *168*
Payne, J. W., 67, 68, 69, 71, 72, 73, 84, *97*, 171, 173, 174, 175, *178, 179*
Pearson, S. W., 185, *195*
Perlman, G., 14, *26*
Peters, M., 150, *155*
Peterson, G. W., 216, 241
Peterson, T. O., 151, *152*, 221, 228, *240*
Pettigrew, A. M., 143, *155*
Pfarrer, R., 32, *33*
Phillip,, , 162, *168*
Phillips, L. D., 91, *97*
Pinto, J. N., 186, 189, *197*
Plaisent, M., 161, *168*
Podsakoff, P. M., 228, 235, *241*
Porter,, 161, *168*
Posner, B. Z., 141, 142, 150, *155*
Powers, M., 201, *207*

Pracht, W., 200, 202, *207*
Pratkanis, A. R., 187, *197*
Preschel, B. M., 219, *241*

R

Radford, J., 91, *97*
Rahn, R. J., 200, 202, *206*
Rallet, A., 160, 162, *168*
Ramaprasad, A., 85, 86, *97*
Rao, R., 160, 162, *168*
Rapport, R., 150, *155*
Rasmussen, J., 85, *97*
Raub, A. C., 186, 187, *197*
Ravlin, E. C., 137, 141, 144, 145, *155*
Raymond, L., 185, *197*
Reardon, R. C., 216, *241*
Renato, T., 141, *153*
Revis, D., 33, *33*
Rice, R. E., 163, *168*
Richardson, J. T. E., 202, 203, *207*
Rivard, S., 219, 220, *240*
Robey, D., 137, 142, 148, 152, *153, 154, 155*, 163, *168*
Robinson, V., 150, *155*
Rockart, J. F., 160, 161, *168*, 183, *197*
Rosenblitt, D., 160, 162, *168*
Roske-Hofstrand, R. J., 15, *26*
Rosson, M. B., 53, *65*
Rushinek, A., 24, *26*, 162, *168*, 185, *197*
Rushinek, S. F., 24, *26*, 162, *168*, 185, *197*
Russo, J. E., 173, *179*
Ryan, J. C., 161, *167*
Ryan-Jones, R. E., 216, *241*

S

Safayeni, F., 160, *168*
Saffo, P., 122, *134*
Saga, V., 216, *241*
Salas, E., 201, *207*
Salaway, G., 146, 147, *155*
Salem, P. J., 162, 163, 164, *169*
Salomon, G., 8, *11*
Sampson, J. -P., Jr., 216, *241*
Sanchez, P., 201, *207*
Sarson, T., 94, *96*
Savelyev, A., 5, 6, 7, *11*
Schatzman, L., 146, *155*
Schechtman, S. L., 171, *178*
Schepanksi, A., 70, *80*
Schkade, D. A., 69, 70, *80*
Schlender, B. R., 32, *33*
Schmitt, 141, 142, 150, *155*

Schon, D. A., 85, *97*
Schrode, W., 200, 202, *206*
Schultz, R. L., 162, *169*
Schumann, M., 127, *134*
Schwab, D. P., 229, *241*
Schwartz, D. G., 86, *97*
Schwartz, J. P., 15, *26*
Scott-Morton, M. S., 199, *206*
Sears, A., 33, *33*
Sena, J., 122, *134*
Sengupta, K., 83, *97*
Sethi, V., 161, *167,* 212, 219, *241*
Shachter, R. D., 86, *97*
Shani, A. B., 122, 124, 130, *134, 135*
Shapiro, D. Z., 130, 131, *134*
Sharrock, W. W., 131, *134*
Shin, J., 70, *80*
Shinar, D., 15, *26*
Shipmand, F., 83, *96*
Shneiderman, B., 15, 17, *25, 26,* 27, *33,* 36, *50,* 93,
    97, 138, 151, *155,* 201, *207*
Short, J. E., 160, 161, *168*
Sibbet, D., 122, *134*
Siegler, R. S., 55, *65*
Silver, M. S., 171, 172, *179*
Simon, A., 160, 163, *168, 169*
Simon, H. A., 84, 85, *97,* 140, 144, *154,* 172, 174,
    178, 179
Simpson, M., 36, *50*
Sims, D., 94, *96*
Singley, M. K., 55, *65*
Slevin, D. P., 162, *169*
Smart, J. R., 161, *169*
Smith, D. C., 37, *50*
Smith, M. L., 225, *240*
Smith, S. L., 14, *26*
Smithin, T., 86, *97*
Smith-Kerker, P. L., 102, 103, *106*
Snapper, J. W., 138, *154*
Solomon, P., 53, 54, *65*
Sparrow, J. A., 201, *207*
Sprague, R. H., Jr., 183, *197*
Sproull, L. S., 143, 144, *155,* 162, *169*
Stabell, C. B., 171, *179*
Stebbins, M., 124, *135*
Stern, M. I., 15, *26*
Stogdill, R. M., 114, *120*
Stone, M. D., 159, *169*
Straub, D. W., Jr., 220, 229, 230, 235, *241*
Strauss, A. L., 146, *155*
Stroud, T., 36, *50*
Stubbart, C., 85, 86, *97*

Stubler, W. F., 161, *167*
Suen, C., 32, *33*
Sullivan, C. H., 161, *169*
Susman, G. L., 146, 150, *155*
Svenson, O., 171, 173, *179*
Swanson, E. B., 185, *197*
Swanson, E. G., 219, *241*
Swatski, J., 33, *33*

T
Talbot, J., 219, 220, *240*
Tappert, C. C., 32, *33*
Tapscott, D., 160, *169*
Taylor, J., 130, *135*
Taylor, W., 175, 176, *178*
Te'eni, D., 83, *97*
Tesch, R., 56, *65*
Thiers, G., 146, 147, 148, *153*
Todd, P., 148, *155,* 161, 162, 163, *169,* 171, 172,
    173, *179*
Torkzadeh, G., 183, 184, 185, 190, *196,* 216, *240*
Torrance, E. P., 203, *207*
Treacy, M. E., 160, 161, 163, *166, 169*
Trice, A. W., 160, *169*
Trice, H. M., 141, 144, 149, *153*
Trist, E. L., 124, 130, *134*
Troutman, T., 174, *178*
Trumbly, J. E., 222, *241*
Turner, J. A., 151, *155,* 160, 161, 163, *168, 169*
Tversky, A., 173, *179*

U
Uecker, W., 70, *80*
Ugbah, S. D., 163, *169*
Uhlig, R. P., 161, *169*
Ulrich, E., 128, *135*

V
Valacich, J. S., 27, *33,* 132, *134*
VanDyke, V., 144, *155*
Vaske, J. J., 161, 162, 163, *166*
Venda, V., 5, 6, 7, *11*
Vernon-Gerstenfeld, S., 188, *197*
Verplank, B., 37, *50*
Vessey, I., 112, *119,* 199, 204, 205, *207*
Vitell, S. J., 137, *155*
Vogel, D. R., 27, *33,* 122, *135*
Volpert, W., 128, *135*

W
Wakahara, T., 32, *33*
Weick, K. E., 160, *167,* 229, 231, *241*

Weinberg, P., 162, *169*
Weiss, I. R., 183, *195*
Weiss, R. M., 144, 149, *156*
Wetherbe, J. C., 183, *196*
Whalen, T., 14, 15, *26*
White, K. B., 142, *156*
Wilder, G., 186, *197*
Wilson, G. D., 144, 145, *153*
Wintrob, S., 159, *169*
Wolf, C. G., 32, *33*
Wood-Harper, E., 145, *155, 156*

Wood-Harper, T., 147, *156*

Y
Yaverbaum, G. J., 160, *169*
Yen, M., 101n, *107*
Young, T. R., 162, *168, 169*

Z
Zmud, R. W., 185, 186, *197,* 201, *206,* 220, 221, *241*
Zuboff, S., 162, *169*

Subject Index

A

Achievement, 145
Action research, 145
Adaptive systems, 53
Alternative decision paths, 87
Analysis of Variance, 10
Animation, 24, 25
Anonymity, 27
askSAM, 56
Asynchronous, 161

B

Belief system, 138
Bounded rationality, 163
Browser, 30

C

Case research, 148
COBOL (common business oriented language), 115
Cognitive effort, 75, 77
Cognitive ergonomics, 129
Cognitive load, 102
Cognitive maps, 83, 84, 85
Cognitive processes, 8
Color, 5, 8
Color cognitive maps, 93
Colorblindness, 5
Communication aids, 84
Communication context, 83
Communication richness, 83
Compensatory model, 68, 69
Competence, 129
Complexity, 7, 69, 71
Computer-based decision aids, 79, 84
Computer-mediated communications, 162
Conceptual model, 38
Concern for others, 145
Constraint of measurement, 231
Construct definition, 213
Construct measurement, 212
Construct validity, 235

Constructs, 211, 212, 213
Content, 212
Content knowledge, 62
Context, 18
Context representation, 83
Context-specific scales, 214
Cost/benefit analysis, 173
Covariate, 19
Creativity, 203
CSCW (Computer supported cooperative work), 122
CSQS (Calgary Surveys Query System), 219

D

Decision accuracy, 68, 69
Decision task characteristics, 71
Decision-making biases, 85
Decision-making effectiveness, 171
Decision-making style, 200
Degree of familiarity, 165
Dependent variables, 230
DIA (divisional information assistants), 132
Distortion, 161
Domain expertise, 201
DSS (Decision Support System), 4, 67, 231

E

E-mail, 159,, 162
EIS (Executive Information Systems), 4
Electronic brainstorming, 30
Electronic voting, 31
Elimination by aspects, 77
ELOC (executable lines of code)114
Empirical, 13, 15
EMS (Electronic Meeting System), 27, 30, 122
End user success, 185
Ethics, 132
EUC (end user computing), 183
EV (Expected Value), 68
Evaluation apprehension, 27
Experimenter effects, 237
Expert strategies, 7

F

Face-to-face meetings, 31, 32, 162
Fairness, 145
Field dependence/independence, 200
Framework, 3,8
Functionality, 83
Fundamental ideology, 149

G

Generic scales, 214
Graphic representations, 199
Graphic,
   analogy, 46
   metaphor, 45
   representation, 43
   style, 44
Group cohesiveness, 111, 112
Group factors, 111
Group Interface, 27, 29
Group
   consensus, 30
   distraction, 28
   idea, 30
   meeting expenses, 28
   time constraints, 27
Groupware, 121, 122
GUI (Graphical User Interfaces), 10

H

Halstead's Effort, 112
Handwriting recognition, 33
Heuristic/Analytic style, 200
Heuristics, 68, 172
Holistic representations, 204
Honesty, 145
Horizontal presentation, 24
Human decision processes, 68
Human dignity, 141
Human factors in information systems, 221, 223
Human rights, 142
Human-factors approach, 84
Human/Computer dialogue, 35
Human/Computer Interaction, 5
Human/Computer Interface, 3, 14

I

Icon, universality, 47
Ideographic approach, 127
Ideology, 137
Imagination, 203
Independent variables, 231

Individual characteristics
   age, 186
   cognitive skills, 199, 202
   cognitive style, 188, 200
   computer anxiety, 188
   computer attitudes, 187, 215
   computer experience, 186
   computer skill level, 187
   gender, 186
   personality, 187
Individual differences, 53, 183
Individual factors, 111
Influence diagrams, 87
Information acquisition, 71, 172
Information channeling, 171
Information completeness, 71
Information display, 199
Information load, 71, 79, 176
Information processing, 172
Information search pattern, 69, 70
Information selection strategy
   alternative, 171, 174
   attribute, 171, 174
Information value, 67, 70
Insider, 147
Integration, 129
Intelligent systems, 54
Interactive cognitive maps, 91
Interface complexity, 30
Interface usability, 105
Interface, iconic, 36
Internal efficiency, 128
IT (information technology), 122

K

Knowledge-based interactions, 60

L

Law of the Plurality of Structure Strategies, 6
Law of transformations, 7
LCSH (Library of Congress Subject Heading), 54
Leader behavior, 112
Leadership, production emphasis, 114
LOC (lines of code), 112
Local optimization, 85

M

Management, 111
Manipulation check, 235
Manipulation device
   keyboard, 32

mouse, 32
stylus, 32
MBTI (Myers-Briggs Type Indicator), 220
Measurements, 211
Measures
   behavioral, 233
   obtrusive, 234
   outcome, 233
   perceptual, 233
   process, 233
   qualitative, 234
   quantitative, 234
   unobtrusive, 234
Mental model, 55, 102
Menu
   depth versus breath issues, 14
   performance, 14
   pop-up, 10
   pull-down, 13, 20, 24
   scroll-bar, 13, 20, 21
   traditional, 13, 20, 21
   tree-structured, 14
Minimal manual, 101, 102
Minimalist design, 102
MIS (Management Information Systems), 3
MPI (MIS professional ideology), 138
Multicriteria decisions, 71

N

Noncompensatory model, 68, 69
Normative theories of decision making, 85
Novice strategies, 7

O

Online data capture, 237
OPAC (Online Public Access Catalog), 54
Open-ended study, 147
Operational ideology, 149
Organizational communication, 160

P

Pen-based interface, 32
Performance Measures, Mean average time, 19
Performance
   information retrieval, 53
   least-preferred icons, 38
   menu structure preference, 15
   object discrimination, 46
   optimal number of menu selections, 15
   perceived ease of use, 15
   response times, 15
   search time, 15

Personal values, 142
Phenomenology, 149
Playback behavior, 59
Political process, 137
PPC (project planning and control), 115
Presentation format, 14, 84
PRIMIS, 3
Procedural rules, 60
Process, 212
Process knowledge
   by induction, 60
   by training, 60
   by transfer, 60
Process tracing, 69
Product familiarity, 18
Programmer productivity, 111
Programmer productivity model, 112

Q

Query, 55

R

Reasoning, 203
Reliability, 128
Repetitively superfluous redundancy, 29
Research method
   content analysis, 56
   experimentation, 228
   interview, 56
   observation, 56
   protocol analysis, 56, 69, 148
Retrieval mechanisms, 54

S

Self learning, 132
Simulation, 69
Skills inventory, 18
Social action, 144
Sociotechnical systems, 122, 124, 133
SQL (Structured Query Language), 101
Structurability, 128
Structure strategies, 5
Subsystem
   business environment, 124
   task, 124
   team, 124
Supplanting function of color, 8
Survey reliability, 221
Survey validity, 221
Symbols, 35
Symmetrical matrix, 176
System familiarization, 159

Systems properties
   complexity, 123
   flexibility, 123
   interviews, 123
   power, 123
   robustness, 123
   user friendliness, 123

T

Task, 74
Task complexity, 173, 202
Task context, 215
Task, information extraction, 4, 17
Team review and design perspective, 124
Teamwork, 121
Telecommunications network systems, 122
Theoretical bases, 14
Theory, 211
Theory construction, 225
Theory of bounded rationality, 84
Theory-based research, 3
Time constraints, 174, 176
Transparency, 128

U

Uncertainty reduction, 160
Usability, 83, 94, 101
User, 5

User acceptance, 162
User learning, 6
User manual, 101
User preferences, 23
User satisfaction, 183, 184, 190
User
   ad hoc, 27
   children, 54
   expert, 7, 53
   failure, 58
   novice, 7, 53, 102
   preferences, 91
   profile, 17
   prototypical, 53
   success, 57
Utility function, 85

V

Verbalization of mental processes, 9
Vertical presentation, 24
Voice mail, 159, 162
Voice recognition, 32

W

WPM (words per minute), 32

Z

Zmud and Boynton criteria, 220